TROOPERS

TROOPERS
Behind the Badge

JOHN STARK

N.J. State Police Memorial Association, Inc.
West Trenton, N.J.

▼

All photos N.J. State Police, except as otherwise noted.
All rights reserved under International and Pan-American Copyright Conventions.
Published in the United States
by the N.J. State Police Memorial Association, Inc.,
New Jersey

Library of Congress Catalog Card Number: 93–85268
ISBN: 0–9637674–0–2

On the cover (l to r):
Troopers Gene Johnson, Annemarie Grant, Michael Siegelski

Book design by Giorgetta Bell McRee

Manufactured in the United States of America
First Edition: November 1993
10 9 8 7 6 5 4 3 2 1

▼

For Col. Justin J. Dintino

The New Jersey State Police Memorial Association:
Maj. Bill Coblentz, Kirby Conlon, John Custodio,
Michael J. Dancisin, Capt. Bernard Gallagher, Evan Jahos,
Lt. Col. Richard Jankowski, Col. David B. Kelly,
Col. Eugene Olaff, Sgt. Edward Rowland, Edwin Stier, Esq.

The Troopers

And everyone connected with The New Jersey State Police

▼

Acknowledgments

There aren't a lot of experiences that one can look back on in life and wish to do all over again. Writing this book was such a pleasure and education. For that, I am grateful to all the troopers I interviewed for their time and patience—for the knowledge and the stories you shared. Thank you.

There are those I must single out who went above and beyond the call: Maj. Bill Coblentz, Ed Stier, Lt. Fred Tavener, Trp. Anthony DiSalvatore; and Lt. Tom DeFeo: if this book has a heart, it's because of him and his love for the Outfit. Thank you.

On the civilian side, nobody was a better trouper than my agent and editor, Barbara Bowen, proof that angels do come if you call them. Your excitement about the project kept me motivated, and I will always be grateful.

I will always be indebted, too, to William Rondina and Giovanni Foroni LoFaro for their extraordinary hospitality. You are as much a part of this book as the troopers. Many thanks, too, to the Paul H. Kaiser Foundation for its generous support.

Finally, a very personal thank-you to Col. Dintino, who wanted a candid book about the difficult work his men and women do. There are very few people who have visions. I was lucky to work for one (and to have the help of his secretary, Gail Carrigan). Again, thank you, Colonel, for *TROOPERS*—"this thing of ours."

Contents

Introduction xiii

1 THE ACADEMY 1

2 PATROLLING THE HIGHWAYS 17

3 A TROOPER IS A TROOPER 41

4 TAKEN BY SURPRISE 51

5 TEAMS—ELITE OF THE ELITE 69

6 BREAKING ORGANIZED CRIME 83

7 DEEP COVER OPERATIONS 101

8 WHEN A MOBSTER FLIPS 119

9 THE WAR ON DRUGS 133

10 SAVING LIVES 167

11 DON'T LET THEM GET AWAY 183

12 MAJOR CRIME: MANHUNT OF THE CENTURY 195

13 CHARACTERS WITH CHARACTER 251

Index 267

TROOPERS

Introduction

When I was approached about writing a book about the New Jersey State Police, I was skeptical. I was a feature writer, and what did I know or care about the Doppler effect in radar or how to administer a Breathalyzer test? My subject was people. For the last six-and-a-half years, I'd worked for *People* magazine, interviewing celebrities in the belief that they led interesting lives and had something to say. Maybe some do. As this project got underway, I found out that it was indeed about people, characters with character. Troopers, I found, have everything to say; and, best of all, no publicists to shield them from the questions. Every trooper I interviewed was given the option: "If you want something off the record I'll turn off my tape recorder." Not one said, Turn it off—ever. As a journalist, I felt as if I'd stumbled into an undiscovered diamond mine.

How could anyone who's spent time patrolling the nation's busiest turnpike not have adventurous, heartbreaking, weird stories to tell? How could they not have picked up intriguing insights into human behavior? I was lucky enough to have been able to do my research on the frontlines, from riding with road troopers to going on raids to sitting in vans doing undercover surveillance. When friends asked, Isn't that dangerous? I'd think, It's something troopers do every day of their lives.

The New Jersey State Police is the most diversified law enforcement agency in the country. When I began my research for *TROOPERS*, I had no idea just how diversified; or how passionately committed each Bureau is to its particular area. "The key word with us is adaptability," says Maj. Bill Coblentz of Intelligence. When New Jersey was one of the most Mafia-influenced states in the country, the NJSP established an Intelligence Bureau and subsequently an Organized Crime Bureau that cleaned up the state. That Bureau has remained a model of effectiveness for the federal and other state governments. Through its restructured Narcotics Bureau, that same intensity of purpose is now being directed against the South American drug cartels.

What does a uniformed road trooper have in common with a plain-clothes detective or an undercover officer who's infiltrated an organized crime family? Again, I was lucky. For the first time in four years, a new class of recruits was put through the State Police's training academy, and I was allowed to observe. Only the physically strongest, the smartest, the most sensitive and adaptable, can survive this grueling program. To earn their badges, all troopers must complete the Academy. After that, all troopers must patrol the highways. Besides bonding them for life, these in-your-face experiences give them the background and maturity to handle more specialized areas of law enforcement. Should an emergency arise, no matter what their duties at the time, all troopers can be called out. All troopers must undergo continual weapons qualification and physical fitness tests. Failure to pass can mean your career is over.

I did not want *TROOPERS* to be about the early history of the New Jersey State Police, as rich as that is. It's been done (and done well) by the late Lt. Leo Coakley, in a book called *Jersey Troopers* (Rutgers University Press, 1971). He chronicles the birth of the Outfit, which was begun in 1921 under the leadership of a twenty-five-year-old West Point graduate, Col. H. Norman Schwarzkopf, who was the father of Gen. Norman Schwarzkopf. I wanted to write about today's troopers, from their on-the-job perspectives. I was indeed lucky to have the support of Col. Justin Dintino, Superintendent of the NJSP. Whenever I needed access to something or someone, Col. Dintino delivered; from being allowed to go on a lifesaving aeromedical helicopter flight—I am the only journalist ever to have been given permission—to interviewing a mobster informant in the federal Witness Protection Program, one who audaciously taped his own initiation ceremony into the Mafia. I found in Col. Dintino a forward-looking champion of civil rights who believes troopers must be well-educated to meet the future: all recruits are now required to have a four-year college education. Col. Dintino put all of his troopers through sensitivity training workshops with minority and gay and lesbian groups. An in-service training program has each trooper returning to the Police Academy to take educational and technical courses.

In life, they say, timing is everything; and that I had, from the entry of the 113th Class to the culmination, after ten years, of the Lamonaco case. (Phillip Lamonaco was a trooper who was gunned down by a gang of white revolutionaries, sparking the biggest criminal case since the Lindbergh kidnapping and setting off the nation's largest manhunt.) This was detective work at its finest, in which the State Police's forensics lab was put to full use—matching spent bullets to guns, analyzing genetic codes in bloodstains.

Besides today's troopers, I was lucky to talk with some of the old-timers and hear their stories from the days when a trooper had to have the colonel's permission to marry. I recall Maj. Hugo Stockburger, who watched the Hindenburg explode—on the dirigible's previous trip to New Jersey he had gone aboard, and later had entertained some of its crew members at his house. There was an afternoon in Florida that was spent with Lt. Paul Sjostrom, the last surviving member of the very first class. No celebrity I ever met could match their stories.

To me, this book is about camaraderie. It's a look at people who truly love their work. In these jaded times, I was continually amazed at each trooper's enthusiasm for what he or she does, and the pride each one exudes in doing it. Maybe because I'm from a big city, I just assumed policemen let themselves get out of shape and yell obscenities over their loudspeakers. New Jersey's troopers still pay homage to their founding principles of "Honor, duty, fidelity." "We continue to instill in each recruit who comes through the Academy: We want to be the best and we're willing to work for it," says Coblentz. No matter what the season, troopers wear wool dress blouses with ties, spit-shine their boots, and keep the badge in their cap brightly polished. One told me, "You'd never know it, but I'm really only five foot eight. But when I put on my uniform and stand tall, creating that V-shaped look, people think I'm six foot plus. I've been called out to bar fights that the local police can't control. But when we show up, everyone yells, 'State Troopers!' and behaves. It all has to do with our image, how we perceive ourselves." Just being around them makes one want to do his or her best. I hope I have.

1 / The Academy

The Badge

Sitting down front, facing the stage of the cavernous War Memorial Building in Trenton, they form a large, flag-shaped patch of blue. "Welcome to the family of the New Jersey State Police," says Col. Justin J. Dintino to the graduating members of the 113th class as he stands before them. "You are now a member of the most elite." Row by row, the recruits are called out of their seats and up to the side of the stage to receive the final and most important piece of their uniform. As each recruit's name is announced, he walks center stage, where he shakes Attorney General Robert Del Tufo's hand and salutes the colonel, who hands him a brass badge—a badge so shiny and new it gleams like gold as the colonel unfolds his fist to present it.

2

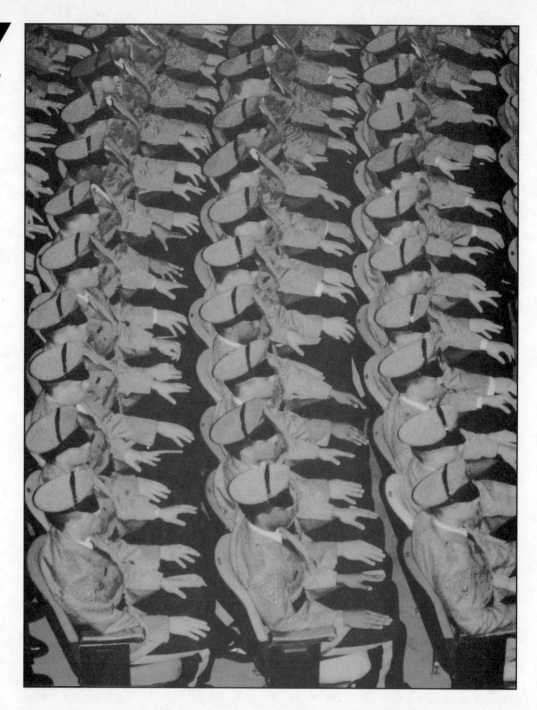

After three months of intense training, the ninety-three surviving members of the 113th class wait to receive the final piece of their uniforms.
(Photo by *The Times of Trenton*, PAUL SAVAGE.)

In 1921, Col. Norman Schwarzkopf (Badge No. 1) founded the New Jersey State Police. Seventy-two years later, Col. Justin Dintino and New Jersey Attorney General Robert Del Tufo present Badge No. 5116 to recruit Joseph Yakup. (Photo by W. KRYSCNSKI.)

4   Leaving the stage, each recruit is now an official New Jersey State Trooper. New Jersey's police training program differs from others in that a recruit doesn't become a part of the Outfit until this final ceremony, and as the graduating members of this 113th Class know—one having been dismissed just two days before—it ain't over 'til it's over. Securing that badge to your cap links you to each trooper who came before, and to all who will come after. Only the fittest are allowed to be a part of that chain, from Col. Schwarzkopf, Badge No. 1, to the 113th's Joseph Yakup, Badge No. 5116.

These new troopers have gone together through an experience so intense that "it creates bonds that last a lifetime, bonds almost as strong as those between child and parent, sister and brother," says Physical Fitness Coordinator Sgt. Carmelo Huertas (Badge No. 3251) from his office at the Academy. Of the 3,732 who took the initial police test for the 113th class, test scores, medical exams, and psychological profiles reduced that number to 128, with 93—or 2.4 percent of the original group—getting badges. Unlike recruits at most police academies, New Jersey's live at the facility during their training, with time off only on weekends and holidays.

Proclaimed one class recruit an hour and a half after his arrival for training at the Academy in Sea Girt: "I'm outta here." He didn't even get a free lunch. "He expected the troopers to be congratulating him for making it that far in the process," says Trooper Anthony DiSalvatore (Badge No. 4610). "He was in for a rude awakening. Often, when applicants are accepted, they think they've made it. Like this guy. He thought we were going to be his buddy and hold his hand for the next hundred days of training. Not the case. Not the case at all."

Anyone who can endure three and a half months in the country's toughest police academy—physically more demanding, they say, than even the Marine Corps boot camp—will graduate as one of the best-trained law enforcement officers in the world. Bullies need not apply. "Most people associate police work with brawn, the bigger the better, a profession that's unsuitable for women," says Huertas. "That's a misconception. Look at Sgt. Benny Castillo, our self-defense instructor. He's five foot four inches tall. We find our best recruit is average built, has good common sense, and can communicate well with the public. They have to project themselves in a positive manner. Sometimes we get recruits here who think their mere physical presence would be enough to quell or handle a situation. Usually they don't last. If I had a choice, I'd take a smart trooper with good physical skills over an Adonis with no brains. Laws are so sophisticated and complicated nowadays that a trooper who isn't articulate will simply put us in a hole."

For that reason the NJSP now requires that a recruit have four years of college. He or she must be between the ages of eighteen and thirty-five years. "There's a big difference between a trooper of today and a trooper of twenty years ago," says Huertas. "The amount of information one needs to graduate out of here today is overwhelming. A trooper has to know just what he or she can legally do and not do. Today's trooper has got to be a psychologist and sociologist, and has to remain active in learning. You can't leave and forget. The Division ensures it through an in-service program that is always keeping them up-to-date."

Besides self-defense classes (boxing, judo, shooting handguns and rifles, wielding a riot baton), recruits must study motor vehicle law, sociology, first aid, accident investigations, psychology, typing, constitutional issues, the juvenile justice code, race relations, and English grammar (there's a weekly spelling test). Besides daily physical fitness classes from hell, recruits must be able to run an eight-minute mile, do distance swimming, and maneuver a troop car as if it were a Batmobile.

Once in the Academy, no one is cut a break. Sadly, time waits for no one. "That recruit pulled a hamstring. If he can't exercise by tomorrow, he'll be disqualified. We can't hold the class back until he can catch up," says Huertas. For the first ten weeks, women are allowed to do modified push-ups. But, after that, they must have strengthened their upper bodies enough to do them like men—several hundred for each exercise session. If she can't, she's sent packing. "It's only fair. No exceptions. People on the road aren't going to give you special considerations," says Huertas. "As I tell all the kids here: white, black, male and female, I hate you all."

6 *The Making of a Trooper*

To understand how this paramilitary organization operates, to know what makes a trooper, one has to go to the source: the Academy. This is where the training takes place that each trooper will fall back on every day on the job. Ask a trooper how he or she survived a gun battle, saved a life, stayed cool undercover, or withstood a defense attorney's relentless badgering on the witness stand, and, like a mantra, you'll hear these words: "I relied on my training."

"Look what a trooper's job entails: irregular hours, lots of stress, and making life and death decisions," says Huertas. "We try to address all of these things through the training program. These kids perform guard duty, getting up at three in the morning. We want them used to an irregular shift, to stressful situations. The job of a police officer is normally negative contact. You don't stop people to tell them they're doing a great job driving their cars. You stop them to tell them they're doing something wrong. The recruits learn that what they do at the Academy correlates with what they're going to be doing out on the road."

Acquiring the right tone of voice for talking to the public, letting them know that you're in charge, comes under the heading of "constructive force." Although not a class, "it's the undertone of the whole training," says DiSalvatore. "A recruit has to acquire a certain body language and demeanor. Rigid. Focused. He or she can't be slumped in the shoulder and not looking someone in the eye. He has to have that I'm-not-going-to-take-any-crap look. He must always be at attention and squared away."

The Academy consists of sixty-five buildings spread over 165 acres on a state-owned National Guard encampment abutting the Atlantic Ocean. When not training State Police recruits, the Training Bureau offers instruction for municipal police officers on a day-by-day basis. Educational courses are continually being taught in such progressive areas as hostage negotiations, sexual assault intervention, drug enforcement, and child abuse prosecution.

Five weeks after the 113th class got underway, enter the gym, where a P.T. (physical training) class is going on. Huertas and P.T. Instructor Tim Fogarty (Badge No. 3387) are putting the men (all of whom have

Recruits live on-base at the Sea Girt facility, considered the toughest Police Academy in the country. The paramilitary training emphasizes teamwork, not individuality. After marching in formation, exhausted recruits stand at attention on their way to mess. (Photo by W. KRYSCNSKI.)

shaved heads) and a woman (out of five, she's the last survivor) through their grueling paces. Right now, they're in the midst of an exercise called "mountain climbing," in which, on all fours, they jog in place. Throughout the class, they take swigs from water jugs that contain a vitamin mixture to replace the electrolytes in their sweating bodies. "Pick it up!" bellows Fogarty, who, at six feet three inches, weighing 240 pounds, joined the State Police after nixing an offer to play with

8 the Dallas Cowboys. At thirty-seven, he still wins the State Police Picnic's annual troop car pull contest. "Bunch of quitters!" screams Huertas, pacing the gym floor. "You are one team," shouts Fogarty. "You are not individuals. This job does not require individuals. It requires teamwork. Is that clear?" "Yes sir!" hollers the class, obviously not loud enough. Fogarty repeats his question: *"IS THAT CLEAR?!" "YES SIRRRRR!"* comes the response, loud as dynamite.

At each class, a recruit is picked to stand on a wooden platform to face the others and lead the count. Recruit David Granitzski, whose turn it is today, has just lost his place. *Fogarty ain't gonna like this.* After being called some names that would make Madonna blush, Granitzski is banished to the back of the gym, where he must complete his jumping jacks with his face to the wall. Although this may seem like gratuitous punishment, there is a reason. The platform is symbolic of a witness stand. If a trooper can't maintain concentration during extreme stress, he or she could blow a case.

"We don't call it punishment," says Huertas. "We call it direction," says Benny Castillo (Badge No. 3172). "Encouragement," says Huertas. "Positive reinforcement," interjects Lester Tice (Badge No. 3672).

Fogarty, you're tough: "I'm easygoing inside," he says, sitting in his office off the gym floor. "They don't know it," he adds, looking out his door. "They're kinda like shell-shocked at this point. One kid, Walsh, I yelled at him pretty good the other day. I jumped up on the stand. Usually I don't do that. He just pissed me off. I'd ask him something, and he had what I call the seven-second delay. That signals to me that he's not sure what he's thinking about. Not clear in his thoughts. As a trooper, you can't have seven-second decisions. You got to go for it. Whatever your gut says. You got to go with your initial thought or reaction. You make a decision, you stay with it.

"Before class, I came down hard on another one of the recruits. He was supposed to hand me a sheet of paper that says who's on light duty today. He forgot it. I said, 'Oh, so you forgot? That means, as a trooper, you forgot the investigation report for the accident! The lawyers want discovery for the grand jury. You forgot all that, too!' Sure, it was only a slip of paper that said Smith couldn't do calisthenics, but the point is, when you're on the job you can't forget to do your paperwork."

"One reason we employ these techniques," says Castillo, "is that when troopers are out on the road, and motorists start yelling at them, they have to stay under control. If somebody is screaming and yelling at you, you have to remain rational to figure out what's going on. Is this motorist yelling at me because he's mad, or is he just trying to distract me so he can do something else? When we're yelling at a recruit, and he or she looks down for a split second—well, that may be the opening somebody is looking for. As the bad guys, we try to be as realistic as possible. If the bad guy would take advantage of a situation, then we take advantage of it."

Just how much *is* enough? "Personally, I'm pretty good at picking up when somebody is breaking," says Assistant Class Coordinator Jim McSorley (Badge No. 3652). "It's my job to get them to decide whether or not they like it here. We owe it to the State Police to weed out anybody who has a negative personality. On the flip side, I don't want to lose a good recruit, so sometimes I back off a little. If you're not in the military before coming here, if you're not used to being told when to get up, eat, and go to class, then it's a hard adjustment. You have to have a certain personality to come into this line of work. The majority of recruits are conservative individuals. It's a matter of getting them into line with our own standards and policies. For the 113th class, I'm the bad guy. It's a role I play, like being an actor. I give out the extra detail assignments. I can give you a tongue lashing like you've never heard before."

Oh, really? "Yeah, but I can also be compassionate," he says, sucking on a cherry-flavored Tootsie Pop.

Overseeing today's P.T. class is the Academy Commandant, Capt. Thomas Gallagher (Badge No. 1934). How does this class measure up?

"At five weeks, the fragmentation gives way to an adhesiveness," he says. "It's now becoming a protective environment instead of a cut-throat one. Recruits are now saying to each other, '*C'mon, you can do it!*' If one becomes weaker, they strong-arm him. The more the instructors are on him, the more they pull the other along. Now, the bonding begins—my classmate is always my classmate. The closer we get to graduation, the more apprehensive they become about going out. It's like going to jail. They look forward to getting out, but they're comfortable in this environment because they've survived. At this point, when they see a classmate isn't giving one hundred percent, that he or she's starting to skate, a negative peer pressure turns on him. They

10 don't want that person to be a part of the class. As things go on, they learn to handle the pressure and have humor about it. They don't take all the insults personally after a while. We are firm but fair. We have to be. If a trooper gets hurt, we don't ever want to hear, 'If only the training program had done its job.'"

Now that everybody's completely, totally wiped out, it's time for the daily 3.5 mile run from the gym to the sand dunes and back. Today's leader is none other than Capt. Gallagher, a marathoner whose idea of a good time is running up the seaboard from Florida to New York. Outside, a belligerent ocean wind is screaming *Halt and About Face!* to the oncoming group. Pity the recruit who's in last place. "Is this the best you can do?" barks a P.T. instructor, running alongside him. "I wouldn't want to be your partner. If I needed help, you couldn't come to my rescue."

Following behind the recruits in a station wagon equipped with oxygen are Troopers William Torowicz (Badge No. 2808), and Wendy Galloway (Badge No. 3700). "Where you going, Gray?" Torowicz shouts out his driver's seat window at one of the runners, who has strayed off course. "They're physically beat and psychologically crushed," says Torowicz. "All they want to do is head back to the barn." The question must be asked: What happens when these zombied-out recruits go home on Friday nights? "With those haircuts?" asks Galloway "—nothing. I call 'em B.C. haircuts." B.C? "Birth control, because nobody'll touch 'em."

"When I came into the Academy in 1982, being black and a woman, I had the double whammy," says Galloway, who teaches social sciences to the recruits. "I was coming into a field that was traditionally white male. But I had a thick outer skin. I kind of knew what I was biting off. My premise was, I wanted this job. I was not here to win a popularity contest."

Although five women were accepted for this class, none made it to graduation day. "Women recruits do have special problems," says Galloway, a former elementary school teacher. "Women do not have the same body strength as men, especially upper body. A woman has to really dig down deep to find the fortitude to do things here she never thought she could do. Men are traditionally more team oriented. A lot of women are not accustomed to being screamed at. But with more women in the military, they're getting used to it. Women do have special biological problems. I can remember times out on patrol when I had needs which are more difficult to satisfy than a man's. I got to know plenty of farmers. When they saw me pull into their driveway they knew I was there for a pit stop. As a woman you make adjustments.

"People ask, What is a female's role on a police force? Some people say, It's working with sexual assault cases, or with children. It's true, they're good in these areas. I think that women can teach how to talk to people. It's nice to have muscles, but, theoretically, this should not be a physical job. If we are the keepers of the peace in society, we

Because laws have become so complex, today's recruits must take extensive educational courses. Trooper Randy Martin of the Telecommunications Unit shows them how to use the National Crime Information Center computer. (Photo by W. KRYSCNSKI.)

12 should never have to put our hands on anyone. A woman knows that with her physical limitations, she has to be able to talk to other people. A man may think, I don't have to talk because I can muscle my way into making people do what I want. That's the difference between a male and female trooper."

What is the most important lesson Galloway didn't learn at the Academy that she can pass on to new recruits? "When you become a police officer in this state, everything you do comes under scrutiny. When the Fourth of July comes and everybody on your block is setting off fireworks, you can't do it. What young recruits have to realize is that everything they do, like the clothes they wear off-duty to go shopping, is noticed. 'Oh, there's the trooper,' someone will say. You may not even know your next-door neighbor, but everybody knows you work for the State Police. They watch your comings and goings, everything you do. You're a trooper seven days a week, all hours."

Since the Police Academy began, residency has been required for recruits, who live rent-free, six to eight in a dorm room. Morning inspection is at 6:30 a.m., lights out at 10 p.m. "Residency gives us a chance to look at an individual for twenty-four hours a day, plus it helps them decide if this is what they want to do for the rest of their life," says Huertas.

Each dorm is meticulously neat, each bathroom antiseptically clean; not thanks to any maid service, either. "They do it all," says Huertas. "We want to instill pride in them. When you look at their lockers, or how they hang their shirts, all those things relate to how one deals with situations on the road. If you fail to check your weapon for serviceability before going out, though it may seem like the most trivial thing at the time, it could cost you your life. You must check your leather. You must make sure there's no green growth on your rounds to prohibit them from being fired. You must check your magazines to make sure they're functional. Your equipment is a part of you. You can't take it for granted. We try to stress that the small details are the ones that are going to get you hurt out there. It isn't going to be that you forgot your gun. It's going to be that somebody grabbed your belt and ripped the holster right off because your leather was rotten."

When recruits arrive, they're issued khaki pants and shirts, and a dark blue cap. As the weeks pass and they do well in their testing, they're rewarded with pieces of their State Police uniforms, such as boots and belts and hats. "They go from having no identity to feeling like a member of the Division. It's a nice psychological tool," says Huertas. "We do it across the board. If they don't perform, we tell them they're going back to their old hats. I tell you, you can see the disappointment in their faces."

At 5 p.m., the recruits line up for mess. Whoever came in last during the day's run is made to eat last. Sorry, no blowing off steam or engaging in smart dinner repartee. Silence and submission are required here, too. *"What are you looking at?"* Huertas yells at one of the recruits chowing down. *"Nothing, sir!"* is the response. After dinner comes study hall. Walk into the large room with long tables, and all the recruits leap up and snap to attention. "Carry on!" are the magic words to unfreeze them. Still, they're not exactly into relaxing. Try talking to them: they all appear to be programmed. Say "Please don't call me *sir*," and the response is, "Yes sir!"

Rufus and Bruce Hay are brothers whose father is a trooper. "He almost fell over when we told him our decision to follow in his footsteps," says Rufus, twenty-six, during a study break. Both Rufus and Bruce have college degrees. Because of the four-year wait between the 112th and 113th classes—owing to state funding problems—they had taken white collar jobs with corporations. Still, when the time finally came, they stuck to their decision to join the Outfit.

These Tom Cruise look-alikes could be twins. "When one does something wrong, we both suffer for it," says Bruce, twenty-four. "'Were you the idiot I gave this to?' an instructor will ask. No sir, it was the other idiot. We both catch it . . . The best part about being here is when a trooper starts talking about an experience he's had. Everybody's face lights up. If you don't understand something they're trying to teach you, maybe something in the juvenile justice code, once they hit that personal story, it all starts to click. You can relate to it."

"Everything relates," says Rufus. "They'll be yelling at you while you're doing jumping jacks. Your legs are cramping up—" "It feels like forever," says Bruce. "You lose the feeling in your toes. Your hamstrings start to cramp. You can barely move. Then they'll start in: 'It's three o'clock in the morning. A guy's trying to grab your gun! What are you going to do? Give up?' A chill runs up your spine and your adrenaline's back. Being here is a plan for life. Before this, I don't remember making my bed two days in a row. Here they teach you how to focus on your goals, how to get from A to B. You bring it home

14 with you on the weekends. The emphasis is on family. You're going to be a part of their family. They say that all the time."

"It's amazing," says Rufus, "there have only been five thousand troopers. There's nobody else like them. You just want to be a part of the organization more than anything in the world."

"V" Is for Victory

It's October, ten weeks after the recruits have arrived. Lined up at the pistol range—under a blue sky with a gold sun—they look different. They have acquired more attitude and self-confidence. They look bigger. Taller. "They're getting that V shape," says Fogarty. "They've lost weight. Toned up. They feel good about themselves. I feel good."

After twenty weeks, it must be difficult to see them leave. "Of course it is," says Wendy Galloway. "They're your children. Your babies. They're grown men with families, but still you call them your kids. You grow very attached to them. You have a great sense of pride on graduation day, that you took a group of people who didn't know a thing about law enforcement and molded them into an ideal. That's what keeps me here, class after class."

With the conclusion of the 113th's graduating ceremonies at the War Memorial Building, the new troopers, in their French blue and cavalry yellow uniforms, march single file up the aisles to the doors. From there they'll go to the basement of the building to pick up their guns, which they're now legally allowed to carry. With their visored caps resting on the brim of their noses, forcing them to tilt their heads back in order to see, they are (except for the experiences that lie ahead) complete. Sounding off for the last time together, their voices fill the auditorium: *"We don't know what you've been told! All we want is the blue and gold."*

FACING PAGE

TOP RIGHT: *Failure to qualify on the firing range means dismissal. Recruits must be able to handle a Heckler & Koch semiautomatic handgun, a 12-gauge shotgun, and an antisniper AR-15.* (Photo by W. KRYSCNSKI.)

BOTTOM RIGHT: *As a packed auditorium of friends and family members look on, the recruits—now troopers—are led out of the Trenton War Memorial Building by Assistant Class Coordinator Jim McSorley.* (Photo by W. KRYSCNSKI.)

15

2 Patrolling the Highways

A City on Wheels

After graduating from the Academy, troopers are dispersed throughout the state to learn to patrol its highways. For two months, all the new troopers ride with a veteran trooper who shows them the ropes. This is another intense bonding experience. "It's a real father thing," says a trooper. "That trooper who trained you is always held in great respect. One of the most emotional days in your career is when, as a young trooper, you're handed the keys to the troop car and told you're ready to go out alone." During the trooper-coach training period, young troopers return to the classroom to get their radar operator and Breathalyzer certificates. No trooper can become a detective, helicopter pilot, undercover narc, organized crime–buster, dog handler, ballistics expert, evidence technician, or anything

17

Locking his beam onto a minivan, a trooper clocks the vehicle at 52 mph. Catching speeders by radar began in New Jersey in 1958. By 1975, it had evolved into the current onboard, lock-on beam system.

else in the State Police, until he or she has served time as a road trooper. They are the backbone of the New Jersey State Police.

When the Outfit began in 1921, road troopers rode horses and motorcycles. Today's road trooper commandeers a white, state-of-the-art Chevrolet Caprice 350, nicknamed the Space Bubble or Electric Bubble Machine. These sleek-looking cars feature LoJack, a vehicle tracking system for finding stolen automobiles; vinyl-back seats for easy cleaning, especially when mopping up blood that could be AIDS contaminated; and the most advanced radio communications system there is—the Motorola 800 Megahurst Simulated Trunk System. As a safety precaution, interior lights remain off when the driver's door is opened. Troop cars soon will contain onboard computers for DMV inquiries and video cameras for recording all vehicle stops.

There are five State Police commands, or troops, in New Jersey. Troop A serves the southern part of the state, Troop B the northern end, and Troop C the central portion. Troop D is solely responsible for the New Jersey Turnpike, the nation's busiest nonstop toll road; Troop E, for the Garden State Parkway. The road trooper's home base is a station; the older ones are called "barracks," even though the longtime tradition of troopers spending their nights there while on duty went out in 1976. Usually, when a trooper arrives at work, he or she will do some pumping up in the weight room, read memos, and talk to the previous shift about what's been happening out there. After donning their uniforms—even in the summer, troopers wear long-sleeved wool blouses to maintain a dress appearance and hide any tattoos—they'll gather and load their weapons, a Heckler & Koch semiautomatic handgun and a 12-gauge shotgun. Wearing a bullet-resistant vest is SOP (standing operating procedure) nowadays.

In the parking lot, troopers will conduct a vehicle inspection of the squad car. They'll calibrate their radar unit with a tuning fork, check the oil under the hood, and open the trunk to make sure it contains flares, a fire extinguisher, and a first aid kit with rubber gloves. They'll turn on the sirens, lights, overheads, and spotlight. The shotgun is secured under the lip of the front seat, and the PR-24, or riot baton, on the left-hand side of the front seat, for easy access when exiting. Lastly, troopers do a Signal 21, or radio check. Many go even further by pulling up the car's backseat to make sure that a passenger from the previous shift hasn't stashed any contraband there.

Road troopers who patrol rural southern, central, and northwest Jersey are often referred to as "cowboys" because of their "can't-wait-to-saddle-up-and-head-out-on-the-road" enthusiasm. Unlike troopers on the Garden State and Turnpike, who mostly issue traffic violations, they are responsible for all aspects of police work, from murder investigations to home burglaries. For that reason, rookie troopers are sent to Troop A, B, and C stations to be broken in. A road trooper must have at least two years' experience before graduating to the Garden

In the early days of the Outfit, troopers rode in style. In his bow tie and breeches (bow ties went out in 1937, breeches in 1958), Trooper Ernest Jesch poses on the running board of his 1928 blue and tan Buick touring car.

This white 1936 Ford V-8 was one of the first marked troop cars.

The 1950 Ford with hand-painted lettering ushered in the black-and-whites.

For an all-too-brief period, troopers on the Garden State Parkway were issued deluxe Chrysler New Yorkers, such as this 1955 model. Trooper John Anderson was one of the lucky drivers.

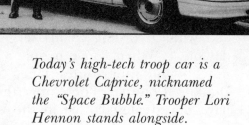

In the gas-guzzling sixties, troopers patrolled in finback Plymouths.

Today's high-tech troop car is a Chevrolet Caprice, nicknamed the "Space Bubble." Trooper Lori Hennon stands alongside.

From 1969 to 1976, the troop car of choice was the Plymouth Fury 3 with 440 magnum engine. "It was the hot car of all time, top of the line," recalls a trooper who drove one. It was the first troop car to have air-conditioning.

22 State or Turnpike. For a road trooper, the Turnpike is the frontlines, a "city on wheels" where, says veteran Paul Morris (Badge No. 3559), "every day is an industrial-strength dose of reality."

Almost all road troopers agree that the worst part of their job is the shift work. Troopers alternate three shifts: 7 a.m. to 3 p.m., 3 p.m. to 11 p.m., and 11 p.m. to 7 a.m. Some say they feel as if they have a permanent case of jet lag. Next on their list of hardships is all the paperwork that comes after each arrest. "You never see that in the movies or on TV," they all say.

The leading cause of injuries and deaths for road troopers is motor vehicle accidents. For safety reasons, motorcycles were phased out in the early 1950s. On the eastern portion of Interstate 78, one can see flags draped with flowers on the embankment where a twenty-four-year-old trooper, Thomas Hanratty (Badge No. 4971), recently was killed while writing a motorist a summons. He was struck by a truck that veered onto the shoulder. "That's the thing that scares you the most out here," says a trooper who worked with Hanratty. "We put ourselves in dangerous positions all of the time. We always have to worry about getting shot. Anything can happen to us at any time."

As the most visible members of the State Police, today's road troopers seem especially concerned with how they present themselves. "People have this thing about cops liking to eat donuts," says Trooper Sean Boero (Badge No. 4597), an ex-Marine who patrols the Turnpike, and who, according to his sergeant, "would rather work than take a day off." "When I give people a ticket," says Boero, cruising along the northbound inner-outer lane, "they'll ask, 'Why aren't you at the Dunkin' Donuts?' The funny thing is, I love Dunkin' Donuts. They have the greatest coffee in the world. I always go there for coffee. I love their donuts, too, but I'll never buy them. Never. Because as soon as I walk in, everyone starts talking and saying, 'Hey, here's a cop coming for his donuts.' So, I'll never get donuts. Never. Unless there's nobody there. Then, I'll get donuts."

"In my high school yearbook, I put 'state trooper' as my goal in life," says Chris Einwechter (Badge No. 4615) of the Woodbine Station. He and his midnight partner, Ralph Steelman (Badge No. 4929), are typical of the new breed of troopers who are always working out to maintain their Academy physiques. In fact, troopers must meet annual physical fitness requirements right up until retirement age, which is

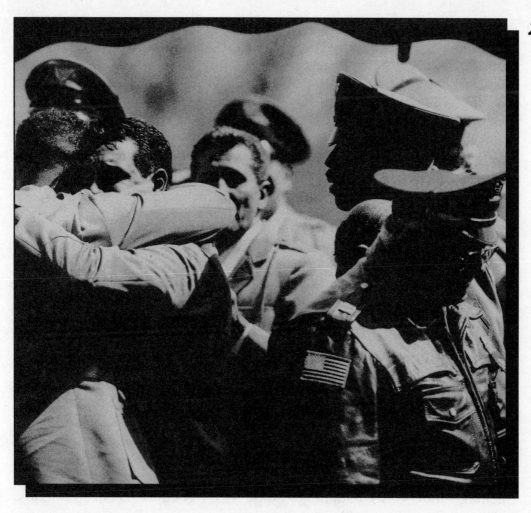

The solidarity of troopers is painfully evident at the funeral of Thomas Hanratty.
(David Bergeland Courier–News)

fifty-five, just like the speed limit. During a break in their overnight patrol, Einwechter and Steelman, best friends who grew up together, pull into the WaWa for oranges and mineral water. "In my yearbook, I put 'to give 110 percent,'" Steelman says. Later, shining his spotlight along the deserted beach at Wildwood at 2 a.m.: "As far as I'm concerned, I'm living up to that."

24   While patrolling the highways, troopers experience the range of emotion involved in their work. "It's the little things, and the big things," says Joe Moure (Badge No. 4648). "One afternoon I stopped four people in a car, an Hispanic family," he says. "The parents were in the backseat. They must have been in their eighties. When I looked in the car window, they had their hands in the air. It made me laugh, and broke my heart. I told them in Spanish, 'Aww, you don't have to do that.' Later, I was sent out to tell an immigrant woman from Eastern Europe that her son had died. She started crying, so I decided to stay with her until her husband got home. When I told him, he started crying, too. I guess they equated me with their son, because they both hugged me and held on to me and wouldn't let me go. Then I couldn't stop crying. That's nothing you're taught at the Academy. Sometimes you have to wing it."

The Phantom Keeps Everybody in Line

At 6:30 in the morning, Trooper James Grant's first order of business is seated in the waiting area of the Bordentown Station. Her name is Mary, and she looks a mess. The divorced grandmother from Trenton didn't take her medication, and has been up for hours walking. "God came to me in the middle of the night and told me to get out of New Jersey . . . *now!*" she says. Though still determined to reach the nearest border, Mary's exhausted, and has stopped by the station in hopes of getting a ride to her daughter's house to say goodbye to her grandkids. "My daughter doesn't like me to see them," she says.

Trooper Grant agrees to take her. Ever the gentleman, he asks Mary, who's in the backseat, "How are you today?"

"I'm fine, except for all the corruption in this state."

As he pulls out of the barracks, Grant proceeds to write the car's mileage down. "It's a rule," he explains. "You have to record all of your mileage when transporting women."

"That's so I can't say you raped me," chimes in Mary.

"That's right," says Grant. "Mary, you do know the law."

Grant (Badge No. 3396), has that bold, "Don't worry, I'm in command, Royal Canadian Mounted Police demeanor" that Col.

Schwarzkopf was after when he founded the New Jersey State Police. With a masters in education from Seton Hall, the distinguished-looking trooper, who is tall and prematurely gray, puts his brains to work every day on the job. He's a master at gleaning information from people, and could give Mike Wallace a run for his money.

Riding along Highway One, he stops two shabbily dressed young women, one white, the other black, who are walking on the narrow shoulder together, in harm's way. Rolling down his window, he asks, "Where you heading?" "We're secretaries going to an interview," says one. "Get in, I'll give you a lift," says Grant, who begins schmoozing them up. Whether they really are going for an interview isn't determined. What is learned in a few minutes' time is that they recently left a battered women's shelter to live in a motel that's infamous for prostitution. The owner, they say, pays them under the table to clean the rooms. At age thirty-four, the white woman already has six kids, all of whom are in foster care. Both have drug problems.

"The general public, juries, judges, they feel as though we coerce people into confessions," says Grant. "I find if you can be yourself, talk to someone on a one-to-one basis, they'll tell you what you want to know." (You won't get an argument out of Sgt. Tim O'Riordan, Badge No. 3046, who also patrolled out of Bordentown. While providing backup on a motor vehicle stop for a local cop, O'Riordan began chatting up the driver of the car. Says O'Riordan: "Out of the blue, and with no change of emotion in his voice, the guy said to me: 'I met a woman last night. I took her home, we did some cocaine and made love. Afterwards, she pissed me off. So I did her in.' I thought he was joking. Still, I brought him back to the station and had his apartment checked out. Inside was a duffel bag containing the woman's severed head and limbs.")

Driving along, Grant displays an uncanny, hawklike ability to spot expired vehicle registration stickers. As for speeders, he stops only one—a granny on her way to work as a school crossing guard. Not even Grant can be so tough as to give her a ticket. She gets a warning. As for creative excuses, Grant says, "I once stopped a woman in Cumberland County. She was pumping her breasts. She had this apparatus full of her milk. I found it kind of disgusting and just backed away from the car, letting her go."

Lunch, at the Mount Holly Diner, is snapping turtle soup, served by

26 Jean, a hard-as-formica waitress with a heart of gold. "Wanna see my Smurfs?" she asks, unbuttoning her top button. Jean recently had the cartoon characters tattooed just south of her name tag. "Why'd I do it?" she asks. The answer was blond, handsome, and thirty-five years old.

"Say, Jean," says Grant, "how about two iced teas." "For Jimmy, none of that machine stuff," she says. "If a trooper wants iced tea, I brew it especially for him." Nothing like a little VIP treatment, huh? "I like being recognized," says Grant. "If you're in here from New York and you need help, you can trust me because I'm wearing this uniform. That's part of what you come into this job for, I think."

Troopers are always talking about how hard it is to stay married. Yet Grant's been wed eleven years to the same woman, Bettyann, a secretary in the county prosecutor's office. "We've known each other since we were twelve years old. We've always been in love," he says. Call Grant a role model. "Young troopers need senior guys like me to set an example. If you want this job to be bad on your marriage, it can. If you allow it, if you're willing to violate the trust with your partner, the opportunities are there. There are men and women out there who like uniforms. Most troopers are young, good-looking, and in excellent physical shape. It'll come to you if you want it. I'll give you an example: a couple of weeks ago I was on midnights, riding with a younger guy. We pulled a car over. As he walked up to the passenger window, he could see that the driver—a pretty woman—had her shirt off. When he got to the window, she slid across the seat, took off her underwear, and said, *"I've been speeding up and down here all night waiting to be stopped!"*

Errant trooper beware. The State Police has its own way of making you toe the line. "If you do something wrong, you're talked to by your senior man, your sergeant, or anyone else who knows what's acceptable," says Grant. "If you continue behaving inappropriately, something may happen, like your locker getting turned over. That's called *The Phantom*. Nobody knows how or when it happens. But *The Phantom* keeps everybody in line."

You hear it a lot from cops, that nobody but another cop can understand them. "That's crazy. It's not true," says Grant, over another iced tea. "My problems are the same as anybody else's. Saying that only another cop can understand you is a crutch that allows you to go out with the other guys after your shift, rather than home to your wife and family. After getting off at 11 p.m., a lot of guys don't want to go home, because the wife and kids are asleep. So, what do they do? They stop out with their six squad guys at the local watering hole. You came into this job knowing it was tough, that you were going to see people dying. If that bothers you, then you've chosen the wrong profession."

Still, it must be very difficult for a cop not to burn out from always seeing the worst aspects of life, from being around nut cases and prostitutes and drug addicts all day.

"We also see the best," argues Grant. "In this job, we can be up in the State House one day guarding the governor, or out talking to a farmer somewhere who's still plowing his field by hand. We get to talk with the most interesting people, like maybe a doctor who's been robbed. You're the first one at an accident scene. You get to decide whether to call the helicopter. In two or three minutes, you're making life and death decisions. It may sound like an everyday, normal routine; but, think about it, you've saved somebody's life. I'm not fabricating this, but after I've arrested people for drunk driving or drugs, I've had them call me up and thank me, telling me that that was the day they hit rock bottom, that they finally made the decision to go to AA, to turn their lives around. I have people thank me all the time for stopping them for speeding.

"In this job, you can't look at the narrow scope. You have to look at the broader picture. You can't focus on the negative. There's just too much positive."

"That second iced tea," says Jean, "it's on me."

It's a Quarter to Three . . .

"The witching hour has begun," says John "Zeke" Maziekien, meaning, if something's going to happen, now's the time. In these predawn hours on the Garden State Parkway, traffic is starting to pick up. All of the bars have closed, and the Atlantic City day-trippers, many fueled on alcohol and disappointment, are hellbent for home.

From 11 p.m. to 7 a.m., troopers must ride with partners. Zeke (Badge No. 3549) and driver Anthony Sempkowski (No. 4109) like it that way. "We keep each other awake and alert," says Zeke. Tonight,

28   Sempkowski's out to reel in some "high rollers"—his term for anyone going over 80 mph. "I'll show you where you can catch some," says Zeke, directing Sempkowski to a favorite "fishing hole," located under an overpass on the Parkway median. In the dark, with the lights off, the car is barely visible. A mere ghost.

For those who fancy video games, this is the best. Maziekien points the radar unit at the oncoming northbound headlights. As a likely candidate for a ticket approaches, Sempkowski and Zeke try to guess how fast the vehicle's going. As the radar beam locks in on a car, Zeke pushes the instrument's handheld clicker to get the precise reading. When a "78" appears, Sempkowski starts to head out, but decides otherwise. "We'll throw him back, wait for something bigger."

Whooosh! An "86" flies by almost immediately. Sempkowski peels out, netting a white Toyota sedan driven by a bespectacled yuppie.

"What's your rush?" asks Sempkowski, an ex-Marine.

"My wife has to go to the bathroom."

"Then why didn't you stop at the rest stop a couple of miles back?"

"I didn't see it."

"Of course not. You were going too fast."

(Troopers are rarely at a loss for words, having heard all the excuses. Having to go to the bathroom is the most popular.)

Heading north across the 180-foot high Driscoll Bridge, which spans the Raritan River, Zeke says, "I had a woman who was afraid to drive over it for fear of hyperventilating and passing out. She had 'bridge phobia.' So, I got out of my car and drove her car across. Of course, when I got to the other side, I realized I had a problem. *I* didn't have a car."   "This bridge is real popular for people who want to commit suicide," says Sempkowski, who knows whereof he speaks.

"I was out with one last year on Labor Day," he says. "I was with that guy for three or four hours. He was a Vietnam veteran. When I got there, he was sitting on the rail, threatening to jump. He told me, if I got near him, he'd do it. I really thought he was going to jump, too. At one point, he was holding on to the rail on the other side. I got queasy just looking down. I had to try and appease him. Out here, you wear a hat of many professions. He wanted to talk to another Vietnam vet, so I contacted the Veterans Association at the Woodbridge Police Department. They happened to have a veteran on hand, who came out to the bridge. After about ten minutes, he got the guy down. But what a mess. We had to completely stop the traffic. Cars were backed up for miles and miles and miles. Finally, we got orders from our troop commander to open up two or three lanes. People were furious. As they drove by the guy they were screaming, *'Jump you idiot! Jump!'* That didn't help the situation."

"I dread working up north at Christmas time, because that's the bridge-jumping season," says Zeke.

Part of a trooper's job on the Garden State is checking out the twenty-four-hour service areas where people can get fast food and gasoline. In one, there's a seventy-year-old man asleep in his car in the commuter lot. "He's there every night, all year round, no matter how bad the weather," says Sempkowski. "His wife won't let him sleep in the house anymore, so he drives out here, puts the recliner seat down, and doesn't leave until morning. It's a sin."

Not everyone at the service areas is after a cheeseburger and fries. Some are hungry for trouble, with all the trimmings. "At the Atlantic City service area, a Chinese gang was robbing men while they used the urinals," says Zeke. "Usually, though, women are the targets," says Sempkowski. "Thieves will wait for women to hang their purses on the hook in the stall. Then they'll reach over, grab her pocketbook, and run. So we suggested they take the hooks off the doors. Sometimes, if a woman is standing in the chow line at the food service area, the thieves will cut a hole in the bottom of her pocketbook so that all the stuff inside falls out, which they'll scoop up without anyone knowing about it. We had a gypsy crew working out here. They'd watch us, know when we'd pull out, wait ten minutes, and then make their hits. They were real good."

Four a.m. and all's not well: Sempkowski and Zeke pull alongside a battered Mercury Sable that's weaving across the lanes. Its three occupants seem nervous, fidgety. (In fact, the man in the backseat turns out to be a member of the Five Percenters, a black gang.) Sempkowski pulls them over.

"The whole thing with a motor vehicle stop is, they know who you are, but you don't know who they are," says Sempkowski before leaving the car. "You can never let your guard down. So you try to use anything you can to your benefit. When I ride at night and have a high-

30   risk stop like this, I usually do stupid things like reach over and open my passenger door and shut it. Or I'll get out, walk around the back of the troop car, and make my approach on the passenger side. The main thing is, Keep the element of surprise in your ballfield."

The driver of the car, who carries no license, gives his name as the person who's listed on the vehicle's registration. Sempkowski asks the driver his age, then his date of birth. As the man stumbles for answers, Sempkowski barks: *"I got a liar here!"*

"That's how I catch liars," says Sempkowski. "I always ask for a person's age and date of birth right up front. If I ask someone who's lying about who they are, they never get it right. Because they're thinking. They can't lie that fast. They start looking in the air, not in my eye, going, 'Uh . . .' After you catch 'em in a lie, you're one up on 'em." After a few minutes of Sempkowski's scrutiny, the man comes clean, giving his real name. Sempkowski issues him three tickets: for having a suspended license (hence not wanting to give his real name), failure to have a current vehicle inspection sticker, and not wearing a seat belt. Sempkowski's parting words: "I catch you out here again and you lie to me, I'm arresting you, taking you in. No get-out-of-jail-free card. Understand?" "Yes sir," says the driver.

Back on the road Sempkowski's suspicions are again raised. "I think we may have a DWI (driving while intoxicated) here," he says, pulling behind a red Jeep, trailing him in his blind spot. "He doesn't know what lane he wants to be in." "They call that white line fever," says Zeke, "doing a tightrope dance." Sempkowski turns on his overheads to pull the guy over. "Notice, he didn't use his turn signals," says Sempkowski. "Drunks rarely do." As Sempkowski pulls up behind the parked Jeep, the driver starts to get out. *"Stay in the car! Get back in!"* Sempkowski announces on his loudspeaker. "When a driver gets out of a car as we approach, it's an indication he's got something in there he doesn't want us to see," says Zeke.

Happy ending: The guy wasn't drunk, just tired, and, as far as Sempkowski and Zeke could tell, had nothing to hide.

But, speaking of drunks:

ZEKE: You know who are really nasty? Drunk women.
SEMPKOWSKI: They'll kick the windows out of the car.
ZEKE: They are the worst. I'd rather go in the ring with Tyson or

George Foreman, get my brains battered out in the fifth round, than pull over a drunk woman.

SEMPKOWSKI: They spit on you. Scratch you.

ZEKE: Man, you can't get a hold of them. It's like, they're bathed in Palmolive Gold. They're nutty.

SEMPKOWSKI: That's the bottom line. Nutty . . .

"We see a lot of weird things out here," says Sempkowski, cruising along. "Like the guy two years ago who threw himself in front of an Atlantic City–bound Leisure Line double-decker bus."

"Oh, yeah," says Zeke, "as the guy jumped out, he threw a coconut cream pie into the bus's windshield. We never did figure out what that was supposed to symbolize."

"We identified him through his dental records. There was nothing left," says Sempkowski. "It was as if he vaporized," says Zeke.

"Once, we got called to the Asbury toll plaza," says Sempkowski. "There were two guys well into their eighties going southbound. The man in the passenger seat was leaning on the driver. I asked the driver, What's up. He starts telling me that the other guy's his friend, that they even live together, but for the last ten or twelve miles, he hasn't been talking. I couldn't believe it. I mean, the guy was dead.

"One beautiful Sunday morning we got a call that there was a naked woman walking along the shoulder of the road past the Garden State Arts Center," says Sempkowski. "Sadly, she had been stabbed, raped, and beaten up, in imminent danger of losing her life. She was an Italian exchange student and didn't speak English. They put her in a car and got her to the hospital. A short time later, some guy jumps off the Driscoll Bridge. So they send me to investigate. The guy landed twenty yards from two fishermen, who pulled him out of the water and brought him back to the boat dock where I was waiting for the body. I thought for sure he was dead. But somehow he survived. I noticed his wrist was slashed, also. Turns out, he did the crime. He'd met the victim at the Arts Center the night before, sexually assaulted her, stabbed her with part of the guard rail, and left her for dead. He knew we were getting close to him, so he felt a little guilty. He's now doing twenty-five years.."

"I'll tell you a spooky night *I'll* never forget," says Sempkowski, as if launching into a Stephen King tale. "It was real foggy out. I was riding

32   with Trooper Kearny. There was this three-car accident with one fatality. The body was lying in the left lane. In the fog, two more cars came by and struck it. As we pulled up to the scene, we saw this Chinese guy with no legs hobbling about in circles, screaming. We thought he'd lost his legs in the wreck, but turns out, he was a double amputee who'd been knocked out of his limbs. He had long pants on and was dragging them through the gasoline. I told the other troopers, 'Whatever you do, don't light any flares, this guy's a human wick!' It was the eeriest sight, what with the fog and all. After we secured the accident scene, I was sent up to the service area to talk to a guy who thought he'd struck something in the road. Sure enough, I looked underneath the guy's car, and you could see the victim's brain matter. Then, under the frame, I saw a suit pocket from the body. That's all there was. I looked inside it, and there was the guy's wallet with three or four thousand dollars in cash inside. He was on his way back from Atlantic City."

Sempkowski and Zeke agree, by far the worst part of being a road trooper is dealing with the car wrecks.

"People do the dumbest things," says Zeke, "like changing tires in dark spots on the shoulder or on a curve. We had one old lady who decided to have a picnic on the grassy median. She was eating her sandwich in the backseat when she got rear-ended by a guy who fell asleep at the wheel. She went flying right through her windshield." "She was a done deal when I got there," says Sempkowski. "People think, just because they're off the road, they're safe," says Zeke.

"Accidents are a big part of the job. You have to be there," says Sempkowski. "You clean it up. Then you think, Jesus Christ, you're glad it wasn't you or a member of your family," says Zeke.

"My first fatal was an overwhelming experience because I got there first," says Zeke. "I was trying to comfort this seventeen-year-old girl who was coming back from her junior prom. She was all covered in blood. I was holding on to her, trying to calm her down. She was cognizant. We were having a conversation. I was guessing she'd be OK. When the first aid arrived, I went out to handle the traffic, to do flare lineup, and get the tow truck to start cleaning up. Afterwards, I went back over to ask how she was doing, and they said she was dead. It was like, how could she die?"

"I had a fatal on Christmas Eve," says Sempkowski. "Try telling some girl's parents that their daughter won't be making it for dinner

that night. Her parents were devastated. She'd just turned twenty-one. **33**
They came out and put a wreath at the accident site."

"I had this young kid who fell asleep at the wheel," says Zeke, "a weightlifter who was the size of me and Tony put together. He was so powerfully built that, upon impact, he broke the seat belt out of its stanchions. When I got there he was walking around, all bloodied up. I sat him down and told him he was going to make it. I said, 'You're a big guy, you'll get through this.' I figured he'd be bruised for a week or two, and that would be it. But he died. We all take life for granted. Out here you learn how fragile it is."

Silent Night

A fierce wind is blowing on this bitter-cold night. The red and green traffic lights suspended above the intersection leading into town sway ominously to and fro, reminiscent of the opening shot in the TV series, "Twin Peaks." Did anyone mention, this is Christmas Eve? "'Tis the season to be holy," says Trooper Jeff Algor, twenty-eight. "'Tis the season for domestic fights, drunks, and ten-finger discounts."

The Fort Dix Barracks sits smack dab in the center of a small, economically depressed burb that features seven bars within its two-block downtown radius.

There's a bar for everyone, almost: bikers, druggies, airmen from nearby McGuire Air Force Base, retired GI's; even a gay bar. Illusions, a neon-lit saloon, features go-go dancers.

"There's no glamour here," says Algor (Badge No. 4594). "A lot of people think this is a punishment station. The O.K. Corral. To me, that's not true. Working here is what being a trooper is all about."

Brown hair, steely blue eyes, chiseled jaw, and athletic body: Algor seems cut from the mold. "I love my job," he says. "I wanted to be a trooper since I was eighteen. Before being accepted, I was a local cop for three years at Spring Lake Heights. At the Academy, I was voted Class Recruit. If nothing else happens to me in life, that was enough."

Troopers assigned to Fort Dix are responsible for helping part-time police departments in and around Wrightstown keep the peace. "These areas have a high amount of welfare. It's a mixed population: whites, blacks, Thais. It's a Heinz 57 variety," says Algor.

34   "I attempted to serve this warrant earlier," he says, sitting in his car before heading out. "The guy's something else. We were called out to his place for a domestic in October. He was drunk and taking it out on his wife and girlfriend, who lives and sleeps with them. Real weird. He tried slugging me and Troopers Healey and Chevrier."

A scenic tour definitely is in order. First stop is a vacant lot behind a bar. "We usually catch somebody doing crack back here," Algor says. Cruising around to the front of the bar, he says, "Last night we saved a guy's life right here on the sidewalk. Fifteen gang members jumped him and stabbed him three times. I'm a hunter. I've never shot a deer that bled that much. The blood looked like it was coming out of a hose from the back of his neck. It was really something."

Next stop, the parking lot of a watering hole down the block. "We got a call the other night that there was a fight going on inside," says Algor. "So we raced right over. We hadn't even gotten out of our cars when the owner came out and told us to get lost, that we were hurting his business."

While driving past the Jamesway, which is chockablock with last-second Christmas shoppers, something catches Algor's eye—an overweight woman in jeans and a sweatshirt. "Is it?" he asks. "It is. It's Brenda Lee." Not the singer, but the town nuisance. "She's continually calling the station to complain about the troopers. One time, she must have called a hundred times. We told her, if she kept that up, we were going to lock her up for harrassment. Trouble is, you have to answer each one of her calls. You have to suck up your gut and go find out what's wrong. There's no call we don't answer . . .

"You should see the master index file we have on her three boys. They're always getting in trouble, but she always defends them, claiming they've done nothing wrong."

So, where's their father? "Don't know," says Algor. "I've never seen him around. But whoever it is, I'd like to buy him a beer. Anybody who could go with her must be really something. That may be the problem. He had a few too many brews . . ."

"Hey, there's Santa," says Algor, as he continues his rounds. Sure enough, a fire truck passes, sirens blaring. Hanging on the outside are not one, but six bearded Santa Clauses. All are waving and yelling, "Ho, ho, ho." Nobody seems to notice, or to care.

Heading out of town along an arrow-straight highway, Algor points out an infamous lounge, a combination dance hall and bar that's twice the size of a bowling alley. "It's a redneck landmark," the trooper says. "You don't want to come here on Friday or Saturday nights, believe me. I couldn't count the times I've been here rolling around the parking lot with people . . ."

"Here's Mrs. Brown's house," Algor says a few minutes later. Earlier that evening, the elderly widow had phoned the barracks to wish the troopers a happy holiday. "She's very lonely and calls us all the time. Usually she says people are stealing the shingles off her roof," Algor says. "Let's stop in and see if she's alright."

When he rings the doorbell, a dog barks. "Come in," says Mrs. Brown, who has a voice higher than Minnie Mouse's. So, where's her dog? "Right here," she says, flipping off a machine. "It cost me $50." Turning the volume way up, she says, "I can make it sound like a Saint Bernard."

Before he leaves, Mrs. Brown asks Trooper Algor for a goodbye hug and kiss. "I don't know," says Algor coyly. "My wife'll get jealous!"

"Ohhhhhhh," squeals Mrs. Brown.

Pulling over a speeder whose excuse is, "I got off late from the funeral parlor," Algor asks, "Do you believe in Santa?"

"Uh, yes," says the driver.

"Well," says Algor, "Santa's just paid you a visit." Instead of a ticket, he hands the driver a warning, and sends him on his way.

"At this intersection, about a month ago," says Algor, "we stopped a car that had a guy and girl inside. She was stark naked and doing a little act for her boyfriend. They'd come out of that bar over there. I guess she felt the moon biting her shoulder. Got all turned on."

Down a deserted stretch of Route 68, a car is being backed into a driveway of a darkened house. "What's this about?" Algor asks, illuminating his searchlight. A very friendly man and a woman get out of the vehicle and approach the squad car. Recognizing the driver, Algor shouts, "What are you up to, Jankowitz?" "We went to his mother's for Christmas Eve, but decided to come home early because of the strong winds," replies the man's wife. "Our swivel trees got blown around. We want to try and straighten 'em out." Unswiveled swivel trees?

"Another important thing you need to be a trooper," says Algor, driving off. "The gift of gab."

A call comes over the radio that a car has just hit a deer. Racing to

36 the accident scene, Algor finds an injured button buck standing alongside the road, frozen with fear. Just then, another squad car pulls up. Trooper Kevin Healey (Badge No. 3482) gets out, draws his gun, and shoots the animal twice in the head. "So, you finally managed to bag one, huh, bud?" asks Algor, explaining that Healey, who's been deer hunting with him all season, has had zero luck.

While Algor's pregnant wife and one-year-old son are spending Christmas Eve with her parents, he shares his holiday dinner with another trooper at the barracks. Over ziti and apple pie sent over by a local diner, Algor and Trooper Danny Ellington (Badge No. 4380) crack up laughing as they recall some of their favorite townsfolk. "I haven't seen Ten Cent Alice in a while," remarks Ellington. "She used to be called Fifty Cent Alice until her price dropped," notes Algor. "No one wants to arrest her," adds Ellington, "because then you have to touch her." Then there's Col. Clink, a retired Air Force officer who, in the dog days of summer, "goes around town wearing at least ten coats at a time"; The Mayor, "not the real mayor, but an old-timer who spends his days directing traffic"; and Sweetsie, a little old lady on East Main Street "who's always baking us pies and cakes."

On the road again:

"I prefer not to have a partner with me," says Algor, heading through town, again passing the fire truck with the waving Santas. "I'm a take-charge guy. I'm not a debate man. I don't like waiting around. I like to find out what the problem is and deal with it. I like to get the people who are screaming and yelling to behave rationally, like ladies and gentlemen . . . You know, people say we beat them up. Never once have I beaten anyone up. It's not my nature. I've had to wrestle people to the ground trying to restrain and cuff 'em. I do what I have to. But I'm not out to hurt anybody. My objective is to do my job and go home . . ."

"Constructive force," he says, turning on the car's interior lights and staring intently at its passenger. "Often, you don't have to do a thing if you look at somebody in the right way. You let 'em know you have full intention of doing whatever it is you're telling them. When you're arresting someone, you can't think, This guy's a lot bigger than me; do I have it in me? If you question yourself, you're done for. You can't show kindness. Kindness is taken as a sign of weakness. People mistake that. You are there to do exactly what the law states. If you show compassion, all of a sudden it's, Here comes the wussy trooper. He's the one who likes to talk to me, who's scared of me."

Spinning his troop car around, Algor decides to stop an oncoming Mercedes 400 for speeding. Before Algor can even turn on his over-heads, the driver pulls over to the shoulder and gets out of his vehicle. He's wearing a fur-trimmed bomber jacket. "Stay inside," Algor announces on his loudspeaker. "People of higher economic status always have to feel they are in charge of whatever situation they are in," Algor says. "Look at his attitude. He gets out of the car like, I'm above this trivial stuff. It's like a bother. I pulled over a well-to-do old lady once who actually said, 'You are nothing but a stupid, menial ser-vant.' I said, 'Really? OK, I'll tell you what. This stupid, menial servant would like an increase in his pay. Could you work on that? Because I don't earn enough to listen to your crap.'"

Since the gas pump at the Fort Dix Barracks is out of commission, Algor pulls into a commercial station. The stringy-haired attendant looks like Cousin It from *The Addams Family*. "Hauled him in once for molestation," says Algor offhandedly. Stopping by the local 7-Eleven for takeout coffee, the trooper asks the cashier if she's been a good girl this year. "Oh, I have," she says, leaning over a rack of candy-flavored condoms. "But my sister's been naughty. And I mean, *very, very* naughty." This is some town, alright.

"Here's where I chased a guy through the woods for three quarters of a mile," says Algor out on the highway. Chasing suspects seems to be a big sport around here. "It is," says Algor. "They feel you're some slow, dumb trooper who doesn't know how to do anything. This is not a brag; it's the truth: anybody I've ever run after, I've caught. I'll run from here to eternity until I catch 'em. I've gone through sticker bush-es, through swamps. They say, 'He's not going through the water,' then, 'Oh shit, he *is* going through the water!' I just keep coming. I usually go into the woods growling and barking. That way, they think I've got a dog with me. To me, this is a game. It's a game I'm not going to lose. And if I don't get you, somebody else will. With all of our equipment, we're going to win."

From killing injured deer to "the time I saved a lady from a bat with a tennis racquet," how is a young trooper ever prepared for the demands of the job? "We have a trooper-coach program," says Algor. "After graduating from the Academy, you're assigned to a road station

38 where you get your feet wet doing all aspects of general police work. You're given an experienced trooper to patrol with. For the first month, he does all the driving. The second month, you take the wheel and get the calls over the radio. If you don't know where you're going, you get out a map and start learning the area. During that two-month period, you do everything around the barracks, including washing dishes. They still play the Academy game with you.

"When I was a local cop my patrolman-coach experience was very different. I remember my first time out. The older patrolman threw me the keys to the car and said, 'Don't hit nothing. Don't kill nobody.'"

Like all other troopers, Algor will tell you the best preparation for the job is experience. "It's the real teacher. And, as experiences go, I've had some doozies over the last five years."

Such as: "I once found this five-hundred-pound lady lying dead on her kitchen floor in the middle of August. She'd been there a while, and her legs were being eaten away by maggots. I've seen some horrible car accidents, too. I remember this guy lying in the street with no face. As his car went around a corner, the wheels caught the curb and blew out, causing him to be pulled out of the vehicle. He went face-first into a tree. His brains were everywhere. The next day, I went back, and there were birds eating what was left."

Does one ever get used to such sights? "Seeing dead bodies and maggots and stuff like that? You just do it. You just do it. You don't think about it. You just handle it. One way we deal with what we see is with a black sense of humor. Like that five-hundred-pound dead lady. I was the senior trooper there. Some of the junior guys were getting their first sniff of a corpse that had been around a few days. The TV was on. The refrigerator door was open. I stood there saying, 'I guess she had a Big Mac attack.' There was a cat in the apartment. So I joked, 'Maybe the cat's got her tongue.' The junior guys are looking at me like, You're messed up, bud. Maybe it sounded insensitive to them, but sometimes you have to use black humor to keep an unpleasant situation from getting to you. You have to blow it off like that."

As a policeman one isn't exactly mingling with the *crème de la crème*. "True, in our jobs we have to deal with a lot of scumbags," Algor says. "They come in all shapes, sizes, and colors. But, once in a while, something we do does have a happy ending. I went to arrest this black guy who had shoplifted a bottle of vodka. He had a room in a welfare hotel. When I got inside, I found out he was a Grenada vet who'd gotten shot over there. He was drunk and had a serious drinking problem. When I found out he was dying of bone cancer, I got a number of a VA hospital in Philly. I then called the VFW in Cookstown, who agreed to give him a ride there. He dried out, and his cancer's in remission. He's called me several times to say, 'Trooper, thank you, thank you.' I told him, 'Don't thank me. You're the one who did it.' Once in a while, you see something wonderful come out of all this misery and B.S."

Good can prevail.

Like tonight. "I can't believe it's so quiet," says Algor as his shift nears its completion. For whatever reason, Christmas Eve proves to be the calmest night of the year at Fort Dix. There are no shoplifters or car thieves to book, no drug arrests, no drunken drivers or domestic battles to break up. Even Brenda Lee hasn't called. For the first time that anyone at the barracks can remember, all is calm and all is bright. It's a miracle. Says Algor: "I guess everyone's at home on their knees tonight, praying, *Please God, don't let the troopers catch me!*"

3 / A Trooper Is a Trooper

A New Outfit

Beginning in the 1960s, law enforcement had to do some major rethinking as minorities and women sought employment in a field that had traditionally been white male and heavy on the macho. In the fall of 1961, three years before Congress passed the Civil Rights Act, the first black graduated from the Academy. In January 1975, three years after the federal Equal Employment Law, the first woman walked across the stage to receive her badge. Presently, 14.5 percent of the Outfit is non–white male, which breaks down to 8.3 percent black, 4.7 Hispanic, .9 Asian, .6 American Indian and 2.4 female.

"When I came aboard in 1967, black troopers were still a novelty," says Lt. Isiah Cherry (Badge No. 2234) of Internal Affairs. "I was first assigned to road patrol at the Hightstown Barracks in central Jersey. I

41

remember pulling over a truck on a back road that had a cracked windshield with a red sticker taped to it, meaning the vehicle had not passed inspection. I issued the guy a summons for the windshield, letting him go on the sticker. Later that day, I was called by my commander, who said the guy stopped by the station to complain that a black trooper had pulled him over. The commander had me issue him the other ticket . . . Not only was I a novelty to the public, but to the other troopers as well. By my example, I tried to show them that people are people. There were incidents, but minor ones. Like the time a trooper brought his kid to the station, who said, 'Daddy, there goes a nigger.' 'Yeah,' said his father, 'but a good one.' But that was it. My experiences have always been, a trooper is a trooper."

From February 13 to June 27, 1980, an experiment took place that has never been repeated by the New Jersey State Police, or any other State Police, for that matter. This was the infamous Ninety-sixth, a class of women recruits only. "It was hard enough getting through the training—" recalls Sgt. Gail Cameron (Badge No. 3482), "—try having all those news cameras following you around while you exercise, study, eat." Out of 116 recruits, 30 graduated, including Sgt. Lori Hennon (Badge No. 3493). "Believe me," she says, "we worked as hard as the men. I say that because that class still has a stigma, as if modifications were made for us. Because of that, I'm not so sure an all-female class should be held again."

Thanks to the women of the Ninety-sixth, female troopers can wear their caps with the best of 'em. "At the end of our training, the Outfit decided to come up with a different style for us," says Hennon. "It resembled a pot without a handle, small-brimmed, about four or five inches high. They asked us our opinion. All thirty of us said, No! We didn't want to be singled out on the road. Besides, having the trooper cap was very important to us. It houses your badge."

Although today's public doesn't think twice about seeing a nonwhite trooper, a woman in uniform "still gets stares," says Hennon. "At the 113th class graduation, I was in full uniform. I heard somebody who got a close look at me whisper, 'Gee, it's a girl!'"

Quiet and thoughtful, Trooper Guy Packwood (Badge No. 4560) joined the State Police in 1987. "I understand that racism is all across society, and I'm sure I've come across a few troopers who may or may not have been bigots," he says, pulling out of the Perryville Station in

In 1961, Paul D. McLemore (Badge No. 1719) becomes the first black trooper.

No preferential treatment was given to the women of the experimental Ninety-sixth class, who had to box, wrestle, even rappel out of a helicopter, to earn their badges.

Recruits (l to r) Arlene Olcheski, Beverly Hillman, and Nancy Potter make State Police history as they graduate from the Academy.

46   his troop car, and onto Interstate 78, which cuts horizontally across New Jersey. "All I can deal with is how they've dealt with me as a person. So far, I've had no direct bouts with racism in the State Police. I think being a trooper has a lot to do with it. Every trooper looks at another trooper as a trooper, whether you like him or not. There are guys I work with who I don't personally like. But if it comes down to a problem on the road, I'll run out of the station in my shorts to back him up."

Probably the most controversial and misunderstood hiring practice was affirmative action, which was in effect from 1975 until 1992, when Col. Dintino was able to prove to the U.S. Justice Department that the State Police had met federal integration standards. "I can't say if the practice is right or wrong," says Packwood. "When I went in the Academy, one third of the class had to be minorities. If that's what they had to do to get people in the Academy, then so be it. If the recruiters hadn't come to my church, I don't think I would have known about the test. Once you're in the Academy, there's no preferential treatment. The standards are the same. Anyone can be dismissed, regardless of race." Responding to a veteran black trooper's charges that younger blacks were given a break on their written tests and are therefore below standard, Packwood is cool. "OK. That's his opinion," he says firmly. "I've always been a good student, so there was never a problem of me passing *any* test."

The reason Packwood decided to become a trooper, he says, is, "I just believe in right and wrong. My mother works for Continental Airlines, in sales, and my father's an electrician for General Motors. I have two sisters, and an older brother, Scott, who's a trooper. My parents instilled good values in us. I'd never do anything to embarrass my family. My grandmother is eighty-something. Her birthday's one day before mine, so we always celebrate them together. She's always telling me about the days when everything cost five cents. She loved seeing my name in the paper when I was playing football. But, graduating from the Academy—that was something really big for her. She came down and saw me get my badge. It was such a big deal for her. The idea of putting any kind of embarrassment on my family; that would be worse than anything for me . . ."

"Some people in life just get turned awry," says Packwood, reflecting on his previous statement. "Like this cousin of mine: we grew up together. We were never apart, from the age of eight on. We played ball together in high school. He was an *A* student. You name a college, and he could have written his ticket there. But we took different routes, for whatever reasons. He chose to get into drugs. I mean, he totally screwed up his life. I loved him like a brother. I tried to help him. But he wound up going to jail for armed robbery. Last year, I was in my troop car, and I passed him on the street. He was wearing one of those monitoring bracelets. I didn't stop. I just kept driving, saddened at how different we'd become."

"Address Me As Trooper"

Trooper Joann Flaherty (Badge No. 4153) patrols much of the same area as Packwood. Via Interstate 78, New York City is about an hour and a half drive from the station, a distance Flaherty measures in sweat and determination. Five years ago, she was a secretary for Shearson Lehman Brothers, going nowhere except to and from work on the Erie Lackawanna. "The men at work were *sooooo* condescending," she says, sitting behind the wheel of her troop car. "Secretaries were garbage to them. I come from a blue collar family, from Harrison, not a real nice town, by Newark. I didn't like the attitude on Wall Street. It's a class system, all the secretaries clawing at each other to see who can work for the top guy, and all the guys clawing at each other to see who's going to be the top guy. I was never going to get beyond what I was."

When a friend told Flaherty she was going to take the exam to be a trooper, Flaherty thought, why not take it, too?

It's a decision that completely changed her life, one she never regretted . . . or did she? "Nope . . .Well . . . Maybe the first two weeks in the Academy I thought, What did I get myself into? My hair was cut real short and I wore khakis like everybody else. So much for my vanity. As a woman, you're used to having guys open doors for you. Forget it. At the Academy I had to do everything the men did. Everything. I got in a lot of fights growing up, but nothing like in the Academy. I got punched so hard in the face by the other men during combat training that I actually saw stars. I was in the 103rd class. Out of thirty

48 or thirty-five women who started, only five finished, which is actually a large number. Sometimes it's none. To be honest, I don't recommend the Outfit for most women. It's tough work."

The most difficult thing about being a woman cop, Flaherty says, is that "you have to do twice as much to be considered half as good. If a guy does something wrong—hey, everybody makes mistakes. But if a woman does something wrong, it's because she's a woman." For that reason, Flaherty goes the extra mile, lifting weights several hours a day. "It's a man's world to begin with. Just more so, on this job. But I knew that coming into it. It's a good job. And there's no pay discrimination. I make the same amount as a guy doing the same work."

As for the argument that women aren't physically as strong as men, constructive force comes into play. "One time, I arrested this drunk driver," says Flaherty. "He was a big guy. I got one cuff on him when he realized what was happening and decided maybe he didn't want to be arrested and started resisting me. I just talked to him. I told him to relax, that you'll be in and out in a half hour. He listened to me. I find you win more fights with brain than brawn. I don't think there are too many people I've arrested that I really could have beaten up if I had to with my bare hands. But they've all thought they would lose if they tried. I once told a guy that if he didn't put his hands behind his back, I was going to get on the radio, and there'd be ten troopers here to kick his butt. Truth is, I didn't have a backup. But if you make them believe it by the way you say it, then, they'll listen to you. Just make them believe it. I don't care if you're six foot four, 250 pounds of solid muscle. There's always somebody bigger and badder than you are. You're always going to meet your match. That's why you have to use your brains."

Mention the phrase "woman trooper," and people think linebacker, Steelers. Better think again, as Flaherty is a beautiful young woman. "Sometimes I get compliments on the road," she admits. "One time, I was driving Interstate 78 in the left lane. There was a truck in the right lane. The driver started looking at me. I mean, flirting with me. I couldn't believe it. I was in a marked car, just like I am now. I was thinking, Who does this guy think he is? So, what do I notice? He doesn't have a New Jersey tax stamp on his truck. So I say, well, I've got a reason to stop him. So I pulled him over. He says to me, 'Hey, baby,' and starts giving me all of this attitude. I guess he thought I was interested in him. Well, I set him straight. I said, '*You address me as Trooper.*' I did a whole inspection of his truck. Besides giving him a tax stamp ticket, I gave him one for having a light out. He wasn't very happy. The message here is, don't flirt with the police.

"Sometimes, when I pull people over, they'll ask, 'What's the problem, honey?' Old ladies will do that. I don't think they mean to be disrespectful, but I always correct them. I tell them, 'It's *Trooper.*' The thing is, when you're on a stop, you have to immediately establish who's in charge. Once you let the other person be in charge, things get crazy. The moment I stop a car I say, 'Sir, I'm Trooper Flaherty.' I'm always polite about it."

The social life of a woman trooper isn't so easy, either. Flaherty's marriage to another trooper ended in a roadblock. "I didn't have a lot of time to spend at home," she says. "If you meet a man and tell him you're a state trooper, some get really intimidated by that. They ask, 'Did you ever arrest anybody? Do you carry a gun?' I say, 'Yes. Yes.' A lot of guys always wanted to be cops. Men want to have all of the authority in a relationship. Yes, I'm a trooper, but I'm not one when I'm off duty. Still, a lot of guys I meet feel intimidated. If I get married again, it won't be to a cop. I'd want a man who is more successful than I am, one who makes more money than me, so he won't be intimidated."

And as for her male trooper coworkers, "I know there are guys on the force who are chauvinists. I've had guys coming up to my face, saying, women shouldn't be on this job. But I know, if I called them and said I needed help, they would do anything to get there, anything to help me out. People don't do that in other jobs. In New York, it was nonstop backstabbing. At my station, we're always kidding each other. That never happened on Wall Street. Like Sgt. Kineran, he's always on my back. There isn't a day that he isn't trying to bust my chops. But I know it's in good fun. If you do something wrong here, you're never going to live it down. You better have thick skin to be on this job. If people know they're getting to you, they keep it up. The guys in my squad are always trying to embarrass me. But I give it right back. One thing I've learned from this job is that men gossip worse than women. They're always going on about their wives, their girlfriends, their sergeants, you name it."

Heading into the parking lot of the station, Flaherty receives a call

50   on her radio. Another trooper has requested backup on a domestic. The calm of the day is suddenly broken as Flaherty peels out, siren screaming. Over narrow, winding country roads—past stone farmhouses and barns, through Norman Rockwell–looking towns—she flies, hitting speeds in excess of 100 mph. She sits bolt upright in her seat; one hand grips the steering wheel, the other, her intercom mike. "Pull over! Out of the way!" she bellows. It's a performance worthy of the Indianapolis 500.

Flaherty, you're good. Really good.

"I know."

4 Taken by Surprise

The First Move

You can stop a thousand cars and nothing happens," says Trooper David Acevedo (Badge No. 4758). "But it's that one thousand and first car that'll give you trouble." While patrolling Interstate 78, Acevedo met Number 1,001: he was attacked by the vehicle's two passengers. All troopers will tell you that what makes their job so difficult, and what the public doesn't always understand, is that they—not the criminal they're stopping—have the disadvantage. "If they're going to take you down," says Acevedo, "maybe they've already planned it out. I think the guys I stopped made that decision while I was pulling them over. As a trooper, you're always in the position of having to defend yourself, because you can't initiate anything. Because I have reasonable suspicions that someone's up to no good, I can't

52 pull my gun out and point it at him. You can't treat people that way."

For Trooper John Jacobs (Badge No. 2659), Number 1,001 meant a bullet through the eye, shot by a member of an outlaw South Jersey motorcycle gang. "The difficulty of being a cop is that you have to wait until somebody else makes the first move," he says. "They know what you're going to do. The guy I was patting down knew as he was turning around that he was going to shoot me. By the time they act, nine times of out ten, it's too late for you to do anything. After pulling him over, I had no reason to hold him at gunpoint just because he looked suspicious. He wasn't under arrest." For Trooper Anthony DiSalvatore, Number 1,001 was drug runners who pumped six bullets into him on the Turnpike. DiSalvatore, who was twenty-five at the time, has the dubious distinction of having taken more bullets than any other New Jersey State Trooper, and lived. For his courage and control under extreme pressure, DiSalvatore was awarded the State Police's highest honor, the Distinguished Service Medal. It was handed to him by Gov. James Florio.

"Looking back," says DiSalvatore, who's still recovering, "I figure, from the moment I stopped those guys on the Pike, they planned to take me out if I gave them more than a ticket. They were part of a posse running drugs down to the Washington, D.C., area. The guy who shot me had just turned eighteen. He had already tried to kill a cab driver and another drug dealer. He had escaped from a detention center in Maryland. No way, did he want to go back to prison."

After finally managing to stop a motorist who would not pull over, Trooper Greg Coffin (Badge No. 4510) approached the seemingly unconscious driver with his gun drawn. "Whether he was unconscious or playing possum, I'll never know," says Coffin. Suddenly, Number 1,001 grabbed the trooper's weapon and pointed it at him. "We go through this extensive training of never letting anyone take your gun," he says. "It was the queerest feeling I've ever had. Suddenly, everything went into slow motion. Wait a minute, I thought. Nobody is supposed to touch my gun. I'll be damned if I'll let him have it! If he does, I'm a dead man. He's got the number-one thing on my uniform. While I was struggling to hold on to it, I felt as if I were being touched in the wrong way, as if I were being violated in a sexual manner."

In the ensuing struggle, Coffin managed to have his left pinky shot off. Sitting in his living room, recuperating, he finds the emotional scars take the longest to heal. "For a long time afterwards I had nightmares," he says. "I'd wake up with the sweats, screaming. Usually it involved a chase. I'd fire my gun and the bullets would travel through the air in slow motion, allowing the guy to get away. People can't say the word 'shooting' to me. They'll call it 'the incident,' or 'the accident,' or 'your injury.' The biggest bridge for me to cross was to say the phrase, 'I've been shot.' I guess, because it makes me sound like a statistic; or that I wasn't as good a trooper as I thought I was. You're never supposed to take the hit. From your Academy days, you're taught to be in control at all times. But how do you always know when it's out of control? I mean, some guy just jumps on your gun. I did nothing to provoke this."

Was it dumb luck or answered prayers that saved Acevedo's, Jacobs's, DiSalvatore's, and Coffin's lives? Neither; though that isn't to say that these didn't play a part. It was their Academy training that they fell back on. For example, if an ordinary citizen is attacked at gunpoint, he or she often will have great difficulty comprehending what happened. Witnesses often give wildly varying accounts of who and what they saw. But notice, in the following stories involving Acevedo, Jacobs, and DiSalvatore, all of them can vividly recall every detail of what went on during their ordeals. It was their ability to remain in charge after being taken by surprise that carried them through.

"How Did I Let This Happen?"

"I was sitting on the median of I-78 two miles from the Pennsylvania border when my radar clocked a Pontiac Firebird heading west in the left lane at 68 mph," says David Acevedo. "It was close to 10 p.m., so I only had an hour left on my shift. I figured, one more for the road. I'd issue him my last summons of the day, then head on in. I pulled out, got behind the car, activated my overhead lights, and pulled the driver over onto the shoulder, near Milepost Two.

"There were two people in the car. I asked the driver, a heavyset, bearded Hispanic in his mid-thirties, for his credentials. He produced a

54 Missouri DL with the name Alfonso Herrerra on it. He said he couldn't find the registration. He did have the title, but the spelling of his last name was different than it was on his DL. I wanted to ask him some questions, so I had him exit the vehicle. I took him to the back of the car, between his car and mine.

"*'Where are you coming from?'* 'New York.' *'Where in New York?'* 'I don't remember.' *'Where you going?'* 'Harrisburg.' *'Who's the passenger?'* 'Uh, Nelson, a good friend of mine.' *'What's his last name?'* 'I don't know.' *'You don't know???'*

"When I get answers like that, my mind starts to go. I've heard scenarios like this before, where the driver doesn't know who he's traveling with. Usually, something's wrong. I told the driver to stay between the cars. I approached the passenger, who was also Hispanic and in his mid-thirties. I asked for some ID. He produced a Missouri DL with the name Nelson Gonzalez on it. He had the same address as Herrerra's. I told him to step out of the vehicle. That way, I could observe him better. When you get somebody out of a car, you can see if there are any bulges in their clothing, if they're concealing a weapon. I had him stand in front of the car. I was facing him, so I could still observe Herrerra. I asked, 'Where ya going?' He said, 'I don't understand English very well.' I said, 'No problem, I speak a little Spanish.' Actually, I speak it very well. But I didn't want him to know that. I didn't want him to know I could understand everything he was saying.

"I asked him who the driver was, and he gave me some off-the-wall name. Since I had conflicting stories, I decided to present Herrerra with a consent to search form, in order to go through his car. I got on my radio and contacted a fellow trooper, John Fortunato, to come back me up. He said he would, but it would take ten or fifteen minutes to get there. Meanwhile, I asked Herrerra to step to the back of my car, where I presented him with the form, in Spanish. After I got through reading it to him from my clipboard, he said he didn't understand it. He wanted his buddy to come back and explain it to him. From my training, I wasn't going to have two strangers next to me. I had to keep them separated. So I told Herrerra to step to the front of my troop car. I then called Gonzalez to come to the back. As I'm reading the form to him, he's saying, 'I don't know. I don't know.'

"With that, Herrerra, who was between the two cars, raises his hands and starts in screaming, 'I'll sign it! I'll sign it!' He starts walking towards me. 'Stay up there!' I yelled, 'Don't come here!' He was hooting and hollering, making a big commotion.

"While my attention was on him, Gonzalez suddenly grabbed me from behind in a bear hug. At that point, everything went into slow motion. I remember saying to myself, How did I get into this position? How did I let this happen? Now I could see Herrerra running towards me with his hands out, going for my throat. As he grabbed my neck, I managed to sidestep. Gonzalez was still on me. Now we're starting to fall. As we're falling, I can feel Gonzalez's hand on my gun. All I could think of was, Don't let him get it. So I put my hand straight down, putting a death grip on my gun. I knew if he got it he'd kill me.

"We fell onto the grassy embankment. Gonzalez was still trying to get my gun. Herrerra was still on top of me, choking me. It had rained that day. It was a dark, cloudy night. All the illumination was in front of my troop car. Back here, there was no light. I could see cars going by, and wondered why no one was stopping. But I doubt anybody could see us. Where's my backup? I kept thinking, I gotta get home to my wife, Wendy, and our four-week-old kid. I've got to get on top of this situation. I've got to regain control. I can't give up. All of this was going on in my head, but time seemed to move very slowly. Those ten to fifteen seconds seemed like forever. I remembered that constable in Texas who was videotaped being shot to death with his own weapon. I knew I had to really fight now. I was in the Marine Corps for four years. Like the Academy, they teach you never to give up. Once you do, it's all over.

"With all my strength, I managed to turn my body slightly, which enabled me to pull my gun out of the holster. Now I'm thinking, I just want them off me. I want them to know I'm in control now. While still on the ground, I aimed my gun upwards, keeping my arm real close to my body. You don't want to extend your arm, because you open yourself up to be grabbed. I never wanted to shoot anybody, but I knew it was them or me. I shot from the hip, in the direction of Herrerra. I continued to roll my body, and fired off a second shot. As soon as I fired it, Herrerra fell. He lay there moaning, 'I've been hit. I've been hit.' As I started getting up off the ground, I noticed Gonzalez running towards his car. I bore down and yelled, 'Get down! Get down! And stay down!' He did. I ran up to my car, reached in, and pushed the emergency button on the radio. Then I took cover.

Emergency squad personnel attend Alfonso Herrerra, who was shot after attacking Trooper David Acevedo.

Backup Troopers Dave Dalrymple (left) and Robert Francis (right) lead the injured, grimmacing Nelson Gonzalez away in cuffs. (Photos by ED KOSKEY, JR., for The Morning Call, Allentown, Pa.)

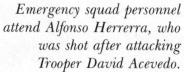

"A backup car from Perryville arrived with two troopers, who cuffed Herrerra and Gonzalez. As they led Gonzalez away, I noticed he was limping and bleeding. Turns out it wasn't Herrerra who got hit by the second bullet, as I thought, but Gonzalez. The bullet went through the back of Gonzalez's leg and lodged in his kneecap. Herrerra got hit by the first bullet, which I thought hadn't hit anyone. It went through his left upper buttock and exited his right lower abdomen. Both underwent surgery that night, and recovered.

"When the guys from Major Crimes showed up at the scene to investigate the incident, they noticed that I didn't have another round in the chamber of my gun, an H&K 9-mm. I think it was because, when I fired the second shot, I was holding the gun so close to my side that the slide wasn't able to go back all the way and eject the cartridge. Had I needed that third round, it wouldn't have been there. Later, when Herrerra's car was searched, they found a pound of cocaine inside. Turns out, he was wanted in Seattle for robbery. Gonzalez had just gotten out of federal prison, having done ten years for attempted hijacking. He was caught getting on a plane with a bomb. He had come over from Cuba in 1980 as a boat person.

"What I learned from all this was to go slower on the job. I'm an aggressive trooper. I like going out there, making arrests, looking for drugs. I really enjoy that. That's my cup of tea. But I've learned now that I have to slow down. Last week, I made another arrest with the same scenario. I pulled over a speeding car at almost the same time of night, in almost the same spot, with two Hispanics inside who were running drugs. Again, they had conflicting stories. This time, though, I waited for backup to arrive before I presented them with the consent to search form. See, when you're trying to explain to someone why you want to search their car for contraband or weapons, you have to stand close to them. You can't be far away. It's at that moment, I've learned, you're vulnerable. It was while I was explaining the search warrant to Gonzalez that he and Herrerra made their move.

"I was up all night doing reports. When I got home the next day, I had big red marks on my neck from being choked. Every bone in my body ached from the stress of my resistance. I'm a strong guy. I work out. I pound ground. I believe in keeping fit. If I didn't, I couldn't have fought those two guys off me. I'd be dead."

58 "Then I Felt the Impact"

"I was patrolling Route 42, which is the North South Freeway, by myself," says John Jacobs. "In the early eighties, we didn't always have partners at night. I was going northbound. About 1:45 a.m., I clocked a Cadillac sedan in the passing direction going 82 mph. Trailing the vehicle were two motorcycles going the same speed. I turned around and started to follow them. When I got within pacing distance, the motorcycles took the next exit and disappeared. I caught up to the white Cadillac and pulled it over. I then called in the stop, advising the station. I proceeded up to the driver, who was by himself. He was a white guy with long hair and a ruddy complexion. I asked for his license and registration, which he was unable to produce.

"He looked a little suspicious, and was extremely nervous. I asked him to step from the vehicle. I thought I would pat him down, make sure he wasn't carrying a weapon. He was wearing a leather motorcycle jacket, a white T-shirt, and jeans. He appeared to be in his mid-thirties. I had him step to the rear of the car, between our cars. I had him place his hands on the trunk, in spread-eagle position. He was illuminated by my headlights. As I was patting him down, I felt a bulge in the left side pocket of his coat. I stuck my hand in and pulled out a penknife. I took a step back and put it in my pocket. Just then, he started to turn around. I thought he was going to say he used the knife for hunting or fishing. That's the usual response when you find a knife on someone. So I was waiting for him to make a comment like that.

"It all happened so quickly. As he was turning to his left, I could see the flash of a muzzle. Then I felt the impact. He had a Charter .38 special on him. It was in the front of his jeans, I guess. When I was searching him, he put it in his palm. The bullet went in below my left eye and hit the vertebrae in the back of my neck. The impact knocked me to the ground. The type of holsters we had then had snaps on them. In the position I was in, I couldn't get the gun out, a Ruger revolver. As I was laying there on the ground, I could see him standing over me. He was shooting, but missing. I kept waiting for a bullet to hit me.

"I managed to get myself up and run across the highway to the grass median. As I was running, I was able to get my weapon out. When I got to the median, I turned around and returned fire. It was then I found out one of his rounds had struck me in the finger, which was part of the reason I had such trouble getting the gun out. At this point, I realized there was blood squirting from my face. I kept thinking, I better get him before I pass out. While I was shooting, he got in his vehicle and took off. It came out at the trial that he apparently had a bunch of dope in the car. Ten minutes after he left the scene, he torched the car to destroy the evidence and the fingerprints.

"I went to my vehicle and lay down on the front seat, hoping to feel better. But I had to sit up to clear the blood out of my mouth and lungs. I draped myself over the steering wheel and called in on the radio. I then unloosened my gunbelt and blouse. I thought for sure I was going to die: at any second, a light switch was going to click off. I thought about my wife and three girls, what they would think when they got the news I was dead. I knew I had to stay awake until the ambulance arrived. I didn't want to die. Not then, not there.

"They rushed me to Cooper Medical Center. They didn't want to operate right away, due to the location of the bullet. It was lodged between the two main arteries that led from the heart up to the brain. The doctors thought that if they hit an artery, I could be paralyzed. But after six or seven days, they decided it would be best to remove it. They were afraid, if someone slapped me on the back of the neck, the bullet might dislodge, doing terrible damage. The operation was a success, though I did lose the sight in my eye.

"When I returned to work they sent me to ballistics. I would have gone back on the road, but my wife made me promise her I wouldn't. At first I had a lot of anger about what happened. This sounds funny, but the anger was at myself, because he got me and I didn't get him. I thought about it a lot. If only I'd felt the gun first, it never would have happened. But I'm not angry anymore. There's nothing you can do about it. You can't change it."

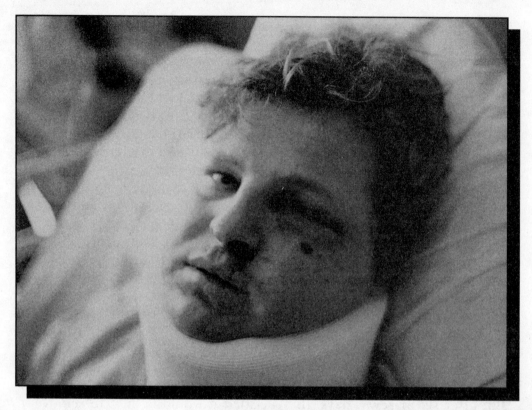

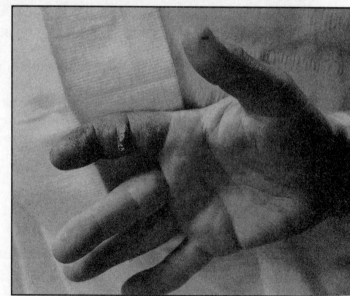

Trooper John Jacobs recovers from a shoot-out with a motorcycle gang member. Jacobs took bullets through the finger and eye.

"Up Until Then, I Was Having a Bad Day"

"When I arrived at the barracks, the temperature was in the nineties and very humid," says Anthony DiSalvatore. "I remember seeing a trooper who had just completed his shift. The sleeves and collar of his blouse were discolored from sweat and dirt. It was so hot, I was thinking about not wearing my vest. Even though wearing them is SOP, a lot of guys don't. But I remembered another trooper who was shot to death on the Turnpike. He always wore his. But on that day, he left it at home to be washed. So I put mine on.

"I wasn't out on patrol very long when I saw a maroon-colored car fly by me in the opposite direction with three black occupants. I noticed it was a rental car by the license plate. I went to the U-turn, swung around, and caught up with the driver. I was going 75 mph, trying to pace him. He was still pulling away. I put the overheads on. After a mile and a half, the vehicle finally pulled over to the shoulder of the road. I called in the stop, approached the vehicle, and asked the driver for license, registration, and rental agreement, which he couldn't produce. 'Why'd you stop me?' he asked. I was sizing up the driver and the occupants. One guy in the backseat was pretending to be asleep. If they all got out of the car, it looked as if I could handle them. I knew I had something. You just know. It's not uncommon on the Pike to lock up three, four people by yourself. By the driver's nervous demeanor and conflicting statements from the other passengers as to who rented the vehicle, I felt it was likely to have been stolen.

"'You stopped me for speeding?'" the driver asked. 'Yes,' I said. 'How fast did you get me?' 'Seventy-five.' 'That's about right. You can give me a ticket.' I thought, I'll decide what I'm going to do here. I asked him to give me his keys and step from the car. I wanted to get us on the shoulder, off the hazardous portion of the roadway. I didn't want to get run over by a tractor-trailer. I don't like standing out there, because a lot of times the truckers try to see how close they can get to you, to see if they can knock your hat off. I've had that happen a couple of times, and it can be dangerous.

"So I questioned the driver as to his origin and destination. I patted him down real quick to make sure he didn't have any weapons. We were standing on the right side of his car, on the grass. I didn't want

62   us to stand between the cars, because if someone were to run into the back of mine, we could be killed. After questioning him, I talked to the passengers. Their stories conflicted. Due to the driver's nervousness, conflicting statements, and inability to provide a rental agreement, I asked him if he'd sign a consent to search form. He said he would, so we stepped back into my troop car, where I explained it to him. The driver has the right to refuse to sign the form, which states that he can stop the search at any time, and that he wasn't coerced into signing it. I think it's safer to do these things in the car, where it's quieter, and you have quick access to the radio.

"When I asked if he would consent to the search, he said, 'Yeah, yeah, I'll sign.' He started to sign one name—his real name—then scribbled it out and signed a bogus one. When he was through, he said, 'C'mon, let's search the car.' I advised him I had some things to do first. While I was radioing in that I was OK on the stop, he kept pulling the door handle, trying to get out, saying over and over, 'C'mon, you gonna search the car, or what?'"

"I told him he could get out of the car now. As we approached his car, he was in front of me on the shoulder, where I could watch him. At this point, we're in between the two vehicles. I told him to go up and sit on the hood of his car. You have someone sit on the hood when it's searched, as a safety precaution. If they get off for any reason, you can feel the vehicle move. Just then, the passenger on the right side opened his door and asked, 'Hey man, what's going on?' The driver replied, 'He just wants to search the car.' Suddenly, the driver and the passenger bolted, running straight ahead, south on the Turnpike. In retrospect I realized, this was a preplanned ambush. As they ran, the passenger in the left backseat exited the vehicle feet-first, holding a red cloth on his lap. I looked at him, then back at the guys who had taken off. In these situations you just let 'em run, catch 'em later. They weren't presenting any immediate danger.

"The next thing I knew, the left rear-seat passenger was coming up over the trunk of their car with a gun. Apparently, he'd had it under the red towel. He said something like, 'Look man, just give me the keys and I'll let you out of here.' I had the keys in my hand because I was planning to open the trunk. Seeing that gun really pissed me off. I looked at him, thinking, Who is this guy? I mean, none of them were very large. If it was just a fight, I'd be OK. I was in really good shape. I was thinking, These guys have no respect for anything. I put my hand on my holster. Next thing I knew, I saw a silver flash, similiar to the ones I'd seen when I'd had my bell rung during the boxing bouts at the Academy. It felt like a hot railroad spike had been driven through my hand. He had shot me at the base of the thumb. I could feel blood pouring out, dripping off my fingertips. I felt like my hand was under a garden hose that had warm water coming out. The impact caused my hand to spin all the way over my head and back around to my holster. I didn't want to look at my hand for fear of being grossed out and going into shock. My mind assessed the situation. *Stay calm.*

"As I drew my gun out of my holster, I was shot again—this time, in the left shoulder. The impact spun me a quarter turn, so that I was facing my troop car. The bullet nicked the top of my vest, going all the way through me. Apparently, the 9-mm rounds he was using were called 'hot shots.' They have a lot of gunpowder in them in order to go through things. At this point, I had my gun in my hand. I wasn't panicking, just assessing the situation. I was thinking, Just let me get some cover, so I can see what's going on here. As I took a step towards the troop car, I was hit in the back by a volley of bullets. Two hit the vest, which saved my life. Another round circumvented the vest at the base of my spine. That bullet entered the lower right side of my back. It went through my intestines, my left lung, hit the first rib on the left side of my chest, richocheted off that, then went through my gall bladder and my liver. Only after taking this scenic tour of my internal organs did it exit out of my chest on the right side.

"I felt as if I'd been pounded in the back by a sledgehammer. The force knocked me to the ground. As I lay there, my mind was racing: OK, I've been shot in the hand, shoulder, and back. Is this guy going to give me a break, or what? This is pissing me off. Get up! Take cover behind the troop car!

"I rose to my feet and took another step towards it. As my left leg was in the air, it was struck by another bullet. The bullet broke my femur. As my foot struck the pavement, the broken pieces ground together. This extreme jolt of pain cleared my mind like smelling salts. I fell back down. Prior to that, I was just having a bad day. But now I saw that this guy was not letting up. I was laying there thinking, Don't

64 try to get up again. It hasn't worked so far. You're lying near an embankment. Roll down it!

"As my body came to rest on the slope of the embankment, I was able to position myself so I could look towards the roadway. The first thing I saw was my attacker walking towards me with the two accomplices on each side, gloating over what they had done. You'd think they were taking a walk in the park, admiring the scenery. Realizing the assailant was coming down to administer the coup de grace, I tried to assess the situation. For a split second I thought, Maybe if I ask him not to shoot me anymore, he won't. But this was not an option. You want to think people are fair, but reason doesn't apply to these guys. The Academy teaches the green recruit to turn any fears he has into fuel. If I didn't want to be worm food, I'd better take charge.

"I got real angry. My trooper training took over. My mind overrode my physical injuries. I stood up. I started shouting, *'I'm gonna kick your asses!'* As I took a step towards them, my left leg hit the ground, and I tumbled. The subject standing to the right of the shooter yelled, *'Shit, the mother's still alive! Shoot him! Kill him!'* The gunman just stood there, stunned that I was still breathing, that I wasn't toast. The accomplice to the left started screaming, *'Shoot him! Shoot him!'*

"While they were yelling at him, he was too perplexed to do anything. My burst of anger, my getting up and confronting them, had saved my life. It bought me enough time to take aim at my attackers. Lying on the embankment, I aimed high, towards their heads. This contradicted our training, which is to aim for the 'Coke bottle,' or a person's upper torso. But I couldn't risk that, because it was rush hour, and I could hit a passing motorist. As I got off my first round, the bullet hit the trunk of their vehicle. The shooter returned fire. Little mounds of dirt were rising on the ground, in front of and beside me.

"While the shooter continued to unload his eighteen-round Mac 10, one of the accomplices fled on foot. The other jumped in my troop car and drove towards the shooter. In the ensuing gun battle, two rounds hit the cruiser. After firing my gun eight times, I dropped the magazine and tried to seat a fresh clip into my weapon. I was barely able to hold the gun in place. I finally released my death grip on the gun. I had had it in my hand since the first round was fired. I reached down to my left ankle for my backup gun. The Velcro straps that held the

No New Jersey trooper has ever taken as many bullets and lived as Anthony DiSalvatore. In the aftermath of the violence, the young trooper's baton and hat were left behind on the Turnpike's grassy embankment.

holster in place gave way with one adrenaline-packed pull. This rendered the gun useless to me, because there was no way I could get it out of the holster with my damaged hand. My attempts to shake it out proved futile. I was completely weaponless.

"As the shooter emptied his gun to put in another magazine, a trucker stopped, got out of his rig, and ran down the hill. 'I'm an ex-cop,' he said. When he saw a gunfight was in progress, he took off,

66 running back to his vehicle, where he called for help on his cellular phone. As I watched my troop car being driven away, I rose to my feet and thought, Oh, no, I'm in trouble now. I'll probably get a blue ticket. That's how your mind thinks from the training. As pain took control of my body, I crumpled to the ground.

"Within minutes, the paramedics arrived. I was laying on the ground, bleeding real bad. As they were taking off my vest, the bullet that went through my back plopped out of my chest. I was having a real hard time breathing, because my lungs were messed up. I went to spit, and a big blob of blood came out. I'd been banged up before. I'd broken my leg a couple of times, and my nose in six places. I used to have a real Italian nose, but now it looks more Irish, more puggish. I was in a car accident once where I bit off a piece of my lip, shattered my eye socket, and broke my cheek. I'm accustomed to pain and injuries. But I was thinking, I really did it this time.

"In a little while, the medical helicopter landed. Someone asked me what my religion was. I said Catholic. Someone said, Get a priest, there's no way he's going to make it. I had just been baptized the year before, and had a real strong faith. I was saying Hail Marys and Our Fathers. That took away some of the pain. The next day, I was supposed to take my dog, Foxy, to be put to sleep. We'd had her since I was a kid. I remember thinking, I was going to beat her to heaven. I was real tired from losing so much blood. I just wanted to close my eyes and take a nap. I told that to one of the emergency personnel. He said that if I did, I'd never wake up. You hear about the power of love; that pulled me through. My father came over from Italy in 1951. He's worked very hard all of his life: Construction. Shipyards. Once, he held down three jobs. Now he's a baker. I'm single, with three older brothers, one who's studying to be a Franciscan. My father's life was centered around me. If I died, it would destroy him. If it weren't for him, I would have taken that nap. I picked myself up by my bootstraps and put my headgear on tight. I knew this was going to be a long, difficult, and bumpy ride.

"They put me in the helicopter, on an IV. The pain was really getting to me. At the hospital, they transported me onto a stretcher. One of the medics was making a siren noise as I was being rushed through the halls, around corners. Just what I needed, I thought, a comedian. In the operating room, they put me on a table that seemed to be high in the air. I woke up that night in intensive care. I had lost six units of blood. I was in the hospital for about a month, going from 170 to 117 pounds, I had so many surgeries. After a few weeks, I developed an infection in my intestine. The medicine they gave me for that is so powerful, it eats away your arteries and veins. They can only give it to you for a couple of days. At that point, the doctor put my chances of living at fifty-fifty. They had to give me a iliostomy, which is similar to a colostomy. Fortunately, they were able to reverse it after two and a half months.

"Before the shoot-out, I was concerned about everything I ate. I got angry with myself if I had a potato chip. Laying there in the hospital, I kept thinking, Why didn't I enjoy some of the junk food I love? Being physical was my life. Now I'm full of scars. I am self-conscious about it, but getting better. This summer I went swimming a little. I still work out, but it affects my shoulder, my knees, my insides. I have to stop because I don't feel so good. But I don't get depressed. I don't feel sorry for myself. I could have been very easily killed, or left a quadraplegic. When I wake up in the morning, it's not a question of how good do I feel, but how bad. But I don't focus on that. We all have our crosses to bear.

"I remember, a few days after the shooting, having this weird dream in the hospital. I was floating down a wide, swift-moving river. It was very blue, with perilous rocks and white rapids. People and things were going by me. In the chaos, people were trying to hold on to anything they could. I reached for a woman's leg, but when I grabbed it, it came off. It was artificial and wooden. I can still hear her laughing. I kept going down the river until I approached a waterfall. I could hear the roaring of the water crashing into the rocks below. I knew, if I went over the falls, I would die. Suddenly, I found myself being yanked out of the river by a hook. When I woke up, I was in the back of a laundry, on a wooden table high off the ground. The owner was an ancient Chinese man. His daughter told me not to move. She said they would put me back together. She said I'd be OK.

"There was no trial. Although my father wanted to see my assailants dead, he didn't want me to be put through any more traumas. A trial could take years. I needed all of my strength to recover. He said I'd been through enough. So, their cases were plea-bargained. One guy got one to five years, with eligibility for parole in a year. The shooter

68 got ten to fourteen, and the driver eight to fifteen . . . No, I don't get angry about what happened, even though what I really wanted in life was taken away from me: to be a road trooper with the State Police. I had been a local cop before being accepted at the Academy. Corny as it may sound, I live in America, and we have it better than any nation in the world. We always have food in the refrigerator. Look, no matter what I've been through, I've still led an easier life than my father."

5 Teams— Elite of the Elite

Super Troopers

During the sixties and seventies, law enforcement found itself in a frenzied rush to keep up with a world in which the flames of violence seemed to have been doused with gasoline. From social unrest—in the summer of 1967, riots left twenty-three dead in Newark—to crazed snipers shooting into crowds, violence was assuming such terrorist forms as hijackings, bombings, assassinations, and the taking of hostages. Realizing it had to be better prepared to meet whatever was out there, the State Police in 1978 introduced a concept called TEAMS, which stands for Technical Emergency and Mission Specialists. This is a group of "super" troopers who are trained in making high-risk rescues and raids. Their skills are many: rappeling off

Because of their intense training exercises and specialized missions, TEAMS members form a close and trusting bond.

Scuba diving in a muddy aqueduct in winter is all part of the TEAMS experience.

With the ever-growing threat of terrorism, TEAMS members practice disarming a sniper and freeing a hostage.

72   buildings and bridges, scuba diving, advanced lifesaving, scaling stalled Ferris wheels to rescue trapped riders, containing hazardous chemical spills, controlling riots and crowds. When a job is considered too dangerous, strenuous, or specialized for regular troopers or local cops, TEAMS is called in.

"The theory is," says Lt. Richard Kitson (Badge No. 2662), who helped found the group, "it is better to have a fewer number of highly trained troopers available than a large number of not-so-motivated ones. You won't read a lot about us, because we do our jobs right. If we botched a sniper incident, it would be all over the media."

To be a TEAMS member is to be, well: "I joined the State Police because I thought they were the elite of law enforcement. Once in the Outfit, I realized that the TEAMS guys were the elite of the elite," says Sgt. Todd Burke (Badge No. 3294) of the C Troop TEAMS unit.

TEAMS members, of whom there are ten per troop, can be distinguished by their special equipment, which includes extra-protective clothing, body shields, riot helmets with built-in whisper microphones, and such high-powered weaponry as AR-15s, which are M-16 variations, and antisniper guns. Rarely do they show up for an incident in plainclothes; they prefer to make a bold impression in their State Police uniforms. TEAMS members are also set apart by their muscular stature. The physical test these guys must pass just to qualify for the unit makes their Academy training seem about as challenging as an Angela Lansbury workout video.

When a rare opening in the unit occurs, dozens of applicants apply. Get this: The twenty or so finalists are made to run, do push-ups, chin-ups, sit-ups, lift weights, and leap off tall buildings in a single bound ("to see if they react to heights," says Burke). Those who survive, after reaching a point of exhaustion, are required to do twenty-five minutes of lap work in a swimming pool. "An average trooper wouldn't even think of applying," says Burke, who looks like Christopher Reeve in his Superman days. Underneath Burke's white dress shirt—à la Clark Kent ready to spring into action—one can see a T-shirt with the State Police logo emblazoned across it.

For one training exercise, TEAMS members had to parachute out of a plane over the Atlantic Ocean, then swim to shore. "Some of these guys," says Kitson, the most decorated member of the New Jersey State Police "keep their socks up with thumbtacks." Pretty intimidating. "We don't like that word. We call it constructive force," says Burke, giving a stare that could make Clint Eastwood blink.

"These guys are always pumped up, with lots of attitude," says a so-called average trooper. "But when you get to know them, they're really great people. The best."

For their work, TEAMS members are not given extra money or higher rank. "It's the prestige," says Burke. "When guys go on vacation they call up asking, 'I'm not missing anything, am I?' You don't want to be left out of a job . . . The kind of guys we're looking for are aggressive and highly motivated, guys who can think on their feet. A cut above." "But don't get us wrong," says Kitson. "We don't look down our noses at anybody." "No, not at all," says Burke. "Never."

"The Ride of a Lifetime"

Lt. Kitson, who has been with TEAMS since its inception, says his most exciting experience was "when I had to dangle from a helicopter in order to rescue a steelworker from the top of a round, 150-foot oil drum. You could see through it because it was being dismantled. The steelworker had had some kind of seizure up there, and couldn't get down. He was just sitting on this eight-inch beam with no guard rails. That was June 21, 1984, in Atlantic Highlands, near the shore. Five firefighters couldn't figure out what to do. Time was of the essence, as a weather front was moving in. In those days, I was just an Indian in the TEAMS unit. The lieutenant in charge conjured up this idea of me and another trooper rappeling down to the guy from a helicopter, hooking him onto a harness, and lifting him to safety. Let me tell you, the idea looked better on paper.

"The helicopter picked up Trooper John O'Neill and me at the Princeton Barracks. After landing in a field, we got out and went to the opposite sides of the helicopter, where we tied ropes around our waists. Then the helicopter took off towards the tower. Once in the air, O'Neill and I were joined together. Now, you have to realize a few things. Whenever you're hanging below a helicopter you get this pendulum effect going. Also, the pilot has a depth perception problem. Our pilot, Charlie Homeijer, had to figure out where we were during

74 all of this. The tower's 150 feet high, and we're 100 feet below him. It was real windy up there with the storm front. Because of the pendulum effect, O'Neill and I kept whacking into the beam in our efforts to get to the guy. We kept signalling Charlie to pull up.

"Finally, we made our way to the steelworker. I had a seat hooked to me to put him in. He was so panicked he couldn't move. I somehow managed to tie him onto me. I found out up there that everybody has a fear of heights, let me tell you. It was real scary. At times those helicopter blades were too close for comfort. When we got picked off, we didn't go straight up, but out like this, for the ride of a lifetime. We landed back at the field, where an ambulance took the guy away.

"I thought to myself afterwards, *What were we doing?*"

Sniper Fire

The need for TEAMS was really brought home after two sniper incidents turned quiet neighborhoods into war zones. In both cases, police were shot at, and hit. On January 8, 1974, a forty-one-year-old contractor named Richard Natale started firing at children in the neighborhood from his cottage near the shore. Reportedly, he was mad at the government and felt this was a way of "expressing himself." On March 28, 1975, as Da Nang was falling, Vietnam vet James Carhart, twenty-three, barricaded himself in the attic of his family's three-story frame house in downtown Mount Holly. After proclaiming to his family that "there are too many churches," the youngest of thirteen children headed upstairs, where he kept an arsenal of weapons. He, too, began shooting at children before turning his gunfire on arriving police officers. By the time Carhart was subdued three hours later, he had managed to kill two policemen, one of whom left behind a pregnant wife and three-year-old daughter. A third officer was left paralyzed from the neck down, and eventually would die from his injuries. A fourth policeman was wounded in the leg. "He must have thought he was back in Vietnam," said his mother, Marion. "That was a law enforcement fiasco, with no organization or planning," remarks Lt. Kitson. Still, had it not been for quick thinking by individual New Jersey State Troopers in both incidents, the carnage could have been worse.

"The Car Was Rocking from Gunfire"

"I was in my troop car when the transmission came over the radio at 12:55 p.m. that two Bricktown police officers had been fired upon on Robin Drive, which was two blocks from where I was," says Richard Dancisin (Badge No. 2283), who's now a detective sergeant at Princeton.

"At the time, I was in the Tactical Patrol Unit, assigned to high-accident, drunk areas. We took our troop cars home with us so, if there was an emergency, we'd be available. It was my day off. I had been called to court that morning in Old Bridge Township. I had just gotten off the Parkway, going east on 88 into the Laurelton circle. I wasn't too familiar with Robin Drive, but I found it. It's a little side street that turns into a dirt road. It's lined with small, identical-looking cabins. As I drove down the road, I observed a parked Bricktown police car. It was empty, with the driver's door open.

"The transmission advised that a sniper was firing from an unknown location. It was a heavily wooded area. I parked in a clearing off the road, about twenty yards from the other police car, and I decided to make contact with the Laurelton Barracks to tell them I had arrived. The radio was mounted on the hump in the middle of the car, which meant, I had to reach over to pick it up. In those days, the radios resembled telephones. To reach the radio I had to duck down. As I did, a shot came through the windshield and over my head, lodging in the headrest. It missed me by an inch. I couldn't hear the gunman fire, so I didn't realize it was a bullet. It sounded to me like bees hitting the car, going zzzzzzzzzzz. But within moments the car was rocking from a barrage of gunfire blasts. It took something like eleven hits. The sniper was aiming right at me with a high-powered .30–.30 rifle.

"I didn't want to get out of the car, but had no choice, as bullets were now penetrating it. My face was covered with blood from all the shattered glass. One bullet missed me by stopping in the armrest. I didn't know where the guy was. If I got out and he was behind me, I would be out in the open, a clear target. Nevertheless, I felt, my only chance was to get behind the rim of one of the tires, knowing a bullet couldn't go through that. I slinked out of the car, taking the radio receiver with me as far as it would stretch. I then called Laurelton

76 Barracks and said, Don't let anybody come down this road. From wherever the sniper is, he's got a clear shot.

"A lot of cars were already descending on the scene, but another troop car blocked them from coming down the street. There were state troopers, local police; even other towns were coming in. I remained crouched behind my car while a Bricktown police officer, Brian Henfey, snuck up to my position. He told me what had happened. As the two Bricktown policemen were checking out the scene, they were fired upon. One got away into the woods and called for help. The other got hit. After getting shot in the left elbow, he ducked behind a tree for protection. But, being such a good marksman, the sniper got him in his right elbow, which was sticking out. Our immediate objective was to get the wounded policeman out of there.

"Staying low, Brian and I got into my troop car. We popped the trunk release button, sending it up. With the trunk as our shield, we started backing up, in between where we thought the sniper was and where we knew the policeman was. Since he was in clear view of the sniper, we wanted to give him protection. Although the sniper kept shooting as we made our approach, we didn't fire back, because we were afraid he might have hostages. Brian had his head hanging out the car door, trying to give me directions. It was like an obstacle course with all the trees. He didn't dare look up. Bullets were richocheting off the trunk. If it wasn't for the downed policeman, it might have been comical. Brian's telling me, 'Go left. Go right.' At one point, I hit a tree stump, causing the trunk to go down. Shots came immediately through the back window.

"With the trunk back up, we reached the officer. He was lying face-down in a pool of blood, his arms under him. He was unconscious and bleeding to death. Brian managed to climb into the backseat, open the door, and drag him inside. We got out of there as fast as we could, delivering him to an ambulance that was parked fifty yards away.

"The sniper then made the mistake of taking another shot while everyone was looking. We could see his muzzle sticking out through a small window opening. Now we knew where he was. Meanwhile, a woman in a neighboring cabin ran outside with her two kids. She told us the sniper was in there alone, without hostages.

"This meant, we were free to return fire. By now police were surrounding the whole area. I was sent around to keep an eye on the back

Trooper Richard Dancisin inspects the damage to his troop car, which was used as both a shield and a rescue vehicle. (Photo by A. DePaola.)

of the cabin. Apparently, the sniper had a five-gallon can of gasoline inside. No one knows if he shot into it, or if one of our bullets hit it, but a fire started inside the cabin. As the cabin was burning, loud-speakers were urging him to come out, that no one would hurt him. Pretty soon, the building was in full flames and starting to fall down. This must have been my lucky day. As the seam in the back of the cabin parted, out came the sniper's arm, which was on fire, as were his fingers. I pried the rest of the building down with my hands and pulled him out. He was a white guy, kinda wild-looking, and very badly burned. I thought for sure he was going to die, but he was taken to the hospital and pulled through.

"A few days later, I went to the hospital to visit the Bricktown police-

78 man, whose name is Dean Washburn. We became best friends. He was very, very grateful to me. He had just joined the local force, having been a captain in the Marines. Even though he served for twenty-five years and in three wars, this was the only time he'd been shot. He was in rehabilitation for five years. They gave him plastic elbows.

"I guess somebody was on my side out there. According to our trajectory study, had I not reached for the radio, that first bullet would have gone right through my neck. Of course, now I wouldn't drive so blindly into a place after hearing the call, 'Shots fired.' I had heard that call many times before, and it always turned out to be firecrackers. One thing that really saved me is how well trained I was at the Academy. I didn't have to think about what to do next. I just did it. I'd been put through these situations before. The trunk idea, though—that, we did dream up on the spot."

"Officers Have Been Shot!"

"While having dinner at the Cinnaminson Diner on Route 130, I got a telephone call that there was a sniper incident on Garden Street in Mount Holly, and to get there right away," recalls former Trooper Jack Grant (Badge No. 2556), who says that even though he's no longer in the Outfit, "one always feels a part of it." (No wonder. The intense, compactly built Grant is the oldest of four brothers, all New Jersey State Troopers. A sister-in-law also wears the blue and gold.) "I was eating with Trooper Jim Kenna, who's now a lieutenant. It was about five-thirty or six at night. I yelled to Jim, *'C'mon, let's go. Police officers have been shot!'* I found the street, which was two blocks off the center of town. It was lined with row houses, one after another. I couldn't get to it because police cars were parked askew, this way and that. So I parked a block away and ran to the scene. The sniper was in a third floor window, firing down. After he'd shoot, a hail of bullets would be returned. As I had been in Vietnam as a Marine, all the gunfire didn't bother me.

"Kenna and I crouched behind a car on the other side of the street from the house. At that time, the State Police had no SWAT teams or hostage negotiators. There was no organization, no central command at the scene. Hundreds of policemen had descended on the neighborhood. Everything was chaos. I had never been to a police shooting before. From where we were, we could see one of the dead patrolman lying facedown in the street. It was William Wurst, a great big guy from Hainesport, who was only twenty-three. He had come to back up Donald Aleshire, a Mount Holly patrolman, who had also been killed. I never saw his body. Aleshire had left the Philadelphia police force with six years on him, because he felt it was getting too rough. The gunman was either very lucky or a hell of a shot, because he got Wurst right through the eye. I wanted to check Wurst out, to see if he was alive, so I had Jimmy cover me. When I got near him, I could smell the defecation, so I knew he was dead. I went back to Jim and told him to hit the sniper's window with some shots while I made a move to the front porch. That's what we did overseas, firing first as we moved from hole to hole.

"I made it to the front door through clouds of tear gas. While I was standing on the porch, a guy who was in civilian clothes showed up. He was Harry McConnell, the chief of detectives for Burlington County. He said he was getting together a team to go into the house and get the guy. I said, 'Count me in.' I can't remember everyone who went in. Besides me and McConnell, I remember there being a Mount Holly cop named Dennis Holba, another state trooper, and a black officer from Pemberton who we all called Bear. There were some guys standing on the porch from the county prosecutor's office. One had an M-1 carbine. All I had for a weapon was a six-shooter, so I said, 'Can I borrow that?' and took it. I felt a lot better having that in my hand.

"Back then, we had no training in how to move through a house. I wasn't even wearing a bulletproof vest. We just went in, down the hallway in the dark. All gunfire had ceased, so we didn't know if Carhart had moved downstairs, or where he was. After securing the first floor, we went into the basement, which was completely dark. It was really creepy walking around down there. After checking it out, we started going upstairs to the second floor. On the way we came to a landing. Off it was a room where we found Carhart's brother, Louis, who was bedridden. He had been left a quadraplegic from the Korean War. We found out later that the rest of James Carhart's family had escaped

80 from the house when he turned violent. After moving Louis out, we continued up the stairs to the second floor. There we saw a flight of steps leading straight up to a closed door. We knew Carhart was in there.

"Some of the policemen fired shotgun rounds into the door. Since I'm small, and it was a narrow stairwell, I decided to lead the way up. I remember saying to the other cops, 'You ready to do it? Let's go.' Just in case he was in front of the door, I fired five or six rounds into it. When I got to the door I tried to crouch down as low as I could, because I figured he'd try and shoot at us. Bear came up and tried to kick the door open, but it wouldn't budge. It was blocked. Finally, with Holba pushing on it, it opened, swinging in from right to left. I started firing low, into the darkness. *Boom. Boom. Boom. Boom. Boom. Boom.* As I did that, I heard a yell, like *'Ahhhh.'* I knew I'd hit Carhart, but I didn't know where. There was no fire coming back. Maybe he's out of rounds? I fired again, and click, I was out.

"All of a sudden, we all burst into the room, one guy holding a light. Carhart was laying under a mattress. I had hit him in the hip. This was the first time I had seen him. He was a white, skinny little guy with stringy hair. The Mount Holly chief of police came running, screaming, *'You killed my officers!'* I just looked at Carhart and walked back down the stairs. I didn't wait to see him cuffed or anything. I handed the M-1 back to the guy outside, who asked, 'Good job?' I said, 'Yeah, good job,' and walked away. I got in my car and drove off.

"As I was heading back to Edgewater Barracks, where I was stationed, I came upon a Burlington Township officer who was wrestling an individual on the ground. I stopped my car to help him. When I was on top of the guy, I suddenly became very, very tired. All my strength just left my body. Finally, another Burlington officer showed up and helped us out. I got up and said, 'Thanks a lot.' Usually, in an incident like this, you'll give each other your names. But I just left. Wrestling an officer, that's a pretty serious offense. You don't come across that every day.

"When I tried to go to sleep that night at the barracks, I was like a wreck, coming down from all that adrenaline. That's when I got scared of what could have happened, going in that house and up the stairs. It was all so fast. *Boom. Boom. Boom. Boom.* You don't have time to think.

You just do it. It's like in Vietnam, when you throw a grenade. Guys fall, you keep moving. Later, at night when you're digging in, you start shaking. You think, I could have been killed there. Same thing here.

"I remember that myself, Jim Kenna, and the other state trooper, Ronnie Robinson, received commendations and a little plaque from the township of Mount Holly for our bravery. In fact, they had a dinner for us. I didn't go. I had a date with a new girlfriend. She's not the reason why I didn't go. To get an award, see, that's just not me."

6 Breaking Organized Crime

Life Drops a Bomb

There was a time in New Jersey when crime certainly did pay. Gangsters, mobsters, wiseguys—call 'em what you will—had a colorful image dating back to the days of speakeasies and bootlegging. With its urban, upscale population, New Jersey provided a lucrative environment for the Mob, including such gangland luminaries as Dutch Schultz, Lucky Luciano, Joey Adonis, Vito Genovese, Meyer Lansky, Bugsy Siegel, and Albert Anastasia, chief executioner of Murder, Inc. Thugs had an almost romantic image. They were looked upon as modern-day Robin Hoods, Damon Runyon–like characters in checkered suits with wide lapels who committed victimless crimes to make a few bucks. Of course, that was hardly the reality, and up until a few decades ago, law enforcement was almost powerless to do anything about it.

83

84   Through gambling, hijacking, loansharking, extortion, bribery, business frauds, drugs, and a host of other illegal activities, racketeering had become a billion-dollar-a-year industry in New Jersey. It was big business in other parts of the country, too, but in no other state was corruption this rampant. Nowhere had organized crime bought off so many public officials, including mayors, judges, county prosecutors, cabinet members, heads of political machines, union officials, and cops. In New Jersey, "the Fix" had become a fixture.

But, as bad as things were, before New Jersey could be renamed New Sicily, an extraordinary confluence of events occurred, culminating in the creation of the most effective Organized Crime Bureau in the United States. It is *the* Bureau, the one that has taught other states and the federal government how to go after the Mob, or, as it's officially known, La Cosa Nostra. In a relatively short period of time, owing largely to some forward thinking by the State Police, a wedge was driven between organized crime members and public officials. Before 1969, both groups were virtually untouchable. But with bold new ways to investigate and prosecute them, a cleanup of unprecedented scale occurred in New Jersey between 1969 and 1975. During this era, hundreds of public servants were indicted and imprisoned, including Newark's mayor, Hugh J. Addonizio. New Jersey has gone from being arguably the most corrupt state in the union to one that has the highest standards of conduct for its public officials.

The first major strike against organized crime didn't come from law enforcement, though, or even some crusading politician. The first bomb exploded September 1, 1967, when *Life* magazine hit the newsstands with a two-part series entitled "The Brazen Empire of Organized Crime." The articles clearly shocked a nation that had no idea how deeply the Mob had insinuated itself into the core of society. *Life* portrayed New Jersey as one of the most racketeer-infested states in the country. Full-page color photographs of Ruggiero "The Boot" Boiardo's baronial mansion in Livingston looked straight out of "House and Gangster." "The Boot" got a big kick out of lining his driveway with Disney-esque statues of his family, with himself on horseback.

According to *Life*, organized crime had even infiltrated the New Jersey State Police. The article talked of how, in February 1963, a meeting was held at an infamous mob hangout in Mountainside, N.J. called The Barn, in which three of Hudson County's most notorious

In 1978, Boiardo was presented with the "Key to the Town" of Kearny, N.J.

mobsters, Joseph Zicarelli, Angelo "The Gyp" DeCarlo, and Tony "Little Pussy" Russo, had gotten together to discuss the rising cost of fixing police officials. Through a well-connected Hudson County politico, they'd managed to have a policeman promoted to a very high rank in the State Police, claimed *Life*. This greedy "well-placed official" had upset his mobster cronies by demanding that his more than $7,000 a month in kickbacks be doubled during the summer horseracing months.

Ruggiero "The Boot" Boiardo's mansion in Livingston, N.J., may just be the epitome of gangster gaudiness. Painted statues of himself and his family line the driveway. (Photo by Bob Gomel, Life © Time Warner.)
A fake Bambi, clay burro, and naked woman on a pedestal decorate his "Godfather Garden."

The interior of Boiardo's brightly colored Venetian palazzo was lit by enormous crystal chandeliers.

A saint under glass observes the many paintings that line the walls of the marble staircase, including an imitation Mona Lisa.

88 *"It Was Like The Dirty Dozen"*

Secret forces were already at work within the NJSP to combat organized crime when the *Life* exposé hit. Five months earlier, on April 1, 1967, Col. David Kelly had formed an Intelligence Unit to gather information on Mob activity. Procedure required that he notify Attorney General Arthur Sills. "I wrote him a letter," says Kelly, who deliberately forgot to mail it. "I had to have the unit. I knew I'd be denied." Until then, nobody thought organized crime posed much of a problem. Even the FBI didn't acknowledge its existence until 1963, when a small-time Mob hit man named Joe Valachi received his fifteen minutes of fame by spilling the brotherhood's secrets to federal agents, and then on network TV.

Even before he took over the State Police, Col. Kelly knew that organized crime had infiltrated his organization. On several occasions he had heard "tainted" FBI tapes of conversations between his own men and the Mob. Kelly held organizational meetings for the Intelligence Unit in the basement of his house, because, he says, "I didn't know who I could trust within my own outfit."

An Army captain who was decorated for bravery while commanding a batallion in France during World War II and subsequently promoted to major, Kelly had no use for wiseguys. "I used to tell the men in my batallion, 'You came here to kill. If I catch any of you stealing, looting, or raping, you're dead,'" says the gruff-talking Irishman, who served as Col. Schwarzkopf's chief of staff in the Army Reserves after World War II.

Shortly after becoming colonel, Kelly received an offer he could and did refuse: it came from a state representative, who would eventually go to prison for tax evasion. "I'll never forget him wanting to get close to me," says Kelly, sitting at his desk at D.B. Kelly Associates, a security company he founded in Somerset. "I was down in Washington when he came up to me and said, 'Hey, hey, you making any money?' I said, 'Yeah.' He said, 'No, I'm talking real money. I got a guy that's gold, who's willing to pay you five thousand a week.' 'Neil,' I said, 'let me tell you something. I'm going to turn my back, and if you're here when I turn around, I'm decking your nose.' He said, 'You dumb Irish son of a bitch, who's going to know who paid Kelly ten years from now? Who's going to take care of your family?' I said, 'Neil, I'm telling you. I'm turning my back.' He said, 'You stupid Irishman,' and departed."

The four troopers Kelly picked to start the Intelligence Unit, says Edwin Stier, former chief of the Criminal Division of the U.S. Attorney's Office in New Jersey, "had been shunned by the organization for years because of their aggressiveness toward organized crime. Kelly pulled these guys from all over the place. It was like *The Dirty Dozen*, where you get guys who've been kicked around but have developed the raw instincts and the informant connections."

Fitting this profile was Justin Dintino, the present colonel, who in 1965 was a plainclothes detective out of Turnersville in South Jersey. "When we started we didn't have anything except an office at Division Headquarters that our lieutenant had to share with a traffic officer," he says. "The rest of us had to work out of our houses. We had no information at all, only an empty file cabinet. That's because nothing had been done on organized crime by the State Police."

From his office at Division Headquarters today, Dintino remembers the not-so-good old days when, in Turnersville, he decided to conduct four bookmaking raids: "Afterwards, a major from Trenton paid me a visit. He brought along the entire Criminal Investigation Section with him to chew my ass out because I was in their territory," he says. "What the hell, they hadn't pulled a raid in South Jersey in years. But they didn't want us pulling raids, either. Back then, Stumpy Orman, who was the Atlantic City kingpin, and Felix Bochiccio, the Camden kingpin, had close ties with members of the State Police. Very close ties. They probably got the word up, 'Hey, you better straighten that Dintino out . . .'"

The first thing Kelly did after assembling the Intelligence Unit was to put its members to work identifying the various crime families in the state and how their organizations were structured. "My assignment was the Angelo Bruno organization," says Dintino. "It took about a year for us to piece together the members of seven La Cosa Nostra organizations working within New Jersey. Besides the Bruno family, we had Gambino, Genovese, Bonanno, Colombo, Luchese, and DeCavalcante. Our Organized Crime Bureau was the first to make the distinction between the Mafia, which is Sicilian, and La Cosa Nostra, or LCN, which is the American version. Anyway, we told the colonel the seven LCN organizations operating within New Jersey had about five-hun-

90 dred members and three thousand associates in the state, and that their number-one activity at that time was gambling. We recommended that the colonel select fifty people for an Organized Crime Task Force (which was later renamed the Organized Crime Bureau). He implemented it within a couple of months, in December 1967. We also recommended some tools we felt were necessary to combat organized crime, such as electronic surveillance and witness immunity."

The Electronic Surveillance Act

So heavy was the fallout from the *Life* articles that in early 1968, the New Jersey State Legislature decided to hold hearings into the supposed problem. It wasn't just the public that was outraged, but legislators from rural counties who'd had no idea how serious things were. The pressure was on. *Something had to be done*, though who knew what. Chairman Ed Forsythe's brilliant idea was to engage noted university professor Robert Blakey, the man who would create the federal RICO statute, to testify and offer his solutions.

Blakey proposed a State Grand Jury Act that would authorize the creation of grand juries on the state level, something that had never been done anywhere before. These juries would be given the power to investigate and return indictments for racketeering activities. Since state grand juries would not have the heavy burden that county ones had, they could do long-term racketeering investigations, involving themselves in cases that crossed county lines.

He proposed a State Commission of Investigation, which would be a five-member, governor-appointed panel set up to investigate and expose organized crime. Although the SCI would have no law enforcement power, it could propose legislative and administrative solutions.

He urged enactment of the Electronic Surveillance Act, which Congress had passed as a provision in the Omnibus Crime Act of 1966. This provision allowed the states and the federal government to use electronic surveillance, such as wiretaps and bugs. Blakey helped create this provision following his participation in Lyndon Johnson's Presidential Organized Crime Commission, the first of its kind ever.

So feared was the Electronic Surveillance Act by civil libertarians that it had yet to be used on any level.

While the Legislature debated these controversial proposals, and while the press waged a relentless campaign to enact them, Gov. Richard Hughes and Attorney General Arthur Sills decided to take matters into their own hands. They called a Mercer County Grand Jury to investigate all this organized crime hullabaloo. If what Hughes and Sills were after was to show that New Jersey really wasn't a cesspool of organized crime, and that after seven years in office they had not ignored the problem, the plan backfired. Badly.

Following the *Life* articles, the second major organized crime bomb was dropped in December 1968. This time, the bombardier was one of Sills's assistants, William Brennan III, son of the Supreme Court Justice. As part of his grand jury investigation, Sills sent Brennan to State Police headquarters to see what the Intelligence Unit had on the Mob. He was given a small desk at which to work. "I was about as welcome there as a case of the clap," he says.

Maybe he was. Maybe he wasn't.

"We made Bill Brennan," says David Kelly, who one Indian summer afternoon had his men slip Brennan a really sizzling file. It involved testimony from John Pereira, president of the Young Democrats Club of Woodbridge, who had fallen victim to a loanshark deal run by mob boss John DiGilio. Pereira, who had brought charges, now claimed that DiGilio and his attorneys—Norman Robbins, a Woodbridge municipal prosecutor, and David Friedland, a state assemblyman—were trying to get the case fixed in court. (Friedland, who later became a state senator, is currently in prison for embezzlement of union pension funds. He made headlines when he tried to beat that rap by faking his death in a scuba diving accident in the Caribbean.) "The file just stunk," says Brennan, who now heads a large law practice in Princeton. "I think they gave it to me to see what Hughes and Sills would do with the information."

Christmas came a few weeks early for the media that year, when Brennan gave a speech before the Sigma Delta Chi journalism fraternity about the Forsythe hearings. Brennan was disillusioned with Sills's investigation and the legislature's hesitancy in passing the Electronic Surveillance Act. Although the Legislature had approved the creation of statewide grand juries and the SCI, Hughes and Sills had yet to set them up. So, when Brennan was asked by an audience member if he thought the New Jersey Legislature had been infected by the Mob, he opened the cargo bay and dropped his bombshell. He said that based on intelligence information he had gone through, he knew of three legislators who were entirely too comfortable with organized crime— although he gave no names. "That statement still rings in my ears after all these years," says Ed Stier. "It made headlines around the state. By not identifying the names, all the legislators were suspect. It caused quite a stir, making the administration even more uncomfortable than before."

Brennan's statement finally managed to break the gridlock in the Legislature. On January 1, 1969, the Electronic Surveillance Act was passed by almost unanimous vote. Who could oppose it? That could mean you were on Brennan's list of names.

So, it appeared that law enforcement now had all it needed to go after organized crime, all but one thing: the support of Attorney General Sills, who still refused to believe just how bad organized crime was. In early January, a meeting was held in the basement of Sills's house in which Col. Kelly, Ed Stier (then chief of the Criminal Division in the U.S. Attorney's Office in Newark), his "gangbusting" partner Peter Richards, and U.S. Attorney David Satz tried to break down the attorney general's resistance. Specifically, Kelly wanted Sills to hire Stier and Richards to work with the State Police in implementing the recent organized crime–fighting legislation. Again, it was Brennan to the rescue. During the meeting Sills received a phone call from one of his assistants with some startling news. At that very moment, Brennan was clutching his files in front of a legislative committee, where he'd been ordered to name names. He had just announced, he had three more! Sills looked at Kelly and asked, "What do you need?"

Joining Forces

Moving into a small office at State Police Division Headquarters, Stier and Richards took over the massive job of setting up the legal and technical procedures for implementing electronic surveillance and administering the State Grand Jury Act. For the next six years, they worked hand-in-hand with the State Police, gathering information, developing informants, and drawing indictments, all in an effort to put cases together in an airtight way. The only thing they couldn't do was try their own cases. But that soon changed with the passage in 1970 of

Gangbusting partners Ed Stier and Peter Richards were the subject of an editorial cartoon in the Asbury Park Press. *(Artist, BILL KING.)*

94   the Criminal Justice Act, which created the Division of Criminal Justice. The Act gave the attorney general the ability to supersede county prosecutors and try the indictments handed up by the state grand jury.

After Mob hitman Ira Pecznik was sentenced to fifteen years for armed robbery, he felt betrayed by his employer, the Campisi gang, a Genovese offshoot. So he told Trooper Joseph Mackin, who helped put him behind bars, that he'd be willing to expose the Campisis for an airplane ticket to Israel. Although law enforcement's initial response was, "this is crazy," the State Police called in gangbusters Stier and Richards. "We decided to step in to change the balance, to see if we could hold more cards than he did," says Stier. After arranging Pecznik's complicated transfer from Trenton State Prison to Monmouth County Jail, then having an apartment constructed for him in a Ft. Dix stockade so he would't go stir-crazy, Stier and Richards, along with Deputy Attorney General Barry Goas, spent fourteen months negotiating with the charismatic hitman. Before going to the state grand jury, they had to convince a reluctant Governor William Cahill to sign an order springing Pecznik from jail so he could be placed in a Witness Protection Program, where he remained until his death. "As a result of this intense effort we were able to take the entire Campisi organization off the steet, at least for a while," says Stier. This was "gangbusting" at its finest.

"It was a very exciting time, because things were being done that had never been done before," says Stier, who was issued a gun and taught to shoot at Division Headquarters. "We were way ahead of everybody else, way ahead of the federal government. All the legal theories—the organized crime–related conspiracies and the misconduct-in-office theories—we were coming up with in those early days were brand new. It was an opportunity to do things that were unique in organized crime investigations. We combined the resources of the State Police, the Intelligence Bureau, the Organized Crime Task Force, the troop detectives, and many others, with a state grand jury. There's still nothing like it in the United States. When Bob Blakey testified before the Forsythe Committee that organized crime could get whatever it wanted at every level of government in New Jersey, he was right. The major success this program had was that it was more effective than if the federal government had stepped in. It was the state doing it, which I think is a much healthier process.

"Maybe a lot of what I'm saying went on then doesn't sound extra-ordinary now, because we're all used to hearing television reports on the way organized crime is fought today. But, back then, each case was a breakthrough. New Jersey became the subject of much study, espe-cially from Bob Blakey and his Organized Crime Institute at Cornell. I went up there and helped train federal and other state prosecutors to do the kinds of things we were doing. In fact, the guy who developed the evidence that led to the prosecution of the Mafia Commission in New York—a major, landmark case—which in turn led to a whole series of prosecutions of New York racketeers, including John Gotti, was Ron Goldstock, who's head of the New York Organized Crime Task Force. He was Blakey's assistant at Cornell. A lot of what he is doing today stemmed from what was learned at the Organized Crime Institute, which, in part, was based on what we were doing in New Jersey."

Without the use of electronic surveillance, it's almost impossible to indict Mob bosses. The very structure of their organization protects them from arrest. Mob bosses, as a rule, do not expose themselves in the commission of crimes. They have underlings who do it for them. What they can be arrested for is conspiracy to commit wrongdoings. Proof of such conspiracy requires the use of electronic surveillance. The irony is, many civil libertarians feel it's a dangerous threat to the public's right to privacy. Even after Congress enacted the Electronic Surveillance Act, Attorney General Ramsey Clark refused to implement it. That was left up to President Nixon, who in 1968 ran on an anti–organized crime platform.

With the public in mind, Stier and Richards were extremely careful in developing their cases. "It was an extraordinary achievement to get the Legislature to enact an electronic surveillance statute, because it really is a very serious infringement on privacy," says Stier. "We had to make sure it was used under only the most extraordinary circumstances and under the tightest controls. We made sure that whenever we used it, we had a solid legal basis. Because we operated from that premise, we were very successful with it. It was vital that we preserve the statute. Had we not been as conscious as we were of the rights of the people who were the subjects of electronic surveillance, I think we would have made mis-takes and stretched the law beyond its limits. It might have been discred-ited and repealed. The law had to come before the Legislature every

96 couple of years for renewal. It had a sunset provision where it periodically automatically expired, which meant we had to go back to the Legislature and make a case that it had been used effectively."

They Talked, and They Talked, and They Went to Jail

The first significant legal use of electronic surveillance in the United States was carried out by the New Jersey State Police, resulting in the imprisonment of the aforementioned infamous "Bayonne Joe" Zicarelli, who bossed bookies, loansharks, and numbers writers in Hudson County. Zicarelli's office, which the State Police succeeded in bugging, was inside the Regal Oldsmobile dealership in Union City.

From the Zicarelli tapes, law enforcement got its first in-depth look into the nefarious inner workings of organized crime. "It was just like out of *The Godfather*, where people were going to Marlon Brando for favors," says Col. Dintino, who helped plant the Zicarelli bug, and who remembers that dark and stormy night when he and fellow trooper Al Piperata broke into Zicarelli's office through a back window of the brightly lit Olds showroom. As Dintino and Piperata stood guard outside the office, Marty Ficke, who was head of the Electronic Surveillance Unit, and four assistants installed a listening device in the light fixture over Zicarelli's desk and put a tap on his telephone.

"Back then, you've got to understand, a lot of people, even in law enforcement, did not believe in La Cosa Nostra, because it was so secretive and so little was known about it. But any nonbelievers who listened to the tapes we got were convinced," says Dintino. "These guys talked about people they had killed way back when. They talked of past wars they had had with Bugsy Siegel, Meyer Lansky, and Dutch Schultz. They talked about prosecutors and policemen who were on their payroll. They talked about who they wanted to make judges and prosecutors. We learned that one individual, John Armellino, who was mayor of West New York, was being paid thousands a month from them. Although we had that tap authorized for fifty days, we had to cut it short. It was too bad, because it was the best of times. But when Zicarelli and his guys started talking about kidnapping and knocking off a guy who worked for them—a professional wiretapper who they thought was doing jobs for a rival—we decided to move in. Even so, as a result of those tapes, a number of politicians and police officials were charged with corruption and other serious criminal offenses. In addition to organized crime members, a lot of people went to jail."

Once they created a break between the Mob and public officials, the Organized Crime Bureau's next stage was to dismantle LCN families, from the bosses on down. Starting with Project Alpha (see Chapter 7) in 1973, the State Police and the federal government began working together on a number of elaborate, headline-making stings that enmeshed scores of racketeers. With Operation Omega in 1979, law enforcement officials proved, for the first time ever in a court of law, that a national organized crime conspiracy called "La Cosa Nostra," or, in English, "This Thing of Ours," really did exist. This historic case saw members of the Vito Genovese family, including its long-time *capo*, eighty-eight-year-old Ruggiero Boiardo, indicted on charges of murder, gambling, loansharking, and robbery.

If ever there was a banner year in organized crime's history, it was 1987. Operation Intrepid resulted in racketeering charges against fifty-three members and associates of the Genovese crime family, while Operation Tigershark brought the same charges, plus ten counts of murder, against thirteen members of the Bruno/Scarfo crime family of Atlantic City and Philadelphia. Tigershark put the Scarfos' cutthroat boss, Nicodemo "Little Nicky" Scarfo, in prison for the rest of his life.

"Tigershark was our shining moment," says Lt. Ed Johnson (Badge No. 2746), who met four times with Scarfo *capo* Tommy DelGiorno to convince him to work for the State Police. "When DelGiorno came aboard there were twenty-five unsolved murders going back to 1978. He identified seventeen of those. He was the main witness against Scarfo and seventeen of his made guys. We'd never seen that happen before. Many individuals have been taken out of the LCN hierarchy, only to have the octopus grow another head. DelGiorno gutted the regime. Up until DelGiorno came aboard, the Scarfo gang had a stranglehold of fear on society. The night he flipped was very dramatic. I was there when higher-ups from the State Police and the Attorney General's Office had a midnight meeting with DelGiorno at Philadelphia's International Embassy Hotel. The idea that he was actually going to walk through that door and spill his guts was unbelievable.

98   "Besides decimating the family, DelGiorno's information brought about the cultivation of other informers, such as Nicholas Caramandi, Nicholas Milano, and Phil Leonetti, who became a witness against John Gotti, and was a prime mover in flipping Sammy "The Bull" Gravano. Because of DelGiorno, we were able, down the line, to decimate another faction of the Bruno/Scarfo family with Operation Broadsword, in which we used another informer, George Fresolone.

"You could say Tigershark effectively broke the back of organized crime in South Jersey and Philadelphia. A void was created, which, slowly and surely, is being filled. But I don't think it will ever reach the magnitude of intimidation we once had."

The Myth of Omerta

Although Tigershark gave detectives the confidence that anybody could be flipped, Col. Dintino knew that all along. "You've got to dirty them up," he says, "make a case against them. Maybe you don't make it publicly. Maybe you go pick them up and let them know you've got something on them. You sit them down and say, 'Alright, I know you're involved in loansharking or bookmaking or this or the other.' You show them just enough, that you're not really interested in them, but in their information. You know, I found it not all that tough to do. For years police stayed away from the LCN, thinking there was no use talking to them. But they're like anybody else. They put their pants on like you or me. This code of silence, this 'Omerta' thing, it's a myth. If you've got a case against them, and you put the pressure on them, you'd be surprised how many are willing to squirm out of it by giving up their pals. I learned that early on in my organized crime career. I was very successful in obtaining information and making cases. The key to my success was developing my sources. As soon as I realized that, I zeroed in on it.

"I'm not saying that you just walk up to a guy and he's going to flip. It takes work to make a case against him. There was a bookmaker I was pressuring, a big-timer who had a number of sports books and whatnot. I was banging away at his operations. I had a couple of lower local sources putting the hurt on him. We went in there and knocked about ten of his bookmaking banks off at one time. Then I did it again. Three months later, again. Then I heard he was going to the loansharks. Between the lawyers and the bail bondsmen, he was hurting. Finally, I gave him a call and had him meet me one night behind some bar. Now, he thought this was payoff time, because he was paying everybody. When I pulled up, he was already there. I made him get into my car. I said to him right away, 'I know what you're thinking. That I'm here for the payoff because I've been knocking your balls off.' I told him the only way I'd get off his back was if he gave me information. That's what I'm looking for, I said. He started talking right away, because he wanted me to be his friend. He was a gold mine. I never made a case when I had to use him as a witness. I didn't want to burn him, though I was able to make a lot of cases from the information I gleaned from him.

"This guy knew Philadelphia and Atlantic City. He had a mind like Einstein. He never wrote anything down. He did everything from memory in case the police should ever grab him. We developed such a rapport that when I called him, he'd get right back to me. He had a code name and I had a code name. He even came to my house a few times. In half a day, he'd give me enough information to keep fifty detectives busy for a month. The secret with these guys is in knowing what motivates them. Money? Rarely. It's fear and self-preservation. You get a guy who is going to face prison time. You show him that you've got something on him, that he's had a previous record or whatever, he's going to be your best source. And, he's going to be honest, too. Because right up front, you tell him, 'Hey, you know, you lie to me once and everything is off.' So, you'll find they're more truthful to you than your own wife."

Having cleaned up the government, and having scored major victories in dismantling LCN families, the Bureau has found a new focus for the nineties. Dintino took the unprecedented step of merging Organized Crime Bureau with the Narcotics Bureau to become what is known as CERB, which stands for Criminal Enterprise and Rackeetering Bureau.

"Narcotics have been our country's number-one problem for the last thirty years," says Dintino, who served on President Reagan's Commission on Organized Crime from 1983 to 1986. "I say our emphasis is wrong. Compared to other organized crime groups, La Cosa Nostra's involvement in narcotics is minimal. If we concentrated on these other groups like we do on LCN, we would be doing a real service to this country, because we would really be attacking the narcotic problem. LCN's big areas are labor racketeering, loansharking, and gambling. And that's peanuts compared to narcotics. Peanuts.

"One of the mandates we had on the President's Commission was to structure out organized crime in this country, which we did. We got into these other groups, such as Asians, Colombians, and Mexicans. We wanted to show it wasn't just La Cosa Nostra out there. From our studies, we found that every state says they have Colombians and a cocaine problem, but not necessarily an LCN problem. Our surveys showed that LCN has 1,700 members and 17,000 associates in this country, yet our surveys showed there were 500,000 members of organized crime in the United States. Still, everybody, including the FBI, the press, and most people in law enforcement, believes LCN controls everything. They don't. In reality, they only control about five percent of the organized crime problem. Since narcotics is the number-one moneymaker for organized crime, it does not make sense to separate them."

As for the future, Maj. Vince Modarelli of CERB predicts, "We will make an impact on drug cartels. This does not mean we are easing up on traditional organized crime groups. We're still going after them as hard as ever. I hope that in the years to come, we're not going to see the headlines for people like Gotti and Scarfo, because before they can reach that kind of prominence, we will have taken them off."

As for the past, William Brennan likens the forces leading up to the creation of the Organized Crime Bureau to that of a "genie in a bottle pushing at the cork to get out." Stier maintains, there was no other time like it in the history of U.S. law enforcement. "We were setting legal precedents with almost every case. New Jersey was a very corrupt state. We were prosecuting public officials and organized crime bosses, which was unheard of. But we did what we did because things had to change," he says. "Organized crime was rampant in other states, too," says Dintino in his usual understated way. "We just chose to do something about it."

7 / Deep Cover Operations

To Live in Their World

Operations Alpha and Waterjack were groundbreaking stings in which troopers were sent undercover—deeper than any had gone before—to expose mob activity in and around the Newark waterfront. Troopers were set up in phony trucking and warehousing businesses designed to lure and ensnare criminals. For periods lasting in some cases almost three years, troopers had to assume wiseguy personas. *Were wiseguys.* Day in, day out, seven days a week, they stayed in character, with no time off for good—or was it bad?—behavior. Alpha and Waterjack proved to be two of the most successful incursions ever undertaken into organized crime in the United States, netting scores of arrests and convictions.

Imagine you're a cop, sworn to uphold the law and serve the public,

101

102 when suddenly you're asked to emulate the very people you're out to get. You're asked to dress, talk, think like them. You're asked to live in *their* world, where wrong is right, bad is good, and even Houdini would have trouble separating reality from illusion. A decade or two after their extended forays into the organized crime underworld, Troopers Robert Delaney (Badge No. 2853), Robert Weisert (Badge No. 2724), and Patsy Aramini (Badge No. 2843) are still trying to put their mental slides in order.

Remember The Alamo

As lightning bolts flash over the swamp behind his house in Florida, where he now lives, Bob Delaney recalls the thirty tumultuous months he spent as the key figure in Project Alpha, which culminated in the first mass arrest of organized crime figures in New Jersey, including mob heavyweights Jackie DiNorscio, John DiGilio, and Tino Fiumara, and the recovery of $1 million in stolen goods.

The son of retired State Police Captain Robert Delaney, Robert, Jr., was approached by the State Police to be the star player in the federally funded project, which began in 1975. At age twenty-five, Robert had been a state trooper for not even two years. A meeting at Division Headquarters to see if he could deliver was scheduled with Maj. Bill Baum for 11:30 in the morning. "But when I got there I was told, the major was tied up," says Delaney, who has the quiet charisma of Tim Robbins or Robert Urich. "So, Sgt. First Class Jack Liddy took me to a nearby pub, where he put four or five beers into me. Later I found out that my meeting was actually set for 1:30 p.m., but they had me show up earlier to see if I could handle myself while drinking. It was a good test. I had to keep my wits about me even though I had a buzz on."

Back then, troopers still slept at the barracks while on duty. Come the middle of the night, Delaney quietly packed his gear and sneaked out of the Somerville Station, ready for his new assignment. Stories quickly spread, half-baked rumors that he'd been dishonorably discharged after going to Florida and stabbing somebody in a fight. Only Delaney's parents and grandparents knew the truth of his disappear-

Resigned 4-9-75

Delaney, R.J.   #2853

*Talk about covering your tracks: the State Police even altered Bob
Delaney's official class photo to say that he resigned from the State Police.*

ance. Still, that was little comfort to his socially active father and mother, who gave up going to police dinners because they couldn't stand
the arch looks and judgmental whispers.

While waiting for the sting to be set in place, Delancy stopped by his
parents' house. Answering the phone, he found fellow trooper Bobby
Scott on the line. "I don't know what you did," he told Delaney, "but

104 I've got some money in my savings account. I've spoken to my wife about it. If we can be of any help . . . If we can lend you some cash . . . If you need anybody to testify as a character witness . . ." "You want to talk about getting an apple in my throat," says Delaney.

He was given the ironical alias, Robert Allen Covert—the name of a deceased child—and a new Social Security number by the FBI. This Robert Covert liked the high life; he wore three-piece suits, drove a Lincoln Continental, and sported a wad of cash for picking up tabs. The ruse was: his parents had been killed in an auto accident, leaving him money to invest that he was putting into the trucking business. Delaney and fellow State Trooper Ralph Buono were set up in Elizabeth, N.J., with a small trucking company called Mid Atlantic Air Sea Transport that had one sixteen-foot truck and a step-up van. They opened their doors and waited for organized crime to take the bait. They might as well have been marlin fishing with a worm. After six months, MAST was phased out. "We had to upgrade," says Delaney. "In the real world where money was being made, our operation was small and insignificant. So Maj. Baum wrote up a new proposal, and Col. Pagano made a pitch to Washington for more money, which we got."

The result was Alamo Trucking of Jersey City, something right out of "Mission: Impossible." Surveillance cameras were mounted behind wall grills, videotaping all that went on inside the three-story offices. Signals were transmitted via satellite to a command center, a phony architectual design firm located in a Newark highrise. To activate the cameras, Delaney would dial a supposedly nonworking number. To deactivate them, he would redial. *"When Trucking,"* read the company letterhead stationery, *"Remember The Alamo."*

This time, the bait took, thanks largely to an informant named Pat Kelly, who was Alamo's terminal manager. Now in Witness Protection, the brilliant, smooth-talking entrepreneur agreed to cooperate with the FBI and State Police after running afoul of the law and facing arrest. Timing could not have been better. Kelly's contacts included such influential mob members as Jackie DiNorscio, Tino Fiumara, and John DiGilio. Kelly offered two irresistible qualities to organized crime: loyalty and the ability to earn big bucks. "Had he been of Italian ancestry, he'd have been a 'made' man," says Delaney, "meaning, he'd probably have been made a member of a crime family."

All the emphasis on physical fitness that Delaney endured as a trooper went out the window when he became the wiseguy owner of a mob-controlled trucking company.

Troopers working on the Operation Alpha sting were issued phony business cards. This was Bob Weisert's, AKA Bob Hesse.

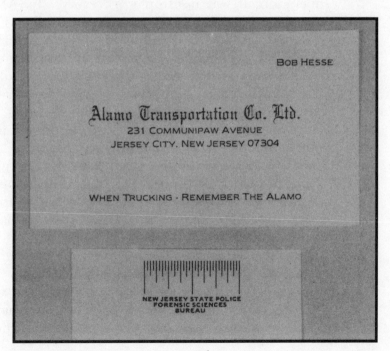

"Kelly *was* the brains," says Bob Weisert, a former State Police under-cover narc who was brought in to ease Delaney and Buono's workload. Weisert was Kelly's assistant, in charge of writing payoff checks to the Mob. These eventually totaled twenty-five percent of Alamo's profits; DiNorscio, DiGilio, and Fiumara each took a third. "Kelly started Alamo with one truck, then tripled it, then tripled it again," says Weisert. "This was all through his knowing how to handle contracts, juggle truck routes, figure out the dropoff and the pickup."

In no time, the company became so successful that it had forty-five tractor-trailers hauling vegetables, seafood, and meat across the nation. There were twenty-five drivers, two secretaries, two full-time bookkeep-ers (who were really FBI agents), even a company softball team. "Alamo was an extraordinary amount of work," says Weisert. "Besides the organized crime guys wanting their kickbacks, percentages, and personal favors for family members and prison cronies, I had to deal with everything from rate questions, to trucks breaking down, to Texas sheriffs pulling our trucks off the road for being overweight. Once, we lost $80,000 worth of shrimp when someone forgot to turn on a truck's refrigeration unit. That kind of insurance claim can kill an undercover operation. It was nonstop work every day. After six months, the ten-sion got so bad I'd wake up each morning and throw up."

Sitting in his office at Division Headquarters, where he's now a Sgt. First Class in Technical Services, Weisert remembers the job as being "very tense . . . There was always someone looking over your shoulder. It was difficult to get up and activate the surveillance equipment. You were always under the evil eye."

During the investigation, Weisert scored a major coup when elusive mob figure and hit man John DiGilio agreed to meet with him to dis-cuss a loansharking deal. The gangster and his driver, Anthony Pacillio, picked Weisert up in a Lincoln Continental. The unarmed Weisert, who was wearing a Nagra on-body tape recorder in his under-wear, was to be protected by an unmarked backup car's crew. "As we were driving around, DiGilio looked out his back window and said, 'Geez, there's a car following us,'" says Weisert. "I nearly had a heart attack. He told Anthony, 'Go left here! Now make a right! Go down this road! Pull into that park!' I thought for sure I'd been found out. Then DiGilio, pointing out the back window, said, 'It's that yellow car. . .' That's when I decided to go to church that Sunday, because no undercover State Police car would ever be painted yellow. It was just some-body in a sports car." What Weisert didn't know is, he *was* all alone out there. "The backup crew had a bumper beeper to keep track of us," he says. "But while they were following us, the aerial, which was attached with a suction cup, flew off on the Bayonne Bridge."

Weisert recalls another incident with a chill. "I was sitting in the conference room of Alamo Trucking when seven or eight workers—tough truck driver types—burst in the door, as white as sheets. We'd sent them to mob boss Tino Fiumara's house as a favor, to do some repair work on his swimming pool. While they were in the midst of sandblasting and caulking holes, Tino came home, all dressed up. He stood at the side of the pool watching them work. All of a sudden, he started yelling at them, picked up a ten-pound sledgehammer, and proceeded to knock his brick, five-foot-high barbecue into the ground. He then threw the sledgehammer into the pool and said he'd kill these guys if they didn't do a good job. They all jumped out of the pool, into their truck, and took off, too scared to go back."

"The fear level I experienced every day was not something an undercover cop admitted to back then," says Delaney, who put on forty-five pounds thanks to a mob diet and no exercise. "I was excellent at going to meetings, kissing on the cheek, and recording the proceed-ings. Then, twenty minutes later, I'd be driving down the street and have to throw my guts up, or hit a gas station because I had diarrhea."

One particular showdown occurred when DiNorscio, who was in Rahway State Prison, sent an associate to Delaney demanding that Alamo pay for round-trip tickets to Disney World for his wife, kids, and mother. "I sent word back to him that the answer was no," says Delaney. The physically imposing associate returned with DiNorscio's response: Pay, or "he'll shut everything down, there won't be nothing moving out of here." So Alamo gave in, paying almost $1,500 in vaca-tion airfares. DiNorscio's family has only the U.S. taxpayers to thank.

Mob-a-phobia wasn't Delaney's only stress factor, either: "I had more fear of getting shot by another cop," he says. "I could picture myself unloading stolen bicycles off a truck when some kid, thinking he's doing the arrest of the century, shows up and overreacts."

"The pressure of never being able to come out from undercover, to not take days off or vacations, was horrible," says Weisert, who shared a waterfront penthouse with Kelly. "I didn't see my parents, have

108   dates, or go to the movies. Once, I managed to take two days off, but spent them in my apartment catching up on reports. I remember spending Christmas alone, too. When I got home at night, Pat would be there staring me in the face. Usually we'd stay up to work on the investigation. Some nights, the wiseguys would drop by to talk about some stolen property or whatever, so I'd have to activate the tape recorders, which were in the ice bucket and planters.

"One night, I got home about nine o'clock, when four or five mob guys showed up wanting to borrow one of our repair trucks, which we let 'em have. I rode with them to a warehouse in Kearny, N.J., where there was over $700,000 worth of stolen tractors and trailers being chopped up by thirty thugs from the Tri-State area wielding blowtorches and sledgehammers. I mean, there I was in a three-piece suit, writing down serial numbers on a matchbook. Looking back, I was crazy to do that. If I had been caught, I'd never have been found. That kind of stuff really wears on you."

And talk about feeling naked. "When you're doing a one-day undercover narcotics job, you keep your identification hidden somewhere in your car," he says. "We had nothing. We had to turn in our ID cards and guns, anything that could prove who we were. One night, I got pulled over in my Corvette by two troopers on the Turnpike. They wanted to look in my briefcase, which I wouldn't let them do. It's hard to tell a cop he can't do something. But I had things in there that could blow the investigation. I convinced them to call Jack Liddy, who told them I was deep undercover. Still, they didn't understand why I didn't have my identification somewhere. They couldn't help thinking like cops. They let me go, but followed me and stopped me again. They just couldn't understand. Where was my ID? We were really very alone out there."

There was the lighter side, though. "These guys emulated the movies," says Delaney. "They went to see films like *The Godfather* to see how they were supposed to act." Delaney recalls sitting in the lounge at the Bellavita Ristorante in Parsippany when thug Joey Adonis, Jr., handed the waiter a handful of quarters for the jukebox. "He wanted to be sure '*The Godfather*' Theme was playing whenever he entered the dining room."

Once Delaney watched a new bartender in a mob hangout almost get his face mashed in after making a homosexual slur. Seems nobody told him about the mob custom of kissing one another on the cheek.

There are no Police Academy classes, no uncharm school for how to be a hoodlum. Delaney and Weisert learned as they went along. "You can't have an 'I' problem," says Weisert, who spent months ingratiating himself with the Mob by fetching them coffee during meetings. "It can't be 'me, me, me.' These OC people want to sit down and tell you about *their* adventures, how many trucks *they* stole, how many people *they* beat up or killed. You can't have a guy at the table saying, 'Aw, that's nothing.' They like to talk and they like listeners. They don't like people with real opinions who can do them one better. The problem is, cops like to ask questions. You can't do that undercover. You have to learn a new technique for getting information, like saying to a guy after he tells you something, 'Ah, *nooo* way . . .' The whole key is to have big ears and a small mouth."

"I've learned that all organizations are the same, whether criminal or straight," says Delaney. "I tell undercover people, the same pecking order you went through as a young cop, you're going to go through as a young member of a criminal organization. You're going to have older guys wanting to tell you war stories. In the world of the State Police, they want to tell you about the high-speed chases they were on, the arrests they effected, the good times they had, the knockaround stories. Just to say you put the cuffs on somebody doesn't make a good story. You got to do a little puffin'. Same with the Mob. The bad guys want to tell you about the hijacks that went wrong, the stuffing of the body in the car trunk, the beating that somebody took. They tell you twenty million things that happened. You find out they only did eight million of them."

"They Took Me Hook, Line, and Sinker"

As the owner of a warehouse set up to store and fence hijacked goods in Elizabeth, Trooper Patsy Aramini secretly recorded more than three hundred hours of mob wheeling-dealing, starting in 1981. Besides the Nagra tape recorder he wore strapped to his leg, his warehouse was

The real Patsy Aramini on road patrol.

equipped with voice and video equipment to record meetings and conversations. His sting, called Operation Waterjack, led to the lockup of a ring of Hudson County truck cargo hijackers, including four policemen.

The hyper Aramini, who seems to have given Al Pacino or Joe Pesce acting lessons, is only too happy to replay his greatest hits. "Listen to this," he says excitedly, turning up the volume on his tape deck. "Here's where they tried to stick me with a load of Buddhas that were part of a stolen load from a Conrail job. I said, 'Stick 'em up your ass! What am I going to do with them?'"

Just as Delaney and Weisert had Kelly to get them established in the underworld, Aramini had an informant whose code name was B70. "Wiseguys," says Aramini, "do not like to meet new people. "B70 was a big-time thief and hijacker. He introduced me as his friend. Only because of him did these guys take me hook, line, and sinker."

Unlike Delaney and Weisert, Aramini never deferred to anyone. As Pat Amato of Amato Storage, he called the shots from the beginning. "I played everything down, like I didn't give a flying whatever," says the marathon runner. "That's why I was so successful. Nobody controlled me. I let them know that through my attitude and mannerisms. I figured this is my friggin' warehouse, my operation. I don't need you. Don't dictate to me, because I'll go somewhere else and get somebody else's stolen property. Once they asked me where I'd been because I was gone for a couple of days. 'Jesus Christ,' I said, 'Where've I been?! I was sick and when I'm sick the world stops! You got that?!' That was my approach, and it worked great."

But, despite his abrasive front, Aramini eventually developed an ulcer, probably brought on when his Nagra body recorder, which can run for three hours, ran out of tape and started making a squeaky noise during a mob hijack-planning session. "I almost went in my pants," he says. "Another time," Aramini recalls, "I used the expression 'PD,' meaning police department, to a rogue cop. It was a careless mistake. Nobody but another cop would say that."

Trying to look cool and keep your guard up at all times isn't easy "After hanging out with these people for a while, eating and drinking and partying with 'em, you tend to get a little complacent," says Aramini, who was poured a strong cup of reality one Sunday morning. "I was on my way to help loot a warehouse with some of the guys, including a corrupt local policeman. While in the car, he made the statement that if another cop caught us, he'd have to shoot him. I said, *'Whoa!'* He said, 'Yeah, I'm not losing my fucking pension and going to

112 As the cigar-smoking Pat Amato, Aramini drove a $100,000 Ferrari. Working with him on Operation Waterjack were Troopers Alan Duranik (left) and Peter Henderson (center). While Aramini and his mob cronies were unloading a shipment of stolen Ralph Lauren shirts and sweaters, State Police busted them. So that mob members wouldn't think Aramini set them up, he too was cuffed, photographed, and locked in a jail cell.

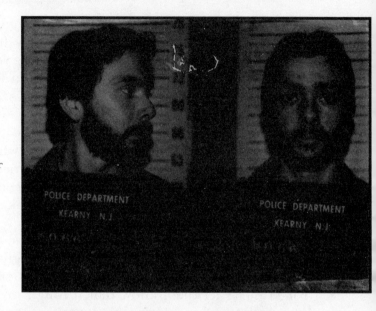

jail.' When he said that, it was like someone coming up behind me and squeezing my balls so tight that my voice changed."

Scumbags Can Be People, Too

Delaney, Weisert, and Aramini all experienced reverse culture shock when, after being undercover for so long, they were finally brought in from the cold. Delaney admits, he was reluctant to drop his flashy, big-spending persona. "I continued to dress like a wiseguy for over a year," he says. He walked and talked like 'em, even defended them.

DELANEY: Look, what you're asking undercover cops to do is become friends with the criminals, so some natural bondings are going to take place. It's almost like the Stockholm syndrome. You're in fear. That fear causes you to want to get close to these guys, so they don't do you any harm. You want to let them know you're a good guy in their eyes. Then, all of a sudden, they start doing nice things for you, like inviting you to their house for Easter dinner, or giving Christmas presents to you because they know you're alone. They open their house to you. You break bread with their family. After two-and-a-half years of hanging around these people, I went from this Irish Catholic kid who never cursed in front of women, to defending these criminals, saying, "Aw, this guy's not so bad. He's not putting bullets in people's heads. He's just stealing." Jack Liddy once said to me, "Just listen to yourself! Do you know what you're saying?" But it's like Patsy once said, "Scumbags can be people, too."

ARAMINI: As soon as we'd do a score, like buying up stolen property, or hijacking a Conrail shipment, we'd all go out and party. Stealing was a very social thing. You're talking day in and day out with the same people. You're earning with them, and they respect you for that. These guys weren't all that different from anybody else, except for how they made a living. Some could be really personable. They'd steal the eyeballs off one guy, and give the shirt off their back to another. If they figured you had money, they'd take it from you. They had no problem with stealing. They were thieves. They lived for today, not tomorrow.

114 Easy come, easy go. The one thing they all had in common was wanting to beat the system.

WEISERT: On the surface, some of these people were very likable, with tremendous personalities. They'd come in the office laughing, always have two or three jokes to tell. Maybe one of them would talk about taking his kid fishing. So you'd sit back and think, Hey, he's not so bad. Then you'd think, Yeah, but last week he told me about how he took a pipe wrench and crushed some guy's skull in.

Back in Uniform

On September 28, 1977, in a series of predawn raids, more than thirty suspects were brought to the West Orange Armory for fingerprinting and booking as a result of Operation Alpha. Delaney and Weisert, in State Police uniform, stood with their hands clasped behind their backs as each man was trundled in wearing cuffs. "I felt like crap," Delaney says. "I felt like I had betrayed a friend, broken a code of ethics. I dropped my head. I wanted to get out of there. As a kid in Catholic school, I got whacked by a nun for telling on a friend. I was taught snitching wasn't right. So here I am making a career out of it."

On June 6, 1983, Aramini's undercover job, Operation Waterjack, ended when eight of his criminal "cohorts" were indicted on charges of conspiring to steal merchandise from the Conrail yard in Kearny and store it in his warehouse. Aramini, in trooper uniform, went to visit them in jail, hoping, he says, "to see if they'd flip. None would." What would Emily Post do in *this* situation? "I put my hand out, and one guy wouldn't shake it," says Aramini. "I felt terrible. Another guy, seeing me in uniform, said, 'Hey, you look pretty sharp. I'm proud of youse.' That really made me feel bad. I told them, 'Listen, I'm not here to apologize for my position. I said, I have mixed feelings about it, but I had a job to do. It's nothing personal.' They understood."

But did Aramini? "I had nightmares afterwards of meeting these guys, of trying to make amends, even apologizing for what I did."

Little did Delaney, Weisert, and Aramini know that the worst wasn't over. Now came the courtroom trials.

Hudson County crime boss John DiGilio kept this photograph on his bedroom dresser, framed. Perhaps he wanted to remember always the Operation Alpha troopers who got him and twenty-nine other mobsters arrested. Back in uniform, Troopers Bob Weisert (standing, second from left), Ralph Buono, and Bob Delaney attend a press conference announcing the mass bust. Standing next to Delaney is Jack Liddy, who headed up the sting. Col. Clinton Pagano is seated, far right. Alongside him is State Attorney General William Hyland.

"It's a unique experience, let me tell you," says Weisert, shaking his head slowly. "I was on trial from 1980 to 1988. By the time we got to the DiGilio trial, where he was finally convicted of conspiracy to commit loansharking, transcripts were stacked five feet high. I spent months by myself in a room reading them and preparing for the trial. Then I'd get on the stand, and the defense would start doing things to throw me off, to trip me up. When I'd walk down the courtroom hall, they'd have a gauntlet of ten to twenty wiseguys lined up, making comments as I passed. They'd bump into me in the elevator, or ask me questions while I was standing at the urinal in the men's room. When I was on the stand they'd be making faces or pointing their finger at me like it was a gun. We're two weeks into one of the trials when DiGilio faked a heart attack and had to be carried out on a stretcher to spend a few days in the hospital. Testifying was hell. The lawyers would grill me in relentless detail about percentages and interest rates and how much they were compounded at. They knew I'd eventually make an error. The lawyers used all kinds of dirty tricks, like having me read a page from a book, then quizzing me afterwards to see how good my memory was. They even robbed my personnel file to see if I had ever been in any trouble.

"Since I was the only witness against DiGilio, I was afraid I'd be blown away in court. During the trials, I lived in a hotel room with armed guards for weeks on end. After the undercover part was over, I got married, but those trials ruined it for us, for any newlyweds. We ended up getting divorced. One day, I was told the State Police had heard there were contracts out on Bobby, Ralph, and me. During those years I was too afraid to go to Hudson County or Newark Airport. If I got an assignment to go there, I got out of it."

"I used to wake up in the middle of the night screaming," says Delaney. "As you'd be washing your hands in the courthouse bathroom they'd come up and spit in the sink. Or, they'd rub their eyes while looking at you, which meant they were going to gouge your eyes out."

Although DiGilio was convicted on loansharking, he never served any time. In the spring of 1988, the hit man's body was found floating in the Hackensack River; he was done in by a mob associate. When troopers broke into his house afterwards, they found, sitting on his dresser, a framed photograph of Delaney, Weisert, and Buono, taken during the press conference that followed the armory roundup.

For Aramini, the only trooper among the three to have been married when he went undercover, the trials also had their scary moments—and not just from fear of reprisal from organized crime members. "My wife came to the proceedings every day for moral support," Aramini says. "One day, one of my tapes was played where a guy says to me, 'You know those two broads we went out with last Friday? We're going out with 'em again this Friday.' I saw my wife look up, the judge smirk, and I thought, Oh, shit . . .

"I was pretty uptight," says Aramini. "One time, I woke up in the middle of the night because I heard noises in my basement. I got up, went to the end table, and took out my gun. I ran downstairs and saw the garage door open. I cocked the gun and aimed it at a person who was standing there, saying: 'Don't move or I'll blow you away!' Then I noticed, it was my wife. She had gotten up to let our two German shepherds out. Whoa, that was a scary moment! From then on, I decided not to keep a gun in the house."

Even though more than a decade has passed since Projects Alpha and Waterjack were wrapped, Delaney, Weisert, and Aramini still have a shaken air about them, as if they'd managed to walk away from a head-on collision. Years later, they're still struggling to get perspective on what happened, to come to grips with its emotional levels. Sure, they received trooper fame from their undercover operations. But, at the same time, they all experienced the profound letdown that comes when life goes back to normal, when one thinks, I can never top this. Yet, despite it all, and knowing what they know now, all say they'd do it again. "We went as deep undercover as anybody could go, giving as much as you can ask from a man," says Weisert. "I feel as if we won the Olympics."

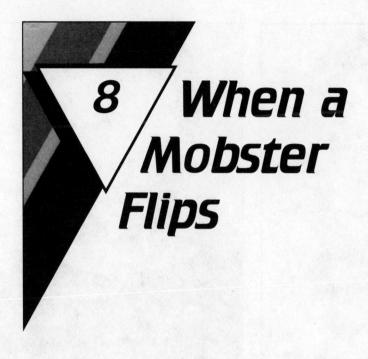

8 When a Mobster Flips

The Informer Hall of Fame

You can ask the *who, what, when, how,* and *why,* but definitely not the *where.* Living someplace in America, under an assumed identity, is George Fresolone, former racketeer and "made" member of the Bruno/Scarfo crime family. The reason he's in the federal Witness Protection Progam with his wife and three children is that there's a contract on his head. He's an informer who spent two years working with the State Police on Operation Broadsword, which targeted the northeast New Jersey faction of the Bruno/Scarfo crime family.

Fresolone did some things no other mob informers have done. After being nabbed, mobsters may sing like Pavarotti, but Fresolone made events happen. During his second year, working hand-in-hand with State Police Detectives Eddie Quirk (Badge No. 2979) and Billy

It was LCN member George Fresolone's secret tapings that bagged Nicodemo Scarfo, Jr. (right). He was acting as a conduit for his imprisoned dad, the infamous Nicodemo Scarfo, Sr. (left).

Newsome (Badge No. 3043), Fresolone secretly recorded four hundred conversations and meetings with organized crime members from six different families. These tapes resulted in the arrests and imprisonment of twenty-two mob associates and seventeen "made" LCN members, on everything from racketeering to extortion to weapons possession. On August 21, 1990, 150 state troopers fanned out across northern and central New Jersey before dawn to conduct simultaneous raids. Among those rounded up were Nicodemo Scarfo, Jr., who was acting as a messenger for his father, who continued to run the disarrayed family from federal prison in Marion, Ill.; Anthony "Tony Buck" Piccolo, the acting boss of the Bruno/Scarfo family; and John Riggi, the boss of the DeCavalcante family, whom authorities had been trying to nail for years.

On July 29, 1990, Fresolone went where no informer has bravely gone before: he recorded his own "Making," or initiation ceremony into La Cosa Nostra, and thus insured his immortality in the Informer Hall of Fame. In one extraordinary conversation, Fresolone taped a gangster offering high praise to the blue and gold. "There's no place in this country that has the State Police like New Jersey," said convicted mobster Joe Sodano, after arguing that New York was a much better area in which to operate because gambling attracted so little law enforcement attention. "I wish we were all born and lived in New York," Sodano said. "[We'd] have plenty of money and a much better shot to keep going . . . But here, the State Police are everywhere . . . They got more different squads. Organized crime. Intelligence. This and that."

For their work, Quirk and Newsome were named Troopers of the Year.

Born and reared in the Ironbound section of Newark, Fresolone grew up with the Mob. As a teenager, he was taken under the wing of Pasquale "Patty Specs" Martirano, a *capo* in the northern New Jersey Bruno/Scarfo family. On August 4, 1990, several days after inducting Fresolone into the LCN, Martirano died of liver cancer. On a sunny day in January '93, Fresolone came to New Jersey to give this interview. For a previous trip to Newark to answer a judge's subpoena he was surrounded by a State Police SWAT team. For this meeting, he's accompanied by Quirk, the detective who convinced him to work for the State Police, and whom Fresolone calls his best friend. The setting is a sparsely furnished modern condo, where everyone's seated at a round dining room table.

Let's start with your childhood.

FRESOLONE: I'm from Newark. Born and raised in Down Neck. My father died when I was ten or eleven. He was a bookmaker. Actually, a

122 numbers operator for the Bruno family. My uncle was the same. They were either around Patty Martirano or Tony Bananas.

QUIRK: The Down Neck section of New Jersey is like the seat or birthplace of most organized crime activity in New Jersey. It had the Genovese, Luchese, and Gambino families. Although the Bruno family was associated with Philadelphia and South Jersey, it had a strong presence in the Down Neck section, which is also called the Ironbound section. It was a traditionally working class Italian neighborhood.

FRESOLONE: When I was a kid, I'd get on my bike and pick up packages for my father's business. I'd put the packages inside a secret pocket in my pants. Other boys had paper routes. I had a numbers route.

What did your mother think about this?

FRESOLONE: She came from Italy. She closed her eyes to it. She passed away in 1988, the year I got pinched. I knew no other life. Nobody told me about going to college.

QUIRK: Your high school yearbook—tell him what you put you wanted to be when you grew up.

FRESOLONE: "Bookmaker." That was Eastside High. Not too many people can say they fulfilled their dreams.

QUIRK: I wanted to be a doctor.

FRESOLONE: I went beyond my dreams.

What was your first break?

FRESOLONE: I was actually dating Patty's daughter for a while. Then I started driving him around.

QUIRK: He was a father figure to you after yours passed away.

FRESOLONE: I was handpicked by Patty. I was his driver. He groomed me from day one.

QUIRK: Godfather to your kids. Best man at your wedding. In the North Jersey hierarchy of the Bruno family, he was a well-respected individual.

FRESOLONE: And, at the end of my career, I was to be the underboss to Tony Buck Piccolo.

What was your big break?

FRESOLONE: I started in the numbers business. Collecting a few dollars for shy accounts they had. I was so involved with Pat, I'd do anything in the world for him. I ate steak with the man. I ate bologna with the man. You know what I mean? We had great times. We had bad times. We stuck together. I wasn't like the other guys. If they weren't making money, they'd go across the street to make ten. Forget the ten. Tomorrow, we might make twenty. That loyalty to Pat is what made me turn and do what I did. I was trying to protect him. He wasn't getting any help from his so-called friends.

QUIRK: Today there is no honor anymore.

Is 'Omerta' a myth?

FRESOLONE: Now, it is. Years ago, no. I grew up with it. Finally I says, hold it. This is not the way it is. The loyalty I have with me and Patty should be for all of our friends. It wasn't like that. It was everybody for themselves. When a guy's in trouble, you help somebody. Nobody cared. Like, fuck you. I thought Patty was a dying breed.

QUIRK: There aren't many like him anymore. An old-timer. Most of the wiseguys I deal with now don't share the wealth. It's a pretty much "me" type of thing. That's why you see more people coming over and working for us. It's easier to recruit people now.

124   FRESOLONE: When I went to jail, they continued to make money from my business.

QUIRK: He had an extremely lucrative bookmaking business.

FRESOLONE: Numbers. Sports gambling.

Why weren't you taken care of?

FRESOLONE: Greedy people. They came first. Fuck George, he's in jail, was the attitude. Let's go spend the money. George's money. I made a lot of money for a lot of people. When I went to jail, my wife had to go on welfare. Patty took care of her as much as possible, but after a while, he didn't have it to give. The others weren't putting in. There's no loyalty. That's what it boiled down to. The only loyalty I believed I had was with Patty. Thank God he died never knowing what I did.

QUIRK: It would have been rough on him had he found out.

Why did you flip?

FRESOLONE: A multitude of reasons. My kids. My family. I had just come out of jail. I didn't want them to go through that again. I was a three-time loser. I go in front of a judge, and he's putting me away under the 2-C law for being arrested in such a short time.

QUIRK: His kids were growing up. It was no life for them. He could end up in jail or dead.

How did the State Police approach you?

QUIRK: I went to George's house in Kenilworth, New Jersey, on June 1, 1988, to arrest him on racketeering charges. We were doing a roundup as a result of Operation Marat, which specifically targeted the Bruno/Scarfo family. We went early in the morning, which is our practice.

FRESOLONE: I was coming home from a monte game with a guy named Slicker. I knew they were there. I could have screwed 'em. I dropped Anthony off. He went and got pinched, and I got pinched. Eddie was at my house waiting for me. He treated me and my family like a gentleman. That's the main reason why we hit it off so well. I mean, I've been arrested before, and they tore my house apart.

QUIRK: You have to treat a person with respect.

FRESOLONE: He didn't touch nothing till I got home. He didn't tell my kids he was a cop. He told 'em he was an insurance salesman.

QUIRK: On the way to be printed, I started talking to him about it. He really didn't want to hear it. It was a nice conversation. Friendly. Nothing heavy-handed. We did him a favor. We got his bail reduced.

FRESOLONE: Then I did you a favor. They were looking for Patty, and he was out of the country on the lam. I said, "Save the time and man-hours. Don't waste the state's money. He's not here."

QUIRK: I went to George's house several times. You establish a rapport.

FRESOLONE: They would come ringing the doorbell, and I'd of been out all night gambling. I'd say, "Leave me alone. I don't want to talk to you." We bickered for a while.

QUIRK: I told him I was looking for intelligence information on the organized crime families. We did our homework on George. We knew he was an integral part of the Bruno/Scarfo family and dealt with made members of the other organized crime families. Everyone trusted him. We met finally at a Toys "R" Us in Scotch Plains one Sunday morning. We talked it over, walking up and down the aisles, for two-and-a-half hours.

What did you tell the State Police you could give them?

FRESOLONE: When I told them what I could do, they didn't believe me. I had to make them believers. They thought I was just rattling off to save my own skin.

Troopers Thomas Semon (foreground) and Thomas Van Tassel escort "the biggest catch of 'em all," the dapper mob boss, John Riggi, to a waiting bus after a raid that netted forty organized crime members. (JOHN DECKER, The Record.)

The plug was pulled on Operation Broadsword when police felt Joseph (Scoops) Licata—shown here in cuffs after his arrest—might murder Fresolone, his rival. Standing guard is Trooper Frank Monte. (WALLY HENNIG, The Star-Ledger.)

QUIRK: In our business, you become a skeptic.

FRESOLONE: Here they were for five years, trying to get John Riggi. Come November, I said, I'll hand him to you on a silver platter. They didn't believe me. But, come November, George handed him over. John Riggi was the biggest catch of all. Something they wanted. Something they could taste. It was like cutting a piece of steak when I got him.

QUIRK: George got us every crime family in Jersey except one.

FRESOLONE: We missed the Bonanno family.

Were you scared taping people?

FRESOLONE: Once you get past the first one, it's easy.

QUIRK: I've done it extensively. In the beginning, you're very self-conscious. You think people can see it. You're sweating. Like everyone else, he was extremely nervous. Probably popped a couple of Valiums. After a while, it's second nature. At the point where George got inducted, he was wearing not one, but two, recording devices.

Where did you hide the transmitter?

FRESOLONE: I have a trademark. I carry a pager. What the police did is, hook up a transmitter inside it.

Why did you decide to pull the operation?

FRESOLONE: Believe me, we could have gone further.

QUIRK: If we did, either George would have gotten killed by Joseph (Scoops) Licata, who had become his rival, or he'd have had to kill Licata. He was very jealous, Mr. Licata.

128 FRESOLONE: Especially because I had become a captain the day I was made.

QUIRK: A field promotion.

FRESOLONE: He knew Patty was sick, and as soon as something happened to Patty, I was going to take his spot. I was going to become the underboss.

When did everyone find out you were the informant?

QUIRK: The day we brought them into the holding facility at Totowa Barracks. We bring John Riggi in. They all stood up, the respect they gave for this guy. He's always dressed impeccably, in suits. Now they're looking around. Everybody knows everybody, but where's George? John Riggi says to me, "You have nothing on me." I said, you know George Fresolone? He says, "Yeah, I know the kid." "Well, he's with us." The color drained out of his face.

FRESOLONE: He knew he was dead. He was history. They said, Tony Buck started getting pains in his chest when they showed him my picture. He almost had a heart attack.

Have there been any trials?

QUIRK: To date, most of the people have pled out, because they know the evidence is damning.

FRESOLONE: See the work I do?

What do you do for a living now?

FRESOLONE: I started my own business. My wife works. We get along.

QUIRK: This is your normal struggling American family.

FRESOLONE: Want to know something? I walk around with $3 in my pocket. I used to come home and put thousands of dollars on the table and tell my wife to take what she needs. But you know what I have now? Fulfillment. Joy. I go to see my kids play basketball and football. I have time to spend with them.

QUIRK: When you're a mob guy, you have to spend twenty-four hours a day thinking of ways to make money.

For a wiseguy, you're very likable.

QUIRK: I never met a wiseguy that wasn't likable. Regular people. Just in a different business.

Like robbing and killing people.

FRESOLONE: You know, hey listen, we don't put a gun in our hand and stick you up and say we're going to take your money. What we do is, gain your confidence and then become your partner. I'm not going to kill innocent people. I'm going to kill one of us.

Your watch, is it gold?

QUIRK: Cost him $8,000.

You wouldn't have it long in New York City.

FRESOLONE: Why? Who's going to take it from me? I'll give you a for-instance. I can't say if I flew here, took a train, or a boat. But I'm somewhere, waiting for transportation, when a person comes up beg-

130 ging money from me. I says to him, "You ain't getting nothing from me. Ain't nobody taking nothing from me."

Whose idea was it to tape your 'Making' ceremony?

FRESOLONE: Actually, they laughed when I told them this could happen. I says, "By the way, there's a chance of me getting straightened out."

QUIRK: Even the colonel couldn't believe it.

What went on?

QUIRK: What happens is, they bring you into a room.

FRESOLONE: Can I explain my ceremony, please?

QUIRK: I was there.

FRESOLONE: You weren't inside, though.

QUIRK: It was in the Bronx.

FRESOLONE: Yeah, the Bronx. My friend, Patty, is dying of cancer. We were having it over at a friend of mine's house, where Patty was staying. The friend whose house it was asked his wife to leave for an hour, that we wanted to talk. There was five of us being made that day, but we had to consolidate everything into one. Tony Buck read the speech. It tells you, you live by the knife you die by the knife, you live by the gun you die by the gun. If you want to leave, leave now. If you stay there's no turning back. Then what happened is, Patty called me up. We get some toilet paper. I cut my hand.

QUIRK: He cut your hand.

FRESOLONE: He pricked my finger.

QUIRK: Your trigger finger.

FRESOLONE: He draws blood with a safety pin. They sterilize the pin each time. They wipe off the blood with a tissue. They put the tissue in my hand and burned it. As it's burning, Patty says, "Repeat after me: *May I burn in hell if I betray my friends in the family.*"

Were your feet getting warm?

FRESOLONE: It was something I looked forward to since I was a kid. This was my ultimate goal. Now I know, once I hit the goal, it's all over with. In a couple of days, I'm history. I'm out of here. This job is coming down, and I'm starting a new life.

QUIRK: He's not George Fresolone anymore.

Did you feel you were betraying family members?

FRESOLONE: Listen to the words: *May I burn in hell if I betray my friends in the family.* My only friend in the family was Pat.

QUIRK: His real friends were sitting outside in Mercedes Benzes, Cadillacs, and an undercover boat, with transmitters all over the place.

Sounds like you had a great adventure, George.

FRESOLONE: It was a great adventure. A lot of fun. I went the whole nine yards. The State Police bought me a car that they bugged.

QUIRK: There'd be times we'd be laughing. Like in Las Vegas. We followed him out there with some mob guys. We were bumping into him. Gambling next to him. Making faces. For a year, day and night, it was

132 George, myself, and Billy Newsome. We lived, breathed, ate, laughed, cried, the whole routine together. We were friends.

Still?

FRESOLONE: O h, yeah.

QUIRK: We talk—

FRESOLONE: Every other day. Me. Him. Billy.

FRESOLONE: Listen, I want Eddie and Billy to retire and come live next door to me. One house on each side of me.

QUIRK: It's too cold in Alaska.

Did you ever think a state trooper would be your best friend?

FRESOLONE: No.

Have your wives ever met?

FRESOLONE: No. Never met. But someday I'm hoping we'll all take a nice trip to Hawaii and relax in the sun.

9 The War on Drugs

Mirrors and Confusion

Located five miles from Division Headquarters in a modern office building is the Criminal Enterprise and Racketeering Bureau, known as CERB. There's no sign on its front door to let you know you've arrived. If you can master the combination on the knob, you'll enter a world where people aren't always who they seem, where secretaries with Jersey accents say things like, "Victah, it's your informant, line three," and where dogs with badges are chauffeured to and from work in their own state-bought Jeeps. This used to be the Narcotics Bureau, until Col. Dintino, in a stepped-up effort to fight the international drug cartels, merged it with the Organized Crime Bureau. No state or federal agency has ever done this. CERB draws upon the State Police's experience in fighting the LCN to target drug sellers. By

133

134 identifying them as major conspirators, they can be prosecuted under the tougher, RICO laws. In the last few years, no area of police work has undergone more rethinking and reordering of priorities than drug interdiction and enforcement. In many ways, CERB is where the nascent OC Bureau was in the late 1960s, up against a seemingly insurmountable problem.

CERB is drugbusters, nineties style. With its combined pool of detectives, and working closely with the Division of Criminal Justice, the Bureau has been formulating the best strategy of attack against the billion-dollar drug cartels, namely, the so-called Cali of Colombia, which is a major supplier of cocaine in the United States.

"I'm challenging the FBI, the DEA. I'm challenging them all and their traditional way of thinking," says Col. Dintino. "For the last thirty years, the number-one problem in this country has been drugs. We're talking about stopping couriers on the highway and seizing millions of dollars. If the LCN were to lose that kind of money, there'd be bodies everywhere. That's the kind of profits we're dealing with. All areas of narcotics dwarf LCN activities. When I had a meeting to talk about bringing organized crime and narcotics under one roof, the idea was met with a total lack of acceptance. Three or four months later, I had another meeting. After a while, people came to understand my reasoning. You've got to change people's thinking, and that takes time. It's especially difficult in law enforcement, because cops tend to see things one way."

CERB is a whole new approach to fighting the war on drugs—starting at the top of a pyramid instead of the bottom. Gone are the days of the street-level buy-busts, where a narc would cuff and haul in a street-level dealer—usually an addict trying to support his habit—for selling him a small amount of dope. Municipal police handle the bulk of those arrests now. Gone, too, are the State Police's highway vehicle searches that civil rights groups claimed were disproportionately aimed at blacks and minorities. "For the first twenty years of the Narcotic Bureau's existence, we were earmarked to interdict street-level narcotics sales. Our new name says it all. We're now looking at the racketeering end," says Maj. Vince Modarelli (Badge No. 2879), who heads up CERB.

Step into his light-filled office. Putting his arm around your shoulder, he asks, "What do you need? I'm gonna take care of you."

"Vinnie worked his way up, starting on the streets in undercover. Nobody knows narcotics better than he does," says a trooper.

Through the latest means of surveillance and wiretapping, CERB's big priority is to learn all it can about the Cali, as well as other drug cartels from Asia, Africa, and the Mid- and Far-East. CERB's ultimate objective is to dismantle the Cali, which has entrenched itself in northeast New Jersey and Queens, N.Y. Since the Cali is so highly structured and diversified, there are many ways to go, and finding the right path has sometimes been a trial-by-error, seat-of-the-pants learning experience. "The Cali has many, many levels," says Det. Charles Cadmus (Badge No. 2734). "This keeps things scrambled. It's all mirrors and confusion. If we get an informant, he's not familiar with his bosses. The cartels are not like the Mafia, which has 'made' members and associates. You can't do a flow chart."

The cartels, which began in the seventies, have evolved into giant corporations "run like General Motors," says Modarelli. They're directed by high-level bosses who remain in South America, and "who we can never get to," says Cadmus. "The Cali cartel members are able to work within the fabric of the Colombian government and social set," says the detective who heads up the twelve-member, round-the-clock Calico surveillance unit, whose identity must remain secret. "One of their biggest leaders is a hands-on guy named Gilberto Rodriguez Orejuela, aka 'The Chess Player,' who owns banks and soccer teams and lives in the city of Cali. He's built four or five police precincts around his neighborhood. The Cali group is that entrenched in the Colombian government and business community."

Cali cocaine shipments are usually smuggled by trucks into the United States over the California, Texas, and Arizona borders. After being warehoused in the Southwest, shipments are transported across country to New Jersey and New York in tractor-trailers by independent truckers who are known as "mules." Once here, the shipments are delivered to midlevel distributors, who are trusted employees of the cartel's top level. So that "mules" can't give information to the police if arrested, shipments are unloaded at dropoff points away from the distributors' warehouses and stash houses. These distributors, in turn, ship the cocaine to lower midlevel distributors across the country, who are responsible for getting it to street-level dealers. The cartels employ coordinators to make sure all the gears run smoothly. Since it is a well-

On January 31, 1991, State
Police drug enforcement
agents confiscated 3.1 million
dollars in shrink-wrapped
bills on a road stop.
*A Secaucus warehouse
is the not-very-glamorous
setting for a cocaine haul.*

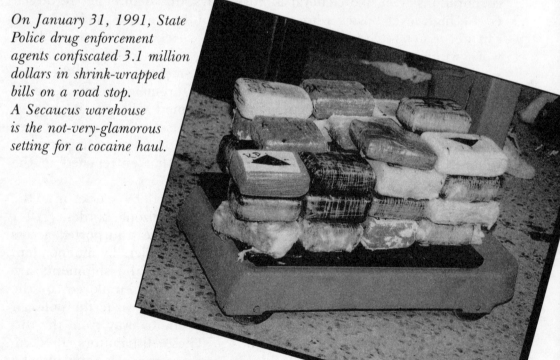

run business, each cell—a cell being a unit of a cartel employing four to six people—keeps books and ledgers of its transactions. To help get profits out of the country, cartel members have set themselves up in hundreds of business fronts across the United States that act as money transfer stations. Savvy to the legal system, they employ lawyers to fight wiretap amendments and to represent them in court if arrested.

"For every step we take, they take one ahead of us. It's a constant battle for new laws and regulations, especially when it comes to wiretaps," says Cadmus. Since drug dealers rely on such modern means of communication as fax machines, computers, and cellular and mobile car phones, wiretap laws are continually being amended to allow detectives to tap into these devices. "I hate to admit it, but we don't know who our enemy is," says Modarelli. "Unlike the Mafia, who flaunts its activities and its money, the cartels are very secretive. They do not employ Americans, drive fancy cars, associate with the general public, or spend their profits here." "Unlike the Medellín cartel, which was ruled by thugs who wielded bats and guns, the Cali cartel is very low-keyed," says the head Cali detective. "If they rub you out, it'll be done so clinically and clean it won't make the headlines."

As for the Cali's profits, "We hear estimates of $2 billion a year, but that pales in comparison to the truth," says Modarelli, displaying across his desk photos of confiscated drugs and stacks of hundred-dollar bills that have been vacuum-packed for easier transportation. "In four weeks, we took almost $6 million cash off 'mules' from this one cell. Four weeks went by before they even knew a dollar was missing. The $6 million was nothing. You tell me a business that could withstand a $6 million cash loss within four weeks and not miss a step. We beat our chests when we take five thousand pounds of cocaine, but there hasn't been a single police action in this country that has been responsible for impacting the cocaine trade at all."

"By 1990, we really became aware that in order to fight this war, we had to be in the street," says the Cali detective, who spends most of his days trailing Cali cartel members around northeast New Jersey and New York. "We had to physically watch these people. Keep an eye on them for extended periods of time. We work with wiretaps and surveillance to put together the whole puzzle of how they operate. This began to happen as troopers became more and more proficient at following people. And we realized it took an eight-to-ten-man surveillance

138 team to follow one car properly. This is not something that's taught in a classroom. To do it right you probably have to break every motor vehicle law in the book, and do it safely. There's an art to following somebody from a distance. We can't use aerial surveillance because the area we're working in has too large a volume of air traffic . . .

"I've been on this job for three years," says the Cali detective. "We are making progress, getting closer and closer to the top rungs." Rather than take down a drug "mule" or money courier, at least right away, Cali detectives will follow him or her for extended periods of time, hoping they'll be led to higher levels of the cartel. Since drug trafficking involves other countries and states, the NJSP works alongside the FBI, DEA, ATF, and other State Police departments. "People said it would be impossible to infiltrate the cartels, but we have. We have Colombian informants," says Modarelli.

When Drug Worlds Collide

Gone pretty much are the "Miami Vice" days when cocaine was shipped to southern Florida and then driven north by cartel family members in "load cars," which are automobiles with hidden compartments. New Jersey is a corridor state, and tons of cocaine are transported across its highways every week. Less than one percent of that is ever found. Since so many get their kicks from cocaine, the Operation Roadside task force tries to interdict those loads by knowing what to look for. "We are unique to the State Police, concentrating on the transportation of narcotics in commercial vehicles—a fancy way of saying tractor-trailers," says Matthew Hartigan (Badge No. 3396). "Tim Grant (Badge No. 3535) and I will sit in a van on a highway looking for certain tractor-trailers. We train road troopers who've stopped a truck for a motor vehicle violation or inspection to engage the driver in a conversation. If the trooper's suspicions are aroused, he'll attempt to get a consent to search." "In order to inspect a tractor-trailer, we must have probable cause," says Grant. "That can be obtained ahead of time through informants and wiretaps."

Operation Roadside began in May 1990. "By reviewing Drug

Enforcement Agency sensitivity reports, we started noticing trends," says Hartigan. "Tractor-trailers were being seized in the Los Angeles area and other western states with large shipments of cocaine—one hundred to one thousand kilograms—and large shipments of money, millions of dollars. We noticed the tractor-trailers were often registered in New Jersey and the drivers maintained addresses in Hudson County. The cocaine and the money were destined for offload and staging areas in New Jersey, which are parking lots, motels, public storage areas, places like that. We found out they were using New Jersey because it gives them easy access to New York City. Lodging and gas facilities are available here without crossing the bridges and tunnels into New York with the trucks.

"We noticed the trucks were being driven by Cuban criminals. The Colombians trust Cubans. Colombians think all Anglos are cops." The truck of choice has been the Peterbilt, either bought by the Colombians for the driver's use, or paid for by the driver from his profits—a cross-country run can bring $40,000. "The drivers are free to do their own trucking business, but when called upon, will deliver their loads as instructed," says Hartigan. "These trucks have fancy paint schemes, chrome wheels, and exhaust stacks. The Peterbilt is a status symbol, like a Mercedes Benz. Originally, company names would be the initials of the driver or his wife. Historically, people who come into this country are intrigued by the Old West and our country's fast pace. So, we're seeing names like Wild West Trucking and Speedy Enterprises. We've had cases where trucks have been outfitted with hidden compartments. Once we found one in the airfoil on top of the rig. There were hundreds of pounds of cocaine inside. False walls are common, too. A forty-foot truck will actually be thirty-nine feet because there's a hollow wall." "The important thing to remember is, this operation does not address legitimate companies," says Grant.

Keeping one step ahead is a constant problem. "That's why they're using more sophisticated hidden compartments," says Hartigan. "U-Hauls are becoming popular, because they don't have to take them to weigh stations. We've also seen a rise in the use of recreational vehicles and campers. We still find all the drivers are Cubans."

Although tractor-trailers are the preferred mode of transportation into New Jersey, "we certainly still have ships coming in with loads secreted in them," says Modarelli. "We've been involved in a number of

140 investigations with U.S. Customs in which cartels have gone to elaborate means to secrete cocaine in various conveniences. We had a case where five thousand pounds were in a load of chocolates sent via Port Newark in decontainerized shipments. We've seen cocaine hidden in hollowed-out fenceposts and in the crankcase of an ocean liner engine that took steam fitters four hours to get into. The cartel didn't ship that load from South America to New York to save money. They sent it to three different ports around the world to mask its origin. So cost means nothing to them. I tell you, I shudder to think of the profits, to think how much cocaine is in transit throughout the world right now, and how much money is going south . . .

"We seized $3.5 million from two couriers in Jeep Cherokees on their way to a warehouse in Philadelphia," says Modarelli. "We found it in hot water heaters. It was the largest cash seizure in the history of New Jersey, made by our hotel interdiction unit after countless hours of surveillance. The launderers had a lathe-type machine that wove this currency into a core of fiber glass. That core was then put into the hot water heaters, replacing the heating elements. They were being shipped in water heaters to South America. Weeks later, they would ship the core that was taken out. It was cost effective. After taking the money out of the water heaters, they would reassemble and sell them. We also had a case in which we interdicted $2 million that was being shipped out of the country inside Nintendo machines."

If a money courier is caught by the police, the cash will be confiscated until he can prove it's for legitimate use—which has yet to be the case in New Jersey. Under the Civil Forfeiture Act, unclaimed money is turned over to the county in which it was seized and is earmarked for drug enforcement. All a courier asks for is a receipt so he can show the distributor that he didn't steal it.

"Find! Fetch!" are two of the scariest words a courier can hear. The State Police has nine narcotics dogs that can be called out to sniff vehicles for hidden compartments containing dope. As the dog's personal handler throws a towel that has cocaine residue on it across a room or into a vehicle, he or she yells, *"Find! Fetch!"* Actually, it's a fake-out, as the handler hides the towel behind his or her back. While searching the room or vehicle for its drug-scented towel, the dog will turn up the narcotics. When suspected drug money is confiscated, a dog handler will hide the cash somewhere in a station house room, such as in a fil-

Trooper Annemarie Grant with Buddy, her live-in narcotics dog.

ing cabinet, desk drawer, or duffel bag. If the dog finds the money, it
means it's been impregnated with drugs from having been around
them.

Often, just the sight of a dog will make someone confess. "One time,
I was at home taking piano lessons from a male teacher who I had
never used before," says Det. Annemarie Grant (Badge No. 3479), who
handles Buddy, a seventy-five-pound labrador. "When Buddy came into
the living room, I told the teacher he was a narcotics dog. The teacher

142 got up from the bench, went over to the couch, picked up his leather coat, walked into the bathroom, and flushed the toilet."

Is the drug war *really* winnable? "They have the big advantage over law enforcement," says Modarelli. "For them, money does not come into play. In law enforcement money *does* come into play. We have budgets and manpower allotments." A long-term "high-level" investigation can run into the millions of dollars. Instead of buying $20 bags of heroin, one is buying hundreds of kilos of cocaine, which can cost between $20,000 and $40,000 each. "If we lose a case in court, we lose the case," says Cadmus. "If they lose—at least it's been the experience in South America—they kill a judge."

Small Victories

"The situation is not hopeless. We just need a change in attitudes," says the head Cali detective. "We're attacking the problem from the top. It's got to be attacked from the very bottom, too—getting young kids not to use it." For that reason, thirty-seven state troopers participate in Project DARE (Drug Abuse Resistance Education), a seventeen-week drug awareness course taught by nine hundred police officers to fifth graders in almost four hundred public school districts around the state. In terms of percentage, that makes New Jersey number one.

"This is my forty-first year in law enforcement, and I've seen it all," says Col. Dintino. "As for priorities in fighting the war on drugs, education and rehabilitation have always been at the bottom end of the totem pole. Those priorities have to change. In November 1988, we sent six troopers to Virginia to be trained as DARE instructors. At that time, there were only twenty-two DARE officers in New Jersey. We're now the lead agency. We teach our own people and local law enforcement officials how to use the program. I feel we've got to employ the same educational strategy to keep kids off drugs as we did with cigarettes. It's going to take ten to twenty years for attitudes to change. But they will. I'd like to see the DARE program become legislation. All kids should have to go through it. That, I strongly feel, should be etched in stone."

"Surveys being done in California are showing that DARE works, that drug use is decreasing among first-time users," says Sgt. James Eden (Badge No. 3183) of the State Police's DARE unit. "One of the really positive things about the program is that the police get to be seen in a different light. They eat lunch with the kids and are with them at recess. Children see a policeman as a friendly officer, like it used to be."

Modarelli joined the Narcotics Bureau in 1978, ten years after it began as a response to the flower children. "We've seen the Bureau change from its number-one problem being the enforcement of psychedelic drugs to the cocaine explosion," he says. "I liken the drug problem to the Vietnam war. When I was doing undercover in the seventies and eighties, risking my life, people didn't want me out there. The drug war was an unpopular one. We did not have the support of the people of this country. In the mid-eighties, there was a public outcry. You saw a change in the drug laws. The Comprehensive Drug Reform Act of 1987 was enacted that gave stiffer penalties for school zone use. Why cocaine? I don't know. But I do know that we the people—our generation—*we* allowed it to happen. It's now our responsibility to do something about it. We created it. We have to solve it.

"The drug criminals will always be a step ahead of our Bureau. But fighting organized crime taught us how to adapt, and that's our advantage."

"Don't Act Like a Cop"

When it comes to undercover work, they all say, Maj. Modarelli couldn't be touched. He was the King. "My wife tells me I was a lot happier out buying dope than I am now," he says, standing an inch from your face. "I loved it. I played everything from an Iranian arms seller, to a wiseguy, to a street dealer. You got to have balls and a good mouth to do that. I never used drugs in my life, never bought or sold them outside of my undercover exploits. I never covered my face with a beard or disguised my looks. Never once was I uncovered.

"It takes a unique individual to be able to work undercover. Not

144 everyone can do it. I have a lot of good investigators who couldn't fill a prescription in a drug store. The biggest thing I try to teach my people is, don't act like a cop. I tell them to act as though you really are a drug dealer, as if you really have a hundred thousand of your own money in the car, and you're not protected by an army of state troopers. You have to leave behind all of your Academy training. Some detectives have such a lust to do their job, they can't interact with the other side. They can't befriend someone for the purpose of role-playing. There's going to come a time when you are going to put the handcuffs on that person, and you're a trooper again. But for the interim, you *are* one of them. You sit for hours in a bar and talk to 'em. Bullshit with 'em about the football game. You do the things detectives aren't supposed to do."

No matter how good Modarelli was, there were some roles even he couldn't pull off. Like being black. Or a female.

Because she could pass for a teenager, road trooper Joann Flaherty was taken out of her squad car and asked to pose as a high school student at Hunterdon Central in Flemington. Her mission: to mingle with the predominately white, middle-class students, to find out which ones were buying and selling drugs. "Only the principal and superintendent of schools knew my real identity," she says. "I had to go to class every day, take gym, even eat the horrible cafeteria food. I had to miss a lot of classes because I had court dates. My teachers thought I was cutting, so I was given a lot of detentions and made to stay after class. It was very frustrating, because I was always a good student. But at Hunterdon they thought I was a punk, because I didn't do my homework or always show up. I couldn't tell them the truth. I had to let them think I was a bad girl."

After two months, Flaherty revealed herself. "I was brought to the principal's office," she says. "I wasn't dressed as a student, but was wearing a business suit. The principal called about thirty kids in. My sergeant was there. He told them: 'You all know who this young lady is, don't you? They all said, 'Yes.' He then said, 'She's a state trooper, and you're all under arrest.' One girl started cursing me. The other kids just sat there with their mouths open.

"Nothing much happened to them. They were all juveniles. They all got suspended. I just hope they got a good scare."

With so much drug activity taking place in inner cities, minority undercover troopers are never short of assignments. "I wanted to do this work since I came into the State Police," says Det. Tim Goss (Badge No. 4834), sitting at his desk, wiring himself up for his morning chores. With his skinhead haircut, maroon silk shirt, and gold chain around his neck, Goss could pass for a pimp. Or, because he's so lean, a hyped-up crack addict. Out of uniform, he's someone you'd cross the street to avoid running into.

"I've worked hard to get informants," he says. "When I first got assigned to narcotics, I didn't know what drugs looked like. They just assumed because I was black that I knew what to ask for. I grew up in the suburbs and joined the Army when I was seventeen. My father was a military man. I had to become streetwise, quick. I began as a road trooper. Problem was, when it came to writing tickets, I was too compassionate. I realized, a guy might be running late for work. Or, a woman who was a single parent living on welfare couldn't afford to get her car fixed to pass inspection. But in narcotics, wrong is wrong. I don't feel guilty for arresting somebody for that."

Many of the people Goss arrests are black or Hispanic. "Sure, they take it very personally," he says. "They feel that I'm betraying them. I had a girlfriend whose brother was kind of screwed up and selling drugs. One day, her mother said to me bitterly, 'So, why don't you just go shoot him?' Basically, they think we work for the enemy."

"After a raid," says undercover detective Victor Sherman (Badge No. 4834), "people start to gather. They'll call me Uncle Tom and tell me if I come back out here, they'll kick my ass. I don't make the laws. The laws say, this is the way it is. This is what I get paid for every two weeks. I try to do the best I can. I let those comments roll off of me."

"When you first come into narcotics, you have high expectations," says Goss, who is single and lives with his invalid mother. "You think you can save the world. But as time goes on, you realize every time you take one person off, there are ten more out there to replace him. It can make you really jaded. When you drive into a drug-infested area to make a buy, it seems everyone's involved, including the old lady on the porch who's doing lookout." The reason he jeopardizes his life each day, he says, "is because you *are* doing something good. There are just a whole lot of them out there." "You may be taking only one guy down," says Sherman, "but that one guy may be selling crack to your sister."

Should a dealer ask an undercover cop to partake in drugs, "I just tell 'em I'm in a rush. Or 'Hey man, it's for my woman'; I use that excuse an awful lot," says Goss. "You have to ad lib," says Sherman. "If you're doing a street-level buy, you don't want to hang around. They don't want you hanging around."

Before heading out of the office, Goss gets a call from one of his informants, whom he puts on the speaker phone. "Where were you yesterday?" Goss asks. "I'm fucked up, man. I was in a car accident." "Yeah? Well I heard you ran your mouth too damn much." "Say, T, I need a few dollars to get my prescriptions filled. Can we meet?" "Not today. I got a job, and I'm late." Click. "There are three reasons someone becomes an informant," Goss explains. "One reason is, they've been arrested and want to work off their charges. Another is revenge. They might have a boyfriend or girlfriend they want to get back at. With that kind of informant, the trick is to get as much information as fast as you can, because eventually they'll change their mind. Another reason they'll become informants is strictly for the money."

"Let's go," says Goss, who's helping out the Bureau of Alcohol, Tobacco and Firearms build a case against a crack dealer who's got a new sideline—selling Tech 22 handguns featuring hundred-round clips. Through an informant, Goss has arranged a meeting with the dealer. While he attempts to buy a gun, their conversation will be transmitted to agents from the ATF. They'll be parked around the corner ready to spring to his aid, should he need it. "This guy has a long history of sticking people up," says Goss, who, though armed, will be alone with the dealer. "You take your chances," he says. "When I first came on narcotics, my mother used to wait up all night for me. Now, she doesn't ask me any questions, and I don't tell her anything."

Pulling out of the Bureau's parking lot, Goss takes out his gun, a Walther PPK, the old James Bond special. "Should something happen, I want you to know how this works. On our way, I'll show you how to buy some dope off the street," he says. Entering the East Trenton ghetto, Goss stops the car and gets in the passenger seat. "You drive," he says. Cruising slowly through the neighborhood on this bleak, overcast day, Goss motions to a young man who nods his head and points around the corner. "He's selling. He wants us to drive over there." As the young man approaches the car, Goss says, "Roll down your window and tell 'em, 'Two.' He'll know what you mean. Two bags of heroin. When he gives you the dope, give him this money." The young man runs up the front steps of a dilapidated row house and returns in a matter of seconds. "How much you got?" he asks. "Forty bucks." Money and product quickly change hands as a minivan with a white driver pulls up to place an order. Kind of like going to the Jack-In-The-Box, only less exciting. "It's that easy to get," says Goss.

Sitting in an unmarkd ATF car in a residential neighborhood, Goss can be heard over a transmitter ringing the gun dealer's apartment doorbell. "It's me, T. I got an appointment." "He's not here," says a muffled voice. "Try in a hour." Goss returns an hour later and gets the same answer. "When you start to do larger-scale jobs, they don't always go as planned," he says. "There's no doubt, he's selling guns. It's just a matter of hooking things up. Maybe he couldn't get a delivery. Or maybe he sold them to somebody else. He doesn't even have a telephone. On this level, you're dealing with real low-life. This isn't the LCN, where if you had an appointment with someone, he'd be there, or you'd never do business with him again."

The job is put off to another day, as "T" and the other undercover agents rendezvous at an Italian restaurant for lunch. Sitting next to Goss is a bearded, heavyset black man, named Junior, from the Trenton Vice Squad. There are two white ATF agents, one of whom's from Texas and nicknamed The Klansman. It's quite a group, one that has the other customers looking scared, especially when the guys remove their jackets to reveal shoulder holsters. "We were in here the other day, and some guys from the governor's office got up and moved to another room," says Junior, laughing. The drug cops all seem to get along, sharing war stories. "Oh, we do have fun," says Goss, "we do." "That's because we're out here doing the dirty work, trying to put away the bitch," says Junior. "We're the peons, and peons always get along."

"Women, money, and liquor," says Goss back at the office, "that's the first thing you're told when you come into narcotics. Women will mess you up. Never have sex with a female informant. Money'll get you, too. You're carrying cash around to buy drugs and pay informants. If you have a thousand on you and you can't pay a bill, it's tempting to think, No problem. I'll just borrow some and pay it back when I get my pay-

148 check. That's how you screw yourself up. And no liquor, that's the other rule." What about narcotics? "Nobody says, Don't do it. They don't have to. It's the understood no-no."

"Ow," says Goss, dewiring himself, slowly pulling adhesive tape off his chest and groin. "No one tells you about this part."

Raid's Here!

It's a nice day for a raid, for breaking down doors and catching people unawares. The nicest part is, it's taking place at 11 a.m. instead of at dawn, when they usually occur. Today's target is a Trenton garage owner named Maximo, who's selling marijuana out of his shop and sending his mechanics into the neighborhood as runners. Authorities want to catch him in action, so 11 a.m., it is.

"Usually, you want to get people when they're asleep," says Charlie Cadmus, who helped coordinate this raid for Trenton Vice. Sitting at his desk, the affable detective could be a social director organizing a surprise party. Instead of, We're bringing the Jello mold or onion dip, it's, We're supplying the battering rams and sledgehammers. Wielding them are the weightlifting super troopers who specialize in knocking doors off their hinges. On a raid, they're called the "doormen." "Doormen like to count how many shots it takes them to get in. Our guys have it down to a science," says Cadmus.

Armed unannounced guests can provide some awkward moments, especially since most raids take place when people are in bed, asleep or whatever. "Sometimes you'll catch them in the shower. You just say to the person, Turn the water off, please. You're under arrest," says Victor Sherman. "It isn't uncommon for people who are caught without warning to go to the bathroom on themselves," says Cadmus. "Once you get in there, the rush, the excitement, the place is dark, you're pulling people out of bed, throwing the bed against the wall—once the rush goes down and the lights go on, it's always been my experience that these guys are very compassionate." "A lot of times we'll go in a house and the occupants will start crying," says Sherman. "The women'll hold their babies and ask, *Why are you doing this to me?* I

After the "doorman" busts the door down with a sledgehammer, the shotgun-wielding point man rushes inside, yelling, "State Police!".

try to explain to them that we're not doing anything to *you*. You're doing it to yourselves."

Everyone who works in narcotics agrees—drug raids are where you see the worst, from abused and neglected children, to houses so thick with cockroaches that troopers have to change clothes to enter and exit. "I went on this raid once," says Sherman, "where the house was

150 filled with bottles of urine. They were everywhere, even under piles of clothes. I know, in prison, inmates will bottle their urine to throw at the guards. That's so, when the bottle breaks, the urine will burn them. But why these people were bottling it, I don't know. One police officer got so sick, he vomited. One thing, I'll never understand: We can catch a dealer who has fifty pairs of hundred-dollar sneakers and twenty leather coats in his closet, plus five thousand dollars in cash in his pocket; and yet, he'll live in a house that's a complete and total mess, where even the plumbing doesn't work."

Today's raid is part of a social experiment called "Weed and Seed" that seeks to cripple the local narcotics trade by "weeding" out dealers in run-down neighborhoods while simultaneously "seeding" these same areas with "safe havens" where youngsters can work or play after school. Because of its heavy drug activity, Trenton was chosen by the U.S. Justice Department to serve as pilot site for the initiative. In the ghettos, authorities have established "special enforcement zones" where community foot patrols encourage residents to inform on suspected drug traffickers. Once a tip is received, the Trenton police meet with other law enforcement officials to determine a plan of action. The State Police is part of the "weed" aspect, which involves a slew of agencies, including the U.S. Attorney's Office, the INS, FBI, DEA, and Mercer County Prosecutor's Office.

Once arrested, those considered significant drug dealers are prosecuted in federal court, where—especially if they're repeat offenders—they face much stiffer penalties than they would in a state or municipal court. "We provide the other agencies, particularly Trenton Vice, with undercover people," says Cadmus. "When it comes time for a raid, what I'll do is get on the phone and call other task force agencies. I'll say, 'We're staging a raid at 6 a.m. tomorrow, and this is how many people we need.' The raid will be under the command of whichever agency developed the case. The lead agency provides the point men, who are the shotgun guys. They're the first to go through the doors and into the house or building."

"It's late. I'll drive you to Trenton Vice," says undercover Det. Karl Douglas (Badge No. 3239), who, being black and Korean, can disguise himself in any number of situations. Today, he'll go ahead of the raid party. He'll be standing on the street in front of Maximo's, keeping an eye on what's going on.

Trenton Vice is located on the fourth floor of an old building in a blue collar section of town. The main floor is a senior citizens' center. After climbing four flights of stairs, one comes to an empty, auditorium-sized room. Towards the end of it is a closed door. Opening it, one enters a much smaller room. Here, fifteen men and two women, of all races, are seated, waiting for their orders. One man who's wearing a Navy pea jacket and knit cap looks like a junkie who'd enjoy slitting your throat. In narcotics, nobody is who they are. These are cops. The good guys.

Standing in the front of the room, pointing to a diagram on the wall, is plainclothesman Mike Mihalik, who developed this case. Through a series of control-buys in which he had informants purchasing drugs from Maximo, Mihalik was able to show probable cause. A judge then issued Trenton Vice a no-knock warrant to carry out this raid.

"Point men go here," says Mihalik, who's briefing the others on the layout of Maximo's house and garage, assigning them their positions. Today's doormen, Dets. Louis Arce (Badge No. 3755) and John Miranda (Badge No. 3797), will be split up—Arce breaking into the garage, where it's assumed Maximo will be, and Miranda into the house. In case the gate leading into Maximo's car yard is locked, Mihalik instructs someone to bring along the bolt and fence cutter. This is a complicated job, since it involves simultaneous raids on multiple locations. "Where will Ben be?" asks Chris Kearns, a municipal narcotics dog handler. "Where the van will be stationed, location 304," says Mihalik. "It's a good thing we're in the area," he says to the assembled group. "It's getting out of control. This will send a message. He's flaunting it. He's dealt heroin in the past. He knows how to manipulate the system."

After a last-minute prop check—"We got the pry bar?"—Mihalik announces, "Everybody suit up"; meaning, put on their bullet-resistant vests. "See you at headquarters," he says.

A raid involves a series of maneuvers until the target, or staging area, is reached. Step one was the briefing at Trenton Vice. Step two is in the parking lot of Trenton Police headquarters. Here Lt. Pete Manetto of Trenton Vice is assigning everyone the undercover vehicle they'll ride in, and in what order. When everybody's positioned, the five vehicles pull out, careful to time traffic signals so everybody goes

152 through together. "We want to go in tight formation," says Cadmus. "You can't have anybody getting lost."

Now comes the next step. After driving across town, the convoy pulls into a bank parking lot to wait for further orders. Broadcasting via radio is Mihalik, who is standing across the street from Maximo's garage. He's just sent his informer in to buy some more grass. The informer scored, meaning, Maximo's there and ready for company. According to Douglas, who's on the street somewhere, the gate is open.

"OK, we're going to roll," says Manetto, who's in the lead vehicle. The caravan moves into the street. Ahead of Cadmus' car is a white undercover van. "It's been used so much, the kids in the neighborhood all know it belongs to Trenton Vice," says Cadmus. "When they see it, watch them start yelling, 'Five-oh! Five-oh!' That's a warning, which comes from the title of the TV show, *Hawaii 5-0.*"

"We're almost there," says Cadmus. "When you see John jump out of the van, you jump, too."

In the time it takes to unbuckle one's seat belt, Miranda has already screamed "State Police!" and power-whammed the front door of Maximo's row house into the next county. The point man has entered, followed by a rush of Trenton Vice officers. Some of the plainclothesmen run directly through the house, while others head upstairs. Suddenly, mild-mannered Cadmus is wielding a gun and yanking open closet doors to see if anyone's hiding inside. In the living room, loud Latin music is playing, keeping time to the blinking lights of a plastic Christmas tree. In the kitchen sink is a half-eaten, badly burned rice casserole. "Hello," says Cadmus to a fluffed-up Pomeranian.

From upstairs comes a Trenton cop with a handcuffed woman, who is Maximo's wife. She looks neither scared nor angry, just inconvenienced. The officer seats her on the couch under a framed map of Puerto Rico. Placed upright against the wall near the front door—or where the door was—is Miranda's sledgehammer.

"Let's check out the garage, see what they got," says Cadmus. Lying cuffed on the floor alongside a partly dismantled Ford Diplomat are Maximo and his two young assistants. The room is monotone, colorless. One of the assistants strains his neck to look up. His eyes are shockingly blue.

"Maximo, any more antifreeze around here?" asks Kearns. "It's got to all be cleared out before I bring Ben in," he explains. "Ben eats everything." That's not all he does. "When he works, he gets excited," says Kearn, "causing him to go on everything."

While Ben sniffs for drugs, Detectives Cadmus and Jerry Camiso of Trenton Vice go inch by inch through one of the workers' bedrooms off the garage. From under the bed come a woman's earring and a hypodermic needle. "I was in a house the other week," says Camiso, "where the plumbing had backed up and flooded the basement. There was human waste everywhere. I was in another house where they had buckets in each room filled with it. I wish I had brought a camera to show this to kids, to say to them, 'You wanna do drugs? This is how you're going to live.'"

"I work honest," says Maximo, who's now standing cuffed against a garage wall with his assistants. "Don't insult me," says Lt. Manetto.

From outside, in a yard where broken-down cars are parked, comes a pitiful whimpering. Through a wire fence pokes a black, wet nose. Inside this caged area is a young dog—half lab, half pitbull—shivering and trying to lick the hand of anyone who gets near. She has no water; no food. Her cage looks as if it's never been cleaned. "Makes you sick," says Kearns. "She's a beautiful animal."

Although a raid has a great opening, the action goes quickly downhill. In fact, most of the spectators who had gathered out front have left out of boredom. Trying to find Maximo's marijuana stash takes the rest of the afternoon. As Ben jumps excitedly around the outside of a 1983 Monte Carlo parked in the yard, detectives try to open the doors, which are locked. Maximo is brought outside. "Give us the keys," says a detective. "I don't have keys for it." "Give us the keys." "I don't have any." "Are these what we're looking for?" asks a detective, producing them. Looking under the car's backseat, authorities find twenty-eight bags of grass—not a major haul, but enough to book him.

As night falls, the participants in today's drama begin to leave the stage, getting in their unmarked cars and driving off. "Another nice day in the big city," says a uniformed Trenton officer who's come to take Maximo in for processing. "I think my mother will like her; she's got ten acres in Hopewell," says Kearns, taking the abused dog out of her cage. Maybe it *is* a nice day.

154 Day in, Day out

"See the brown porch railing? That's his place, the guy we're eye-balling," says Det. Number One, driving his white minivan past a row house on a narrow, congested street in Union City, N.J. (Because the undercover troopers' names cannot be revealed, they have been assigned numbers for this interview.) This could be any city in South America, actually. Salsa music blaring from car radios. Guys in sunglasses and leather trench coats. Even though it's January, young women are still crossing the intersections wearing Spandex minis.

"This guy we're watching, he's a high-level money man for the Cali cartel, in charge of collecting, counting, and getting the money to where it's going," says Det. One of the Calico unit. "We've been tapping his phone for a while. He's trying to get through to Colombia for further directions. The money was supposed to go out yesterday. When he gets his orders, we'll follow him. After he passes the money on to somebody else, we'll let him come back to Jersey free and clear. We'll follow the other person for a while, see where he leads us. Maybe to a warehouse. Maybe Kennedy Airport. You never know where you're going. The white car sitting there with the woman inside—that's Barb from the County Prosecutor's Office. She's with us . . .

"We'll park here for a while, in this lot" says Det. One, who must talk loudly to be heard above the ear-stinging static of his portable radio. "Just kinda sit here, wait for the jerk to make a move. That's how it works in surveillance. Things stand. Things go. And when they do you're going a million miles an hour. We work with the New York State Police, who join in with us when we get out of the Lincoln Tunnel. They have our radios, so they know we're coming. When we go across New York City, we stop for few red lights. We have Kojak lights to put on our roofs, but rarely use 'em. What good are they without sirens? I knocked a clothes rack onto the sidewalk the other day . . .

"There's never been a unit like Calico in the State Police," says Det. One, who's been surveilling cartel members for almost three years. "We're getting closer and closer to the top rungs of the organization. Traditionally, in police work, you do one job with a twenty-day wiretap. If you don't get enough information, you get two ten-day extensions. In the end, you lock everybody up and do your reporting. Everybody goes back to their normal stations. Here, we watch the same people day in and day out for years. You can't read the paper or reach down for something on the floor. What if the guy makes a move? How do you explain to the other guys who've been out here every day that you missed him? It can't happen. Everybody asks me, how long am I going to be working this job? I say, probably for the rest of my career."

Dressed in jogging pants, sweatshirt, and Adidas, his black hair pulled into a ponytail, Det. One isn't exactly a recruiting poster for the Outfit. His nicknames include "Fat Joey," "The Animal," "The Butcher," and "Uncle Buck," after the John Candy character. "This is not the glamorous side of the State Police," he says, eating a takeout lunch of rice, beans, and yucca root. "You gain weight sitting here. I've put on sixty pounds since I started. There is no taking time off for the health club. I used to run seven, eight miles a day." Could Det. One be the agent who Maj. Modarelli said "eats with his toes"? "If he said it about somebody, then it's me," says Det. One, "I guess, 'cause I'm an interesting character." But no less a trooper: "Since I was six years old, I wanted to be in the State Police. My father is a local police chief. I love the Outfit. It's an honor to be working here . . .

"I don't care what anybody says. I've been in narcotics for ten years. It changes you," Det. One says. "When you're a road trooper, you meet some decent people. Here, the only decent people you meet are other cops and public service employees. All you meet on the streets are scumbags. A lot of people have told me I've changed. I know I have. My wife says I've changed big time. She says I've become rude and obnoxious. I don't have the patience to put up with things. I have to catch myself sometimes. I have to hit myself on the head and say, Stupid, you can't be that way. Come back to reality."

Pulling alongside Det. One's parked van is a Camaro. Inside, talking to the New York State Police on a portable radio, is Det. Two, the head of the Calico team. "Scenario one is, he'll pass it off to the girl," he can be overheard saying. "If it goes to Miami, they got a lot of ways to get it out of there. Stick it on a cigarette boat . . ."

Putting down his radio and looking out his window, Det. Two says, "This is like Desert Storm for these Colombians. They come here on a mission. They're on details, maneuvers. That's what it sounds like when they talk to their cartel family members back home on the phone."

156   Away from the CERB office and out of his suit and tie, Det. Two, who's wearing sunglasses, a leather jacket, T-shirt, and jogging pants, looks too cool. "He's the brains," says Det. One. "He plans what we're going to do." "The Brains" holds up a brand-new yellow hot water bottle for Det. One to see. In surveillance work, one can't always get out of the vehicle to make a pit stop.

Before joining the Calico unit, Det. One worked as a street-level narc. "*Narc*, nobody uses that term anymore," he says. "I've played everything from an arsonist to a hit man. There's nothing like the challenge of going out there and putting something over on somebody. Becoming a good friend of his, and then saying, I got you. It's hysterical. They'll always say, *I knew you were a cop! I knew you were a cop!* Then why'd you sell me the dope, you fool?"

"I never carried a gun undercover. It always made me uncomfortable. I didn't need it. I always got over on people. That's not to say, I wasn't nervous. If you don't have those butterflies in your belly when you go out there to buy dope, if you don't have that little tingle and twitch every time, then it's time to give it up, because that's how you get hurt. When you have no fear, you let your defenses down. Every time I went out, I couldn't eat beforehand. A lot of times, you got to sit in a bar drinking all night with these skeezies. I don't drink at home, I tell people, I only drink at work. But no matter how gooned you get, you gotta always have it in the back of your mind to watch out, to be aware of the risk . . .

"I had a gun put to my head one night. I don't talk much about that. It's not good to talk about it . . ."

But you love this work.

"I do. I *really, really* do."

Pulling alongside Det. One's van, where Det. Two, who's since left, was parked, is a Yellow Cab with a broken roof light. "It's Boo Boo," says Det. One. "Looks like a cab driver, don't he? He's with us. Everybody in our unit has a nickname. We're always ball bustin'. Goofin'. It keeps things going. We call him Boo Boo Bear 'cause he's so lovable you always want to hug him. I also call him Blinkin' Bob, 'cause he's got this facial thing. Whenever I come down on him, he squinches his nose and eyes. We also got Ajax the White Tornado, Mohawk, Bongo, and Pee Wee Herman. We call our leader Five Four, after the last two digits of his badge number. We got this Spanish guy, too. But he doesn't want a nickname, so it's better we leave it alone. I mean, some people are sensitive."

"I get to take this cab home at night," says Boo Boo Bear. "My neighbors all laugh at me. That's what makes the job kinda fun. I got the best job in the State Police. It's like being a kid and playing cowboys and Indians, or cops 'n' robbers. It's having fun with a bunch of good guys and doing the right thing." "Show 'em your bottle," says Det. One. Grinning, Boo Boo holds up an empty Evian bottle that says "Calico Restroom" on it.

"We're gonna take a drive," says Det. One, "catch up with ya later." Tooling around Union City, the detective points out hidden cameras that are focused on suspected cartel residences. The images are beamed back to Calico's headquarters, which are located in Secaucus. "You never know what you're going to have to do in the State Police," says Det. One. "There was a big tree in that vacant field that was blocking our transmission on a trailer, so I cut it down." Det. One points out an apartment building: "We were in there last week to arrest a money launderer we'd been following. The place was empty except for a counting machine. I found $400,000 in a false ceiling. Three million had moved through there in one week alone. When I found the money, the guy says to me, 'Shoot me now. My life is over.'"

Parked in the back lot of a Burger King is a canary yellow Chevrolet with two guys inside who are wearing suits. "They're from Major Crimes. We like to meet here sometimes," says Det. One, introducing Jack Repsha (Badge No. 3443) and Chris Andreychak (Badge No. 3754). "Say, Uncle Buck," asks Repsha, "have you heard anything from your informant, the cokehead cop?" "He got a mental discharge and is gathering shopping carts in a supermarket parking lot," says Det. One. "What a fall, huh?" "I still laugh," says Repsha, "when I think how we were out on that job together, and you took that wicker fan chair from somebody's garbage. Who woulda ever thought you were a cop, walking around with that stupid thing on your head?"

Heading into the lot across from the money launderer's apartment, Det. One pulls alongside Det. Two's car. "Still nothing," says Det. Two, AKA Five Four, the head of the Cali detail.

"People think surveillance is glamorous," says Det. One. "After several days in the back of a van, you want to start scratching the other guys' eyes out. I was on surveillance in Monmouth County. It was the hottest day of the year. I stripped down to my underwear and was covering myself with ice cubes. It must have been 130, 140 degrees in there." "You got to love this work to do it," says Five Four. "During the 'Miami Vice' days, guys wanted to get into narcotics. But after sitting for twelve hours and realizing they had to come back tomorrow to do it all over, they lost interest. They realized that all this job was going to get them was old and gray." With that, Det. Two drives off.

The afternoon is almost gone, and the money counter still hasn't gotten his instructions. Det. One has moved to another lot down the street. While waiting for something—anything—to happen, a Firebird pulls up. The driver is wearing very dark shades. "It's Oak," says Det. One. "That's our nickname for another one of our guys." "This job keeps you on your toes," says Oak. "One minute you're sitting here, and the next thing you know, you're running like a maniac. You're going parallel with somebody and he makes a right. Then you got to go like mad to catch him. We got to coordinate all this on our radios at the same time. It keeps us good, though . . .

"Well, see you later," says Oak, peeling out. "Nice having you on the set." "That's what we call our locations—sets," says Det. One. "We're called the players."

Two local cops approach Det. One's van and knock on the window. "If you guys are doing surveillance, you're doing a lousy job," says an officer. "OK," says Det. One, putting it in gear to leave. "See, in surveillance work, a guy can sit in a car by himself and nobody notices him. Like Five Four, who was crouched down in the seat. A guy and a girl can sit all day or night and nobody'll say anything. But two guys together—people call the cops. They think we're casing the neighborhood . . .

"Let's call it a day," Det. One says, "I don't want to miss wrestling practice. I'm coaching. I'll show you our plant."

Calico's headquarters are located on the second floor of a mini-mall, through an unmarked door with a sign out front saying "We're not buying anything." Inside a dreary-looking room are wiretap machines, dial number retrievers, and TV monitors. Sitting in front of a computer is Det. Three, who's wearing jeans and a sweatshirt covered with spackling paste. "It's my job to enter all of this stuff into the computer. To print out the log so we can go over what conversations were said," he explains.

"Sure, it's tedious work. I sit here all day. Sometimes all night. But I don't mind, because the end result is worth it: putting away somebody who is violating the laws of this state and country. That's why we all do what we do."

A Bust Gone Good—A Bust Gone Bad

Probably the most unpredictable area of State Police work is trying to bust drug dealers. Frustration comes with the territory, so a trooper must have tremendous patience. It can take months of elaborate preparation to set up a sting, only to have the seller not be at home that day or not show up for the buy. Busting drug dealers is certainly one of the most dangerous areas of police work, as undercover troopers are continually putting themselves in risky, vulnerable situations. Nerves of krypton are required. Yet there's nothing like the high of a successful takedown, when the masks are dropped and the final words are spoken: *"State Police, you're under arrest."*

The drama of this kind of work ranges from high comedy to profound tragedy. While working at a narcotics office in Bergen County, Capt. Juan Mattos (Badge No. 3938), who's now in charge of Affirmative Action at Division Headquarters, set up his workplace as a radio station. Posing as a smooth-talking Latin DJ who wanted to retail drugs, he and his coworkers busted two wholesalers who came to sell him a kilo. "It's why," says Mattos, "they coined the term *dope*."

The flip side of that perfect bust was one that left a State Police narcotics detective dead in a shoot-out. Had it not been for Sgt. Brian Caffrey (Badge No. 3295), who brought a situation that erupted into violence under control, the death toll could have been higher. For standing his ground, he was awarded the Distinguished Service Medal. At six foot three, with shoulders that should have a Wide Load sign preceding them, Caffrey makes for a frightening presence when breaking down doors. "Actually," he says, "I like to smile when I enter."

160 La Musica de State Police

"We had been talking about coming up with a different method of an undercover operation," says Mattos from his new digs at headquarters. "Something unique. One day, we were coming back from lunch, when we looked at the radio tower in back of the police station and said, why don't we pose as disk jockeys? Radio Station WNJSP, 1921 on the dial? I was always imitating other people at the station for laughs, so a radio voice was no problem.

"As call letters, I know WNJSP is one too many. But it was such a novel idea we couldn't resist. If you just say 'WNJSP' it doesn't sound right. But if you say it like this—'W ENNNNNNNN JSP'—it works. There is no 1921 on the FM dial, the year the State Police was founded. But a lot of dope dealers are stupid. I know, too, from past experiences, that greed makes anything possible. When you wave money in people's eyes, they become blinded by it and the potential to make more.

"Det. Victor Irizarry said that he had developed an informant who was providing him with a lot of good information. I ran the idea by him, and he thought it was a good one. On the morning of February 18, 1986, I was one of the first to arrive at the station. It was snowing and the road conditions were bad. I got a call from Vic saying that his informant had found two dope dealers who wanted to come to the station to meet me, thinking I was a DJ. Oh really, I thought. We should bring the informant in and find out what was what, which is routine. When Det. Brian Walsh came in for work, I told him he'd have to go to Union City to pick up Vic's informant, then bring him back here so we could debrief him. Find out who he's got, so we could set our buy.

"After Brian got the informant, I took him into Lt. Fred Martens's office. (Martens is now executive director of the Pennsylvania Crime Commission.) Brian told me he had two guys who went for the radio station bit hook, line, and sinker. As we're talking, I'm looking out the window. Suddenly, a 1981 blue Olds starts pulling into the driveway. The informant says to me, 'Oh, my God, they're here!' 'They're here?' 'I told them where the location was, but I didn't think they would come.' As they were pulling in, they got stuck in the snow. Just then, a marked troop car started to pull in and gave them a push. We got on the radio and said to the troopers, 'Please leave the area. We have a narcotics investigation ongoing.' They turned around and left.

"'Quick!' I told all the guys. 'Get everything off the walls that has anything to do with State Police, including the clock. I'll go out and stall them.' They were two Hispanic guys, casually dressed. I go outside, 'How ya doin'? I'm Paco,' I say in Spanish. That was the language we spoke in. Paco is short for Francisco Santiago, which was my undercover name. 'The cop helped us out in the driveway,' one said. 'Oh, yeah,' I replied, 'they pass by here a lot. You can park over here. Come on in and I'll show you the operations.' I brought them into Lt. Martens' office. Sure enough, everything had been removed from the walls. I sat behind the lieutenant's desk.

"We're having a conversation. 'You've probably heard me on the radio,' I say: *La Musica de Paul McCartney. Saludos amigos, This is Paco ... .'* I tell 'em, being a DJ doesn't make a lot of money for me. I want to distribute drugs. They tell me they've got cocaine, marijuana, whatever I want, in whatever quantities. I'm thinking, this is outstanding. They're thinking, this guy's so cool. One guy said to me, 'I've heard you on the radio, man.' I'm going through my routine, saying, 'This is going to work out well. I feel very comfortable with you guys and I like what you're telling me.' I was trying to loosen 'em up, make 'em feel at ease. Get to know 'em. Could they really provide, or were they just talking a big story? Normally, it takes more time to set things up. But I didn't have time. I had to think quick. Improvise.

"I said to them, 'I'd like to get a kilo of cocaine.' This guy, Juan, says, 'We can do that.' Now I knew they were mine. The moment they start to loosen up is when you've got them under your control. 'Where?' I asked. He opened up his leather jacket and pulled out this big brick of cocaine! I mean, that I never expected. I didn't react. 'It looks good,' I said, opening up the package and inspecting it. Crystalline. Very solid. Juan said he'd sell it to me for $34,000. 'Eighty percent pure,' he said. 'Outstanding,' I replied. 'As long as the cash is good, we'll come here and deliver it.' 'I like it. I like it,' I said. 'We can do business.' "As we were talking, I could hear the other detectives laughing outside the door. They couldn't believe this was taking place in the station. I told the dealers, let me have my friend bring in the

162 money, then they could leave. So I got on the intercom and called Det. Larry Churm. I said, 'Would you come in here with the package . . . you know, the one with the money?'

"Larry knocked on the door, then entered with three other detectives. They all just kind of stood around. Finally, Juan, who did all of the talking, said, 'Paco, where's the money?' After a while, I said, 'Look, my name ain't Paco. It's Det. Mattos, and I'm with the State Police.' They started laughing. Ha. Ha. Ha. 'You're funny,' said Juan, 'now give us the money and we'll be out of here. Stop kidding, man.' 'I ain't kidding.' I pulled out my ID and said, 'State Police, you're under arrest.' Tears of laughter turned to tears of sorrow. They were in shock.

"We processed them in the other room and took them down to the Bergen County Jail. I was down there a few days later to talk to another informant. I asked him if some guys had come through who'd been busted selling dope in a police station. I didn't tell him I was the one who did it. The informant said, 'Those two idiots? Jesus Christ! They were humiliated something terrible. They can't show their faces.'

"I'd been in narcotics for seven years when that bust happened. I knew I was being transferred in a month. I felt it was a kind of poetic way to leave. I had made my mark. 'This is Paco: W *ENNNNNNNN* JSP, 1921 on your FM dial.'"

"I Kept Yelling 'State Police!'"

"Nine days before my wedding, I was asked to go on two back-to-back raids that the South Region Narcotics Bureau had planned," says Brian Caffrey. "They were raiding a methamphetamine P2P lab in Washington Township, just south of Camden. After that they were raiding the lab owner's apartment in Westville, about twenty-five minutes away. There's a lot of drug activity in that area. The lab owner was a white male in his fifties, an Italian-American with organized crime connections in Philadelphia. He's dead now, a heart attack in prison. I was selected to attend these raids because I was experienced in them, and because they needed a uniformed trooper at both scenes.

If you don't have a uniformed trooper going through the door first in a narcotics case, they might think you're another drug dealer coming in to rip 'em off. They wanted to establish right off the bat that we were State Police. I was in charge of using the sledgehammer to take the front doors down.

"That afternoon, we had a briefing with members of the narcotics people in the basement of the local Deptford PD. Members of the County Prosecutor's Office were there, too. We also had troopers in unmarked cars monitoring both locations. Search warrants had been obtained, and we were ready to go. I asked if there was a possibility the guy had a weapon. Sgt. Newbury said yes. I had to know, because as the senior trooper out there, I wanted to make sure everyone wore their bullet-proof vests. I didn't know it then, but the guy had been charged with beating an individual to death with a pool cue in Pennsylvania, and was a suspect in another attempted murder case. He was thought to have shot an individual in the head with a .22 rifle over a drug deal. Although the victim lived, he couldn't identify the shooter. During the raids, we recovered that weapon.

"Det. Rich Mursheno and I drove to the lab in a marked car. He was at the wheel. I was in the passenger seat so I could get out right away with the sledgehammer. The lab was located in a little ranch house on a hill, in a nondescript, semirural area. While one of the troopers sneaked around the back, I went to the front door with a couple of the detectives. One of them was Albert Mallen. I remember him kidding me, asking, 'You want me to get that for you?' when we were at the front door. After opening the screen door, there wasn't much room to maneuver the sledgehammer. We didn't have to knock because we had no-knock warrants. It took me three swings to break through the frame of the door and enter. The whole time, I was yelling, *'State Police!'* Meanwhile, the other trooper had broken in the house through the back. The owner wasn't there, but we knew that, going in. We didn't want to raid his residence first, because he might call the lab and say, 'flush it.' We wanted the evidence.

"Inside, we encountered an individual who had been sleeping. We handcuffed and arrested him. The different rooms of the house had microwaves for cooking and drying the stuff. Chemicals were everywhere. The house smelled like cat urine, which is how you know someone's cooking P2P into methamphetamine. That's the odor. After

164 securing the location, we headed out. I remember Al kept trying to bust my stones: 'Hey, super trooper, you want me to handle the sledgehammer at the next job?' We were laughing, getting in our cars.

"When we arrived at the Westville location, Det. Sgt. Bob Linden was waiting outside the guy's apartment with an investigator from the prosecutor's office. The apartment was in a two-story older building near the railroad tracks. It resembled a town house. There were two identical apartments: one upstairs, one down. He owned them both, but lived upstairs. As we got out of our car, the guys in the unmarked ones got out of theirs. Everything happened simultaneously. Holding my sledgehammer, I ran up the outside stairs to the second-floor landing. Det. Gerry Lauther was behind me. At the same time, the other guys were taking out the door below. We were all yelling, *'State Police!'*

"There wasn't much room for me to swing the sledgehammer, especially with Gerry there, so I kicked the door. It sprung right open, then came back as if something was behind it. I opened it again and saw an individual standing there. I dropped my sledgehammer, pulled out my weapon, and told the guy to put his hands in the air. He kinda looked at me, then glanced down the hall. *'Get your damn hands in the air!'* I yelled. He did.

"I entered the room and pushed the guy against the wall. Gerry got on top and pinned him there. It turned out that he was there to put some stuff into the guy's computer. That's how the dealer kept track of his drug transactions. As I was standing in the living room, I heard a round being chambered into a shotgun. I had one in the car, and I thought maybe Mursheno had come up the stairs with it. I turned quickly to look back at the doorway, but nobody was there, so I turned back around. Standing in the hallway, wearing only boxer shorts and glasses, was Dominick Schiavo, the owner. He had come out of his bedroom closet with a 12-gauge shotgun leveled at my waist. He was maybe twenty-five, thirty feet from me. He starts yelling, *'Get the hell out of here!* We're yelling back, *'State Police!'* He's screaming, *'I don't give a fuck who you are, get out of here! Get out of here!'*

"My first thought was, I've got to get out of the way of that shotgun. I immediately grabbed Gerry. I pushed him and the guy he was holding out the door and onto the landing. Then I jumped out. Bob Linden was passing the other guy down the stairs. Gerry was crouched down, partway in the doorway. He was kneeling behind a sofa, taking aim. With my left hand on the doorjamb, I peered around into the room. I could see the guy's elbow sticking out from behind the wall that separated the living room from the bedroom. I could see him swing out with the shotgun. Now I'm thinking, This son of a bitch is going to shoot me! I yelled, *Drop the gun!'* then yanked my head back.

"He fired off a round, taking off the doorjamb where my hand was. The splinters ricocheted into my arm. That round passed in the eight to nine–inch space between my left hand and my face. I could feel the blast as it whizzed by. Another round hit my weapon, which I was holding straight up in my right hand. The round went shewwww and ricocheted off the ceiling. The force of the blast sent my hand reeling back. I thought, this son of a bitch hit me! It just kind of stung, like birdshot. I remember thinking that because I hunt a lot.

"As I stepped back onto the landing, Al came charging up the stairs and into the room. I think he had his gun out. I just remember glimpsing him over my right shoulder. He got hit in the eye and the nasal area by the buckshot. I saw him fall forward. I immediately reached into the room, grabbed him, and pulled him onto the landing. It was then I could see he had a huge hole in his face, that he was in really bad shape. I laid him back and started yelling, *'Call an ambulance! He's been hit!'* I was trying to drag Al over to the stairs. Yet, I knew I couldn't leave Gerry in there alone. At one point, he fired his weapon empty. I was trying to give him a clip. At the same time, I was thinking, I gotta get Al out of here because he's hit bad. I tried to feel his pulse, but there was nothing. Blood was pouring out of his face. It was all going so fast, yet in slow motion. I was confused. I was thinking, Everything's gone to shit here.

"As Schiavo was trying to get off a second blast, I reached in and fired. The bullet hit him in the hand, causing the round to miss us. Schiavo ducked back behind the bedroom wall. Gerry kept firing right through it. We saw the shotgun fall on the floor. That's when I yelled, *'Come out with your hands up!'* As Schiavo came into the living room with his hands above his head, Gerry got him against the wall, then on the floor. Schiavo was all shot up, blood coming out of his chest, arms, and legs. He was saying, *'I didn't know you were cops!'* I'm only in full uniform. We've only been yelling, *'State Police!'* I proceeded into the bedroom, checking out the closet to make sure no one was in there. I remember seeing a crossbow.

"People's initial reaction was, Why didn't you shoot the creep? You know he just killed your buddy, who has a wife and three kids. It goes through your head. It definitely does. As cops, we all like to think that if we had the chance, we'd shoot somebody who killed one of our own. Gerry and I looked at each other, wondering what the other was going to do. But I couldn't shoot him in cold blood. I knew then that if I did, I'd be no better than he is.

"Afterwards, I was sitting with Gerry on the couch downstairs. As I was taking my vest off, my leg started shaking uncontrollably, just jumping up and down. My muscles were reacting from all of the adrenaline that had been coursing through my system.

"A few days later, some of the guys took me out for a bachelor party at a bar. I hadn't slept for three days. I kept thinking about the shooting. What if I had done this or that, would things have turned out different? I kept thinking, if he had moved that shotgun a quarter of an inch, he would have increased the angle and hit me in the face. I had gone to visit my father after the shooting, and he started to cry, he was so shaken up by how close he came to losing me. I made it through the funeral, which was on August 31, and my wedding, which was September 7 at my parents' house. It was the hottest day in September. My wife and I were supposed to go to England for our honeymoon. But I was afraid to leave the country, of having a breakdown. So, for our honeymoon, we went to Maine instead and bought furniture. We were sitting in a restaurant one night having dinner when I started shaking like a leaf. I started getting really depressed. We decided to visit some friends of mine who lived there. They were a great couple, with kids. They insisted we stay with them, which is what I needed. We had a real good time, looking at mountains and stuff. It took the edge off for a while.

"Every day for two years I obsessed about that incident. I pondered over it. I relived it."

10 / Saving Lives

It's All About Helping People

"I am not a hero. Any trooper would have done the same thing." You hear that a lot from members of the State Police. Maybe it's because they're so well prepared for emergencies that they don't consider saving lives to be anything more than "just doing my job." They cannot graduate from the Academy until they have earned a First Responder card. From splinting broken bones to dealing with anaphylactic shock, from handling head traumas to administering CPR, troopers must have a wide range of first aid knowledge; and for good reason. At some point, every trooper is called upon to help a person in desperate need, be it clomping through a frozen ice pond where someone has fallen through, or pulling a trapped truck driver from his burning, exploding rig. For that kind of heroism, done on his off

167

168 hours (proving a trooper is always a trooper), Walter Perski (Badge No. 2402), was left permanently disabled.

Lt. Donald Dalpe (Badge No. 2195) and Trooper David Chirico (Badge No. 4953) were on patrol, when all of a sudden they found their bravery put to the mettle. "You know, as a policeman, you put up with a lot of shit, what with all the domestic disputes and bar fights," says Dalpe, who rushed into a burning house to save a sleeping family. "Then, on the other side, you have the politics of the job," he says. "Most of the guys in the Outfit are pretty macho and won't admit or talk about it, but basically, when you come down to it, this job isn't about shoot-outs and chasing suspects. What it's all about is helping people. That's what makes all the other stuff worthwhile."

Says Chirico, who stands six feet tall and is 235 pounds of solid muscle, and who rescued a child from a submerged automobile: "It wasn't a question of, Oh my God, should I go into the lake or not? That doesn't enter your mind. You just do it."

Their stories, presented here, plus a ride on an aeromedical helicopter flight to save an accident victim, is the real stuff heroes—make that *troopers*—are made of.

"I'm a Trooper and Your House Is on Fire"

"It was a night like any other," recalls Lt. Donald Dalpe from his office at Division Headquaters. "At the time, I was a road trooper stationed in Somerville, with a wife and three kids. We lived in the barracks then. Those were the best days. You had your family at home on weekends, and your other family at work during the week. The hours were long, but they were great times. Great times. On June 19, 1975, Trooper John Hook and I were sent to answer a burglar alarm at a Bridgewater machine tool factory. We checked it out and were on our way back to the station. I was driving. It was about two or three in the morning. Normally, we'd go back via Route 22 or the Interstate. But, for some reason, I decided to take the back streets of Somerville. That's when I spotted a house on fire. It was a split-level, suburban-type house. The whole outside was covered in flames. A Bridgewater patrolman named Charles O'Neill arrived at the same time we did. Since I was the senior trooper, I told my partner John to get on the radio and call for assistance.

"I jumped out of the car and ran to the house. O'Neill did the same thing. We got to the back door and tried to open it, but couldn't get in. It was locked. I don't remember who did it, but one of us kicked the door in. As soon as we did, air got into the house, and it really started to go up. We rushed inside. We were in the kitchen area, I think. It was hard to tell, since the whole downstairs was covered with thick smoke. I didn't even think. I just charged ahead, screaming, 'Is anybody in the house?' I went through what must have been the living room until I came to a staircase. I knew I had to get up those stairs to where the bedrooms would be. As I started to go up, I saw a white, middle-aged woman standing at the top of the stairs in her nightgown. She was screaming. I mean, she was hysterical. Petrified. And not because of the fire; she didn't even know her house was burning up. She thought I was a robber or something. As I proceeded up the stairs, I kept saying, 'I'm a trooper and your house is on fire!' But she wouldn't calm down. I remember having to grab her and shake her to stop her from screaming. There was no time to be wasted.

"By now, the smoke was getting pretty heavy upstairs, and you could feel the heat from the fire below. I don't know if it was a combination of me screaming and her screaming at the top of her lungs, but her husband and kids woke up. There were four kids standing in the hallway, having come from various bedrooms. Her husband was still in bed. I went in the bedroom and he started screaming at me, *What's going on?! What are you doing in my house?!*' I was yelling back, *Your house is on fire! We don't have much time!*' It took me a while to convince them I wasn't an intruder, even though I was in uniform. Through all this commotion, I can still remember the sound of the air conditioners going. The smoke was getting really bad, and it was getting extremely hot. Besides their four kids, the couple had a six-month-old baby. The wife must have gone and gotten the baby, because she was suddenly standing there, holding it. We gathered everyone together in the parents' bedroom, and I told the couple we had to leave right away. They didn't want to. I said we had no choice; *we're going.*

"I grabbed the baby from the mother. I knew, if we were going to do anything, we had to do it now. There was no time left. I told everybody to hold hands, that I would lead them out. I took the oldest

170 child's hand. I'm not sure what order everybody was in, but I remember the father being at the rear and the mother somewhere in the middle. As we started down the steps, I began to realize just how hot it was. By now, the smoke was so dense, you couldn't see anything. I was having real problems breathing. As I was pulling them along, holding the baby in my arms, I kept yelling, *'Keep moving! Keep moving!'*

"It was then I felt a surge. The kid whose hand I was holding, and another kid, were suddenly pushed up next to me. I knew then, the chain had broken. It was a terrible feeling. It really was. I started yelling for the others, but couldn't see where they were. I was starting to be overcome by the smoke and could feel fear setting in. I was losing air and becoming disoriented. I didn't know which direction was which. I was trying to navigate from memory. I knew that I had gone through a kitchen, a dining room, and a living room. The stairs were on the left. So, coming down, I knew I had to go to the right, then continue going right until I got to the back door. But when the chain broke—the heat, the smoke, me reaching for the kids, worrying about where everybody else was—I completely lost it.

"All I knew was, I had to get the hell out of there. I started moving forward, but I lost my balance and fell down the rest of the steps. When I felt myself going, I clutched the baby real tight in my arms. I went down on my back. I was laying there at the bottom of the stairs with no idea where I was. I could hear the kids screaming. But there was nothing more I could do. I knew we weren't going to make it. I remember thinking, Shit, this is it. I had no more air to breathe. You know, it's funny, but at this point the panic went. I became calm. My thoughts were clear.

"I had no idea I was only three feet from the front door. As I was laying there, I suddenly heard loud voices. Firemen were yelling, *'Where are you? Where are you?'* They were outside, but couldn't get in because the heat and smoke were so intense. Finally, they reached in, grabbed us, and pulled us out.

"When I got to safety, I was told that the mother, the father, and all the other kids were alright. The parents knew the house. So, when the chain broke, they headed out the back door. Later, when I posed with the family for a newspaper photograph, the father told me, he was afraid to leave the upstairs bedroom. He thought it was the safest spot. But he said when he felt my big arm, he knew I was in charge, that he should put his trust in me. I never thought of myself as having a big arm. But that's what he said. Although Officer O'Neill had to get out of the house after we were separated, he kept dashing back in until everybody else was out. We were both taken to the hospital for smoke inhalation. I was having great difficulty breathing. There was a heavy burning in my lungs. But I didn't care about the pain, I was so relieved to be alive.

"Had we not arrived when we did, all seven members of that family would have been dead in a matter of minutes. I can't tell you what it's like to have saved someone's life. There's nothing like it. The only thing that's ever come close to it for me was the time I delivered a baby on the Turnpike. That feeling was pretty good, too.

"They Said Someone Was Inside the Car"

"I had just come on duty, so it was after 3 p.m. when the station detailed me to a possible drowning," says Trooper David Chirico from his station in rural northwest Sussex County. "It was at the High Point Country Club, which was maybe thirty seconds from where I was on County Road 653. I headed over, pulling into the gate. Passing the security booth, you go around a good-sized pond, then turn left onto Shore Drive to head counterclockwise around the main lake. That's where the first green is, and where the car had gone off the road.

"From the reports of witnesses, the car had been traveling the speed limit, which is 25 mph. A mother who lived in the housing complex which was situated around the golf course had been driving with four kids in the car. Three of them, two boys and a girl, were hers. She had just picked them up at the school bus stop on 653, or Clove Road. As she was driving back into the country club, her door flew open as she was going around a curve. Nobody knows exactly why, or what happened, but she apparently leaned over to shut it and fell out of the car. Obviously, she didn't have her seat belt on. The normal thing for anyone to do would be to put on the brakes, stop the car, then shut the door. I don't know why she didn't do that.

"Two of the kids were in the front and two in the back. It was an

172 older, two-door, white Ford Granada. Right after the mother fell out, the five-year-old boy in the front seat came flying out, too. I don't know if he was pushed or jumped or what, but he was uninjured and walked home. He wasn't related to the others. The driverless car went on around the curve, then proceeded in a straight direction. It went off the road, down an embankment, and across the first green, which is on water's edge. As the car went into the lake, the other boy in the front seat, who was about ten, managed to jump out.

"When I pulled up to the scene, there were about thirty people standing around. The car was ten or twelve feet underwater. When you come to the scene of an accident, or stop a vehicle on the road, you call the station and let them know. But when something like this is happening, you don't have time for that. You can't risk the twenty seconds it might take. Everyone was pointing to the lake. They said someone was inside the car. For some reason, when the car hit the water, the little girl popped out. Someone, I think, had swum out and gotten her. The car was maybe twenty-five feet from shore. It's a manmade lake that drops off quickly. Had the car traveled another ten feet, it would have sunk thirty feet.

"I jumped out of the car fully dressed, in uniform. I started unbuckling my shoes to go in the water. I didn't know who was in the car, or how many. Adults? Children? A woman came over and told me she was a court clerk. Would I like her to hold my gun? This may sound like an odd thing, but there's nothing worse than you going into a lake and saving somebody's life while some maniac gets ahold of your weapon and shoots nine people. I kept it on. I entered the water, swimming out to where two gentlemen were treading water. They were just above where the car was. One was around my age, thirty. The other, who was in his fifties, had been going under to see what he could find.

"I am a strong swimmer. People say, it was lucky I arrived on the scene, and not someone else. But any trooper would have done what I did. That's just what you do. Everyone's standing around, waiting for you to take charge. You get there, instantly assess that something's not right. The next thing you know, you're in the water. Knowing instinctively what to do comes from your training. I was in the Marine Corps, where I had a "S One" swimming-lifesaving rating, which is the highest you can get. We also did swimming at the State Police Academy. They had me suit up and jump into the pool, wearing a lead diving belt that weighed sixteen pounds. That's the approximate combined weight of your rounds, handcuffs, weapon, vest, and all. As I was crouched in a ball trying to get my shoes off, I found myself standing at the bottom of the pool. That's how fast you sink in all that gear. I had hoped during training never to find myself in that real-life situation. Yet, here it was.

"I had a quick discussion with the gentleman who'd been going down to the car. He said the passenger door was open. He'd checked the front seat. He'd heard there was a little boy in there. When the car went in, it kicked up a lot of mud. The water was so murky you couldn't see anything in it. The way I went down was feet first, following the younger man's legs. That way, I knew I could find the roof of the car, then feel my way to the door. That's exactly what I did. When I got next to the open door, all I could think of was how dark it was in the car. I told myself, you could get caught in there, especially with your weapon on. Just remember how to get out. Don't lose your bearings. Don't get panicky. I went in the first time mainly to get familiar with what was there. I patted around on the front passenger seat, which was a bucket seat. I also felt around the steering wheel. I was under thirty seconds before coming up. I can hold my breath longer, but when you're so excited, your breathing capacity is limited.

"Once above water, I took a deep breath. I relaxed my body so I would sink with everything on. Again, I followed the guy's legs down. This time, I went in the door and knelt on the front passenger seat. Logic told me that if the boy was in the back of the car, he had to be sitting in the seat. That's the way you think. In reality, it turned out, he was bobbing on the roof, almost over the back shelf area.

"I made six or seven dives in all. On my next to last dive, I touched something in the backseat which I thought was a nylon duffel bag. As I was trying to pull it out, it got stuck. I had to go up for air. This time, one of the other guys dove down. He came up and said he had gotten ahold of the boy, who was wedged between the seats. I dove down head first, straight to the door. It was easier to find the car with each dive. Just as I was entering the car, my hand felt the boy's foot coming out. I tried pulling him, but he wouldn't budge. I wasn't sure if his

174 head was getting banged or his arms were caught behind the front seats. It was getting more and more difficult to keep pulling him, so I released and tried pulling again. I had to let go and come up for air. As I did, his body, which must have been moving, came out of the car, and he popped right up with me.

"The first thing I saw was his face, which gave me a terrible shock. His eyes were rolled back. His nose was very, very blue. His tongue was swollen and sticking out. His face was bruised. He was eight years old, and weighed maybe seventy pounds. He was wearing a nylon jacket, which is what I mistook for the duffel bag. I kept him afloat with my hand so his face wouldn't go underwater. My strongest stroke is the sidestroke, which is what you use in lifesaving. But I couldn't support him alongside my body. With all the weight I had on me, I was afraid he'd pull me under. Getting the twenty-five feet back to shore was a struggle. Every time I'd try to reach for water to take a stroke, my head would go under. It was exhausting.

"When I got to shore, there were two girls waiting to do CPR and mouth-to-mouth. One was a lifeguard at the pool. The boy wasn't breathing and didn't have a heartbeat. As soon as he came out of the water, his mother, who had been at the scene watching, took off. There was some question as to whether she'd been drinking. It turned out later, she had a negligence factor with her children. But I'm not going to second-guess her leaving the scene. If you're in shock, you'll do anything. I can't say. The girls worked on the boy for about two minutes without getting a response. I was still standing in the water when the ambulance arrived. The paramedics put a mouthpiece on his face and rushed him to the hospital.

"He lived, but is messed up. He has brain damage and only responds to his mother. For a while afterwards, I kept thinking, if only I'd gotten him on the first or second dive. If only I didn't have to keep going up for air. Maybe I could have gotten ahold of him then. Or maybe, just maybe, it would have been better if I hadn't found him, what with the condition he's in now, in bed for the rest of his life, unable to talk. Is that better than dying?

"I never heard from the mother. I understand she and the kids moved to another area. I didn't expect her to thank me. That would be confronting the person who brought to the light that you screwed up. I try to put the experience in perspective. You're not expected to be praised when you do something good. It's just one of your duties, part of the job description. I figure, I can make someone's day better, or I can make it worse. I prefer making it happier for people."

Summoning Helicopters for the Critically Injured

Since the State Police's aeromedical program began in 1988, there have been almost four thousand lifesaving flights aboard State Police helicopters. "Two years ago, the Atlantic County coroner wanted to know why he didn't have as many deaths as before," says flight paramedic John Rogers. "The obvious common denominator was the helicopters. They work." The program, which operates on a seven-day, twenty-four-hour basis, is divided into two parts: Southstar, which covers southern New Jersey, and Northstar, which is based in Newark and handles the northern end of the state. Helicopters can be summoned by any emergency medical service or mobile intensive care unit, and will carry patients to whatever hospital is best equipped. Usually it's one of the state's three level one trauma centers, University Hospital in Newark, Robert Wood Johnson University Hospital in New Brunswick, and South Jersey Hospital/Cooper Medical Center in Camden.

"We fly the most sophisticated helicopter there is," says Southstar State Police Pilot Rick Arroyo (Badge No. 3756), referring to the shiny white $6.5 million Sikorsky S76B sitting in the landing pad. Both Southstar and Northstar have this craft, plus a smaller Bell LongRanger 206 helicopter for backup. The two-engine Sikorsky requires two pilots, cruises at 180 mph, and can carry (in a crunch) two patients on stretchers. It has such super-deluxe features as a computerized flight management system and built-in storm scope that's able to detect an embedded thunderstorm two hundred miles away. Although the workspace the medics have in the Sikorsky is only seven feet by five feet, it's far roomier than the LongRanger. Being a pilot takes concen-

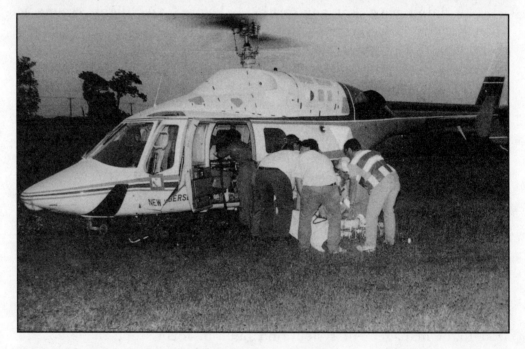

*The State Police's aeromedical program uses two types of helicopters,
the sophisticated, two-engine Sikorsky S76B (above)
and the smaller Bell LongRanger 206 (below).*

tration: "You can't turn around, even when you hear the patient screaming over the whir of the engine," says Arroyo. "It could affect your decision. You have to isolate yourself."

Although most of the emergency calls are for car wrecks and transporting critically ill patients from one hospital to another, they can be for almost anything, from suicides to drownings to stabbings. Recently, Arroyo, along with copilot Al Van Doren (Badge No. 3824), paramedic Rogers, and nurse Shannon Coyle, were awarded certificates of honor for the lifesaving rescue of a twelve-year-old boy who had slipped through the ice on a frozen lake. While the pilots hovered the Sikorsky a few feet above where the ice had broken, Rogers reached out—with Coyle holding tightly onto his legs—and pulled the boy in. "All I had to do was open the door and hang out. Rick and Al are the heroes," says Rogers. "We're not heroes," protests Arroyo. "We were just doing our job. It was teamwork. This whole program is teamwork. And, by the way, I think it should be SOP that John has to hang out of the door on every flight."

If you think it would be exciting to be a passenger on one of the flights, don't. "If we fly you, you won't remember ever having taken the trip," says flight nurse Ann Norton. "That's how bad off you'll be." "Drive carefully," says Rogers to a mechanic leaving the helicopter pad. "We don't want to have to come pick you up."

"Are We Ready to Rock 'N' Roll?"

While the rest of the world is quaffing champagne and ringing in the New Year, tonight's aeromedical flight team—helicopter pilot Rick Arroyo, copilot Ted Heim (Badge No. 3781), nurse Linda Whitworth, and paramedic John Rogers are eating takeout dinners, drinking large cups of black coffee, and watching the Miami-Alabama football game on TV. "Anything could happen tonight," says Arroyo, taking a microwaved burrito out of the oven. "Probably get some MVA's (motor vehicle accidents) about 7 p.m., after people have gotten out of their office parties," says Rogers. "Definitely after midnight," says Whitworth. "Then again," says Arroyo, "we may get nothing. You never know around here. Could be quiet."

On this New Year's Eve, it's business as usual at the Southstar program, located in Voorhees, next door to West Jersey Hospital. This is where the crew members spend their shifts, waiting for a radio call that will have them airborne and on their way to an accident scene in less than six minutes. Sorry, no ducking out for errands or meeting a friend for lunch. The quarters here consist of a TV/eating room, a ready room where dispatches are received, a kitchenette, bathroom, and bunkroom. As rooms go, they're pretty drab—even the fake Christmas tree by the water cooler is missing a few branches. Yet the digs seem warm, due entirely to the camaraderie of the flight crew.

After all, theirs is a familiarity that's been forged through the extreme intensity of what they do for a living, which is to save lives in emergency situations. "From the time the accident occurs until you get the patient to the hospital is called the golden hour," says paramedic Rogers. "That's when patients often die of shock. What we try to do is reverse that shock, from accident to surgical intervention." With the Southstar crew members, it's teamwork or nothing. Helicopters are too small to carry egos.

The sun hasn't even taken its final bow when, at 4:46 p.m., a dispatch comes over the radio from Gloucester County Communications, which fields emergency calls for southern New Jersey. "We're on standby for a shooting in Salem County," says Arroyo.

The next five or six minutes will determine if it's a "fly," meaning, the helicopter will be put into service, or a "stand down," meaning, it won't be called out. Several factors come into play: Ground medics at the scene must decide that if the victim is not immediately flown to a level one trauma center, he or she could die. The average transportation time from accident scene to Cooper Medical is a mere ten minutes. Arroyo will make his response based on the weather: there must be a minimum thousand-foot ceiling, at least two-mile visibility, and no approaching storms. "It's a fly," he says, after receiving a computer printout from the National Weather Service.

By now, the nearest fire department is at the accident scene securing an LZ, or landing zone. All year long, Southstar and Northstar crew members train fire departments for this delicate task. A minimum 110-by-110-foot plot of land is required (although the Sikorsky is capable of dropping into a fifty-by-fifty-foot area), and must be clear of any overhead wires— "our number one-enemy," says Arroyo. "You can't see them on a black road landing at night." "Ready for your longs and lats?" asks a voice from Gloucester County Communications.

Crew members are not told the victim's name, age, or sex before heading out. "That's so we don't make judgment calls," says Arroyo, who, like everybody else, wears a dark blue, flame-retardant flight suit. "If we thought it was a four-year-old girl instead of an eighty-nine-year-old man, we might try to rush ourselves, or take a chance in bad weather. Safety is our big concern. Unlike other helicopter rescue programs, we're not flying to make money, so we don't have to go up."

First out the door are Arroyo and Heim, who start the Sikorsky's engines. After inspecting their orange trauma bags and adjusting their crash helmets, Rogers and Whitworth run across the tarmac, ducking low to avoid the helicopter's spinning blades as they enter the bird's midsection from different sides. Inside, they strap themselves in, their backs to the pilots. Between the medics is the stretcher. Time seems to freeze during the four minutes it takes for the Sikorsky's engines and rotors to get up to speed.

At 5:52 p.m., six minutes after being put on standby, the helicopter begins to rise, then races southwest towards Salem County, over shopping centers and gridlocked highways, bouncing slightly as it hits the turbulence from a passing 737 coming into Philadelphia International. Up here, one feels like a Wagnerian Valkyrie, transporting the fallen to Valhalla. Through microphones in their helmets, Rogers and Whitworth communicate with each other and the pilots. The medics put on surgical gloves and unfold towels, readying themselves for whatever lies ahead.

One can't deny, it's a beautiful evening for flying. Directly ahead, on the Delaware River, sits the Salem nuclear plant, its ominous towers backlit by a salmon-colored sunset. As the helicopter banks to the left, one can see part of a rural field that's been set off by red lit flares. "The ground is marshy, stay left of the LZ," radios a voice to the pilots. Coming into the landing zone, one sees a pickup truck, its bed area illuminated by the headlights of a four-wheel vehicle. The scene looks surreal, dreamlike. A policeman is walking around, talking on a portable radio. Paramedics are in the back of the truck, frantically working on whoever is lying inside.

While Arroyo and Heim stay aboard, Rogers and Whitworth run to the victim—whose hunting boots are sticking out over the truck's tail-

180 gate—with their trauma bags and a cardiac monitor. Upon arriving, the Southstar nurse and paramedic are in charge of the scene. The victim is a man in his thirties, with red hair and a bushy beard. Blood, more brilliant than tonight's sunset, is gushing from a hole just below his neck. "Looks like he got hit by a shotgun," says the policeman. The victim is unconscious and has no radial pulse. "We can't find an exit wound," says one of the ground medics to Rogers and Whitworth. "*Whoa!*" screams Rogers, when he sees one of the victim's hunting buddies peeling out in his Jeep, heading in the direction of the helicopter. "*That's the landing zone! No way! Get back!*"

Standing there, one has that awkward feeling of having flown too close to someone else's reality. "*Help him! Help him!*" sobs a hysterical good old boy, collapsing on the ground. "He's my neighbor. He went ahead of us while I was herding the deer in my truck. I found him just lying there. Oh God, please, please get him to the hospital in time! Please don't let him die!"

After inserting an endotracheal tube in the victim so he can breathe, Rogers and Whitworth inject him with Anectine and Norcuron, drugs that cause temporary paralysis. That's so he won't have convulsions or spasms aboard the helicopter. "We don't want a patient kicking the pilot or knocking a door open," Rogers explains.

"Are we ready to rock 'n' roll?" he asks.

The medics lift the patient off the back of the truck on a longboard, then slide him into the helicopter.

The flight to Cooper Medical Center lasts eight minutes. On the patient's chest sits a pulse oximeter, which monitors his heart rate and oxygen saturation in his blood. From the helicopter window, one can see a dazzling fireworks display over Philadelphia. Inside the helicopter, another display is taking place. As the patient was loaded inside the aircraft, his IV tube got knocked off. Blood is everywhere. As the helicopter dips to and fro, the blood on the floor comes and goes in waves, covering the soles of everyone's shoes.

As the helicoper lands on top of Cooper Medical Center, a trauma team of doctors and nurses is waiting to take over. In their green surgical gowns, masks, and gloves, they look like tarnished statuary come to life, angels of a sort. While Whitworth stays behind to sop up some of the blood with towels, Rogers accompanies the Cooper team to the trauma admitting room, filling them in on the patient's condition as they rush down corridors, in and out of elevators.

Fifteen minutes later, Arroyo, Heim, Rogers, and Whitworth are back at Voorhees. "We sure had a bleeder," says Arroyo, looking at the outside of the helicopter. Sure enough, the blood had been sucked out of the doors and spray-painted everywhere, from back rotor to windshield. Two hours later, Arroyo and the crew are still scrubbing the helicopter with buckets of peroxide.

Later that evening, when their shifts end, Rogers and Whitworth are replaced by flight nurse Genevieve Deltieure and paramedic Rick Rohrbach. All Southstar and Northstar medics are trained at West Jersey Hospital, and hired through a state grant.

How do you ever get used to seeing so much tragedy?

"Everybody asks us that," says Rohrbach. "They want to know how we can take being on the frontlines. I don't know how to answer that. Either you do the job, or you can't."

"You detach yourself," says Deltieure. "But then, there's always one or two or three that hit you, that you keep thinking about. Sometimes, driving home, one case will keep coming up. So, I put on the radio to get it out of my mind. It's usually something that shouldn't have happened, like someone being so depressed he commits suicide. Or a kid being killed. The other day, we were transporting a twenty-four-year-old woman with a bad heart condition from one hospital to another. She had an eight-month-old baby and everything to live for. We knew she wasn't going to live more than twenty-four hours. During our final approach to Cooper, she went into cardiac arrest and died. Those get to you."

How many die and how many live?

"It's about fifty-fifty," says Deltieure.

"It's not like on that '911' TV show," says Rohrbach. "I don't like any of those rescue shows. They don't show reality. They're very one-dimensional. They always have a happy ending."

A few hours pass, and all is still. As midnight approaches, Rohrbach takes a telephone call from Cooper Medical. "The gunshot victim, he's going to make it," he announces. On TV, people are cheering in Times Square. They're hugging and kissing each other and singing *May auld acquaintance be forgot and never brought to mind . . .*

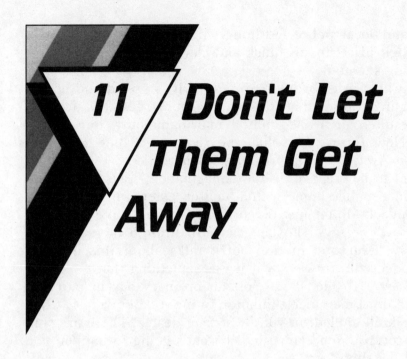

11 / Don't Let Them Get Away

Putting It Together

Muscular strength, being pumped up, isn't what being a trooper necessarily is about. The job takes brains, the wherewithal to outsmart your opponent. When Richard "Archie" Roberts (Badge No. 1863) heard that two bank robbers had fled Flemington in a getaway car, he figured out a few things—like, they were probably headed to Newark, and probably changed vehicles, which would have delayed their travel time. With that information, he went looking for them—and found them, which resulted in his being named 1976's Trooper of the Year. Kevin Tormey (Badge No. 4123) was a rookie road trooper when the call came over the radio that an escaped murderer was in the area. Like Roberts, he went looking for the suspect, and nabbed him after a brilliantly choreographed chase that involved

184 other troopers and local police. Although they both got their men, Roberts paid a high price for his quick and clever thinking. He almost died in the ensuing shootout.

Then there's Cliff Coyle (Badge No. 2370), who stopped and boarded a drug smuggling trawler that was heading out to sea. His derring-do adventure resulted in a $32 million marijuana bust, one of the largest ever in New Jersey, for which he received a Blue Max, the Meritorial Service Award. "While working for narcotics, I did a lot of cases where I had to be creative, use my imagination," says Coyle, who lives by himself in a mobile home with a built-on extension, in the middle of the Adirondack Mountains. "Even my wife won't come here. She prefers New Jersey," he says, shoveling a path through the snow so a visitor can enter. "Everyone in the Outfit talks about this incident where I commandeered a trawler as if it was something that took a lot of bravery," he says. "To me, it was just an ordinary day in narcotics where you had to do some quick thinking. To me, real bravery is when you get a gun or knife pulled on you by a drug dealer. Those are situations you can't control. You can't predict what's going to happen. On this one, I called the shots.

"I Had to Think Fast. I Made Up a Story."

"I was the buck sergeant on duty at the Somerville Station on Route 22," says Archie Roberts. "It was towards the end of the day. I had been on patrol earlier, and had returned to the station at the end of my shift to do some paperwork. I was still in uniform when I heard a broadcast over the radio that there had been a bank holdup in Flemington, and that the two robbers had jumped into a getaway car.

"I decided to head out. As I was traveling southbound on 202 in an unmarked car, I was observing cars going north. I figured, by now, the robbers would have dropped off their original car, gotten in another one, and been on their way towards Newark. Sure enough, I noticed two black males in a car traveling at a high rate of speed coming towards me. The one on the passenger side was pushed way down in the seat so I could only see the top of his head. I thought this was an unusual situation. So, I crossed over the grass median on the highway, sped up alongside them, and signaled them to pull over, which they did. I then pulled behind them, got out of the car, and approached the driver. As I got closer, I could see the guys fit the radio description, so I more or less figured it was them. With every step closer, I worried that I was a target.

"I had to think fast. I didn't want them to know that I knew who they were. Since I had noticed that one of the car's taillights was broken, I made up a story. I asked the driver if he'd recently been in a shopping mall parking lot, because someone had just reported being backed into. I needed to check it out. I told him I needed to ascertain that he wasn't the guy who did it. I asked for his automobile registration, which he gave me. I said I needed to go back to my car and that they could go shortly. Back in my car, I knew I was in a situation that was tentative at best. I was worried, because if I stayed there for too long, it would tip them off that this was more than just a routine stop. I got on the radio and called for help. In a matter of minutes, Trooper Paul Likus pulled up in an unmarked car. He parked in front of my car, got out, and approached the driver. I think what saved everything is that he was in civilian clothes.

"As they started sizing up Likus, I opened my car door, got out, and crawled around between their two cars. I was mostly worried about the passenger, what he might do. So I reached up, grabbed the door handle, and whipped it open. I put my gun to the guy's head and pulled him on his rear end onto the ground. I then stood him at the side of the car with his hands spread out and started searching him. He was wearing a large-brimmed Banana Republic–type hat and a suit jacket. As I searched him, I hit something in the pocket of his jacket and thought he had a baseball in there. I can't forget that. As I started to go down the side of his leg, I suddenly realized it was no baseball. It was a hand grenade. As I came up, he whipped himself off the car and shot me in the arm. I never saw the gun, which turned out to be a .380 Walther, which is a small automatic pistol. All I know is, I was pedaling backwards from the power of it. Realizing what had happened, I grabbed my gun and shot him twice in the stomach, then twice in the chest. We both fell onto the ground, only a few feet apart. He managed to get up. He tried shooting me again, but his gun jammed. It wouldn't go off. Luckily, I'd been shot in the left arm, so I

186 was able to pull my gun around and fire off my fifth shot. It missed him. I fired again. My sixth shot caught him in the face, and I saw his nose go off. But even that didn't stop him. He still stood there, trying to shoot me with his jammed gun.

"I tried to bring my right arm around to take out some bullets to reload. That's when I realized my left arm wasn't working at all. I saw that my shirt and pants were filled with blood. I thought, Holy shit, I'm bleeding to death! I jumped up, leaving my gun on the ground since it was worthless to me. I stumbled towards my car to get myself to the hospital, but kept falling down. I saw another off-duty trooper and two bystanders running towards me. They picked me up and threw me in the back of my car. The bystanders—one of 'em turned out to be the mayor of Bridgewater—drove me to the hospital. One sat in the back with me and helped me make a tourniquet to stop the blood. By the time we reached the hospital, the floor was an inch deep in blood. I remember telling them, 'I'm dying.' Somehow, they got me into the emergency room. I looked at my arm, which had busted out of my police shirt. I knew I was in deep shit. I remember saying, I've got to have something for the pain. The doctors gave me an injection and started putting tubes in me. I lost consciousness during the X-rays.

"The guy that shot me was brought to the same emergency room. We were operated on at the same time. We were in intensive care together. Lying there, I'd have to watch him giving me the finger. My five bullets did less to him than his one did to me. His bullet traveled up my arm to the rib cage and lodged in my lung, resting on top of my heart. It's still there.

"I was sure it was the end for me, being shot. All I could think of is how remiss I'd been in my life, how, if I died, my wife and kids would be in dire financial straits. I've seen it happen a number of times, with other troopers. I've delivered those death messages. You go back later on to see the survivors, and the family unit is crushed. I was thirty-two years old at the time. I had just bought a house. I had been a road trooper for eleven years. I thought I had control of my life. I had control of nothing. After that incident, I couldn't go back on the road, so I left the police and became an accountant, though I later came back to the Outfit in a desk job. To this day, I still relive that incident over and over in my mind, every time I drive down a highway. If that guy's gun hadn't jammed, I'd be dead. Why I didn't die, I don't know. At least I

With Trooper Archie Roberts and the bank robber he apprehended in the same hospital fighting for their lives, State Police Detective Thomas Walker inspects the shoot-out scene—a panama hat, bloodstains, and the trooper's gun will be used as evidence.

wasn't paralyzed. I'd rather be dead than that. For years I had night-mares, waking up in the middle of the night. That incident changed me for good. It took away my youth. I used to be a fun, happy, inno-cent guy. I mean, I still laugh and joke, but I have a very dark view of things now. My wife says that, too. Looking back, I realize that a part of me was left on that highway."

188 "Now I Knew, He Had to Be the One"

"On March 7, 1987, I was getting gas at the Totowa Station," says Kevin Tormey, who's now a plainclothes detective in the Fugitive Unit. "It was about 2 p.m., around the end of my shift. I heard over the intercom that there was a murder in Paterson. It came over SPEN, which is the radio frequency that our stations and the local police use to communicate with each other. According to the report, a male Hispanic with a goatee had just walked into the Lakeview Diner and killed a guy with a shotgun. It turned out to be a love triangle thing. After the shooting he took off in a blue car with a darker-colored top. The report said to be on the lookout.

"I decided to head out on Route 80 westbound, taking a position in the Milepost 53 barrier cut. I thought I'd give it fifteen minutes, and if I didn't see anything, I'd head back in. Twelve minutes later, a blue Mercury Cougar with a brown vinyl top, heading west, went by at 78 mph. I noticed the driver had a goatee and was wearing a coonskin cap. I pulled out and started to follow him. Realizing it was high-risk, I radioed for backup. SPEN immediately broadcast that to everyone. When I got behind the guy, I called the license tag into the station. It wasn't in the computer, which meant it wasn't registered.

"We were having quirky weather that day. It was in the seventies, odd for early March. So, everyone was out, and the traffic was heavy. I was observing this guy, who was traveling along with the flow and not doing anything wrong. I was thinking, He may not be the one we're after. As I drove along, I passed a Montville police officer in the 49 cut who was also obviously on the lookout. Since I couldn't call him on my radio, I signaled to him with my hand that I was watching this guy. He gave me the high sign and came out. I let the suspect pass the 48 Exit, knowing it was two-and-a-half miles to the Route 46 Exit. I figured, I'd wait and pull him over there, as it's kind of desolate.

"When I activated the overheads, he cut immediately to the right shoulder and took off. Up till then I wasn't sure, but now I knew. He had to be the one. I activated my sirens and took off in pursuit. As I did, he cut back across all the lanes of traffic and onto the grass median, which he crossed. He was now heading east in the fast lane. In order for me to cut across the median and spin around the other direction, I had to put my mike on the seat. I remember, it slid onto the floor. I was leaning way over, trying to retrieve it with my right hand, turning the steering wheel with my left. The Montville cop followed right behind me. I'm traveling east now, when the guy cuts across the median again. Again, I follow, as does the Montville cop. We're still going eastbound, only now we're in the westbound fast lane, heading into the oncoming traffic! We're doing like 85, 95 mph. Fortunately, people saw us coming towards them and shifted to the right, except for a few vans who swerved into the median. Meanwhile, Trooper Bobby Wetzelburger was up ahead, trying to slow traffic down as we came towards them.

"We had gone east for a mile and a half when the suspect saw Wetzelburger. So he cut back across the median into the eastbound fast lane again. I cut across, too. When I slowed down to cross the median, the Montville cop got ahead of me, then pulled alongside the guy. By now, another troop car had arrived, and was paralleling me in the middle lane. From where I was, I could see a head just sticking above the seat on the passenger side of the suspect's car. I didn't know if this other passenger was a gunman, or what. Turns out to have been the suspect's six-year-old son, but we didn't know that at the time. After another couple of miles, the guy started to lose control of his car, and swerved into the Montville cop. The collision sent the guy reeling into the median, where the wet grass caused him to bog down and come to a halt. I stopped my car, grabbed my shotgun, opened my door, and took position. As I did, two troop cars pulled up behind me. The Montville cop was out of his car, running towards the guy. I started yelling, *'Don't go near him!'* and, to the driver, *'Put your hands up!'*

"The guy obeyed, sticking his hands out the window. As the Montville cop opened his door, I rushed over and stuck the shotgun right in the guy's face. I banged him with it a little because I was so pumped up. He wouldn't move, so we had to drag him out. He resisted arrest, so the other four troopers jumped him and wrestled him into the cuffs. Just then, in perfect timing, another troop car arrived from the station. We threw the guy in the backseat and the car took off. As it sped away, I remember standing in the median—surrounded by cars that had stopped to watch—and having this great adrenaline rush. I felt drunk from it. It was like when I played football in high school and our team won the state championships. I was ready to play another six games in a row. I had taken this job a year and a half ago expecting excitement, but not this much. Three months earlier, I had saved two people's lives in a burning car; and now this. I had chased down and apprehended a murderer. Standing there, I don't think I've ever felt better than I did that day."

"I Pulled Alongside Yelling, 'Policia! Policia!'

"I had worked all day Thursday, then stayed up all night with agents from the Drug Enforcement Agency doing surveillance on two trucks parked at the Exit 11 service area on the Turnpike," says Cliff Coyle. "We had information that they were picking up a Colombian drug load from an ocean trawler. At 6 a.m., the trucks finally moved, taking a circuitous route to the Lincoln Tunnel Motel in North Bergen. Something had gone wrong for the drivers. Either they got lost trying to find the boat, or the person who was going to take them to it didn't show up. By Friday afternoon I was exhausted, and went home to get some sleep. I was about to climb into bed when the phone rang. It was this guy Don Mason from Customs. 'Hey, Cliff,' he said, 'We just found out, the boat the trucks are supposed to be meeting may be docked in Perth Amboy.' I knew the boats pretty well from my cases, so I said, 'C'mon, let's go.'

"As I met Mason under the Garden State Parkway, near the Raritan Toll Plaza, my adrenaline started to pump. We drove to Perth Amboy, where I checked all the boats at the dock. We didn't know exactly what we were after, just a large, suspicious-looking vessel. Hmm, not here, not here, I thought. Then I remembered a fishing vessel I had once followed called the *Guillitano S* that was tied up in South Amboy, near the railroad yard. I thought that might be a good place to look for drug runners. We went over there, and I spotted a 110-foot trawler tied to a dock that fit the bill. I couldn't read the name on it. So Mason had the DEA send a plane out to read it. It was called the *Seatia*.

"At 5 p.m., I got word from the DEA that the boat we were after was supposed to move by eight o'clock. I was going to get our marine police boat, but there wasn't time. So I called this South Amboy cop I knew named Thomas Brinamen and said, 'Hey, look, I need a favor. I need a little boat.' He said, 'OK, I'll get you one.' A couple of minutes later we met at the South Amboy Post Office. This friend of his had a fourteen-foot Boston whaler with a twenty-five horsepower Evenrude on the back. Brinamen said I could have it, providing I let him go with me. I didn't care. I had nobody to talk to out there. All I had was a DEA radio.

"Brinamen and I launched the boat by the Raritan Yacht Club. We went out on the bay where the Raritan River meets the Kill Van Kull, which separates Staten Island from New Jersey. We went up and down the Raritan trying to get a look at the *Seatia*, using the yachts and sailboats as cover. The *Seatia* was tied up to an old wooden pier. Perpendicular to it was a tugboat called the *Julian*. Eight o'clock came and went, and nothing happened. At eleven o'clock, Brinamen's partner, Bobby Point, decided he wanted to come out with us, too. So we went to the yacht club and picked him up. It was dark now. He was wearing camouflage gear and carrying a shotgun. All I had was a Smith & Wesson five-shooter on an ankle strap.

"During the night, strange things began happening. A tractor-trailer pulled into the railroad yard. Crew members from the *Seatia* began unloading large bundles of something or other into the TT. Some of the bundles were being put inside an abandoned school bus, for storage reasons, I guess. We didn't know exactly what it was at the time, but it turned out to be pot. We cut the engine of the whaler and rowed as close as we could to the *Seatia* without being noticed. We tried to get a better vantage point by pulling up to a pier where a huge barge and an abandoned World War II liberty ship were moored. The barge was pumping something into the harbor, which we suspected was toxic waste. We got out of our whaler and tried walking across the rotted pier. I didn't know that the pier was a seagull condo. Suddenly, a flock of 'em took off, making a horrible racket. The more we walked, the more gulls took off. We decided to backtrack, afraid the birds would give us away, or one of us would crash through those rotten boards. We then took a new route, going hand over hand alongside the barge. From here, the *Seatia* was maybe seventy-five feet away. I told Brinamen and Point that since I had been a lifeguard and could swim for miles, I was going to hit the water and swim up to it. Brinamen said, 'You do, and you'll come out bald.' I said, 'Whaddya mean, I swam here as a kid.' He said, 'Don't go in.' I didn't.

"At three in the morning, we saw lights coming into the yard. It was a pickup truck, which unloaded drums of something or other onto the *Seatia*. We later found out they were 55-gallon drums of gasoline. At four o'clock, the TT started to pull out. I got on my radio and called Matty Marr, a DEA agent who was doing surveillance on top of the PSE&G building in the railroad yard. He notified his department, who moved in on the TT after it crossed the George Washington Bridge into New York.

"It seemed this night was never going to end. I realized I had had no sleep for three days. I was dying of hunger and thirst and everything else. But what else was new? Any big case I worked on over my thirteen years in narco always took three days. That's just the way it was. Just before dawn, the lights came on in the wheelhouses of the *Seatia* and the *Julian*. Suddenly, the tugboat started pulling the trawler out into the channel. I got on the radio and told Matty, *They're getting away!'* He said, 'Well, there's nothing we can do. You do what you have to.' 'Are we ready?' I asked Brinamen and Point. 'Yeah, we're ready,' they said.

"We began to follow them out, the sun coming up. Rub-a-dub-dub, three men in a tub. I know it sounds crazy, us in a fourteen-foot dinghy trying to stop a trawler full of Colombian drug dealers. But in the State Police, you're taught in the Academy to not waver. A good trooper has to think on his feet, make quick decisions, act. A few miles into the channel, the tug cut the *Seatia* loose. We managed to pull alongside the trawler. I looked up and yelled, *'Policia! Policia!'* I had my detective ID out, which I was thrusting in the air. Well, they weren't about to stop. They were hellbent-for-election to get out of there. Then the lights went out in both wheelhouses, and the game began. They tried to crush us between them. Four times they attempted to ram us. Luckily, the whaler wasn't a console. Since the engine was in the back, I could turn it on a dime. That's what saved us. We were able to scoot out from between them, like a fly on the water. I wasn't about to turn around. I followed alongside the *Seatia*, telling Bobby Point, 'I got the wheelhouse covered. If anyone sticks anything out of the fantail, you got it. Blow them out of their socks if you have to.'

"As we were running in and out, all around the ship, it suddenly stopped. We were now five or six miles out in the channel, off Princess Bay in Staten Island. The next thing you know, a white flag appeared. After some choice words were exchanged, I yelled up for the crew to drop a hawser line off the side. A hawser is a large rope that's used to tie boats to docks. I told everyone to move to the back of the boat. Meantime, I looked over to see the *Julian* turn around and start heading straight at us. I wasn't about to be sitting there in a little dinghy. I grabbed hold of the hawser line and began climbing up it, hand over hand. They teach you rope climbing in the Academy. You never know when something's going to come in handy.

"When I got to the top of the line, I figured I'd bought the funny farm. It was me against whatever. I tried to put my head down as I went over the side, in case I was fired at. When I got on deck, there were twelve Colombians standing in the back of the boat. With my gun drawn, I told them to lay down, spread-eagled. They obeyed. Meantime, I could hear the drone of the engine. Was someone in the engine room? I didn't know what was going to happen next. I proceeded to the galleyway, all the while yelling, *'Policia! Come out now, or I'm gonna blow your heads off!'* Since no one came out, I stuck my gun in the hallway and let a round go off. Bing. Bing. Bing. Bing. It echoed like crazy against the steel walls.

"Remember I said they'd been fueling the boat all night? Gasoline was all over the decks. No one had washed it off. As I made my way down the hallway, I slipped and fell. I proceeded to slide a good fifteen or twenty feet. I couldn't stop myself. I slid all the way to the stairs that led to the engine room below. I went right down those stairs on my rear end, hitting each one like Daffy Duck. Pow. Pow. Pow. Pow. Pow. When I got to the bottom I yelled, *'I'm gonna kill you for this!'* I could only thank God the engine room was empty, as was the wheelhouse, and the crew quarters. I picked myself up off the floor, then ran back upstairs—my heart was going like crazy—and out onto the deck. By now, Bobby Point was there, holding the crew at bay with his shotgun. I went over and said, 'You're all under arrest.' It sounds amazing that they all surrendered. They could have easily outpowered me. What I had going for me was the element of surprise. They thought they were home free. Then, all of a sudden, we came out of nowhere. They didn't know what else they were going to be confronted with.

194   "After we secured the boat, the Coast Guard showed up. They had intercepted the *Julian*. With the whaler tied behind us, they took the *Seatia* to the Naval Reserve Center in Perth Amboy. As we were heading in, I noticed ten cases of beer on board. I was so thirsty, I had to have something to drink. I was dying. As I got off the boat, I had a bottle of beer in each hand. I was waving to my boss, who said, 'Oh shit, Coyle, here you go again.' I didn't think to put the beer bottles down, even though the news cameras were rolling. I was then driven back to the dock at South Amboy, where sixteen others involved in this drug smuggling operation had been apprehended. They were all standing together on the pier like bowling pins. You know those plastic balls you see floating on top of fishing nets? I couldn't help it. I grabbed one and rolled it at 'em, yelling, *'Alright!'* As the ball struck 'em, my boss looked at me and said, 'Coyle, get out of here. Go home and get some sleep.'"

12 / Major Crime: Manhunt of the Century

They Never Go Home Until the Job Is Done

Poke around the detectives' desks in the Major Crimes Unit, and you'll probably wish you hadn't. "We're following this case," says Det. Jim McCormick (Badge No. 3551), who that morning received in the mail a provocative photo of a voluptuous young woman dressed as a French maid, bound and gagged and sitting in a chair. Across her image, the sender has scrawled all the sicko things he'd like to do to women. If that doesn't send coolant through your veins, then try digging into another detective's briefcase: there, you'll find a color, eight-by-ten coroner's photo of a fifty-eight-year-old executive who's been completely dismembered. "He's the second man who's been found surgically cut up, wrapped in designer sheets, and left in plastic bags on the Turnpike. We think we're dealing with a serial killer who may be stalking men in New York gay bars," says Lt. Fred Tavener (Badge No. 2314).

196   These detectives, all sixteen, are considered New Jersey's finest experts in homicide investigation. "Major Crimes is probably the most prestigious unit in the State Police," says its supervisor, Lt. Robert Scott (Badge No. 2223), "investigating seventy to eighty cases a year. Troopers are always trying to get in." The Unit's responsibilities include taking on complicated cases from prosecutors' offices, assisting local police in solving homicides, and investigating any assault or murder on or by a state trooper. To be considered for the Unit, one usually has to have been a trooper for at least six years, and to have worked several of those years as a station detective. Each State Police barracks is assigned a station (or road) detective who's in charge of helping investigate crimes in the surrounding townships.

"The difference between a station detective and a major crimes guy is this," says Scott, holding up his left hand as a visual aid. Touching the tips of his outstretched fingers, he says: "In solving a crime, a station detective goes from this point to this point to this point. You can run around from peak to peak checking on the crime and not get anything. It's the little things that always get 'em. Here's how our people do it" Making a continuous, smooth line, Scott traces the tips, sides, and valleys of the fingers on his left hand with his right index finger. "It's almost like a game," he says. "If you beat me, I lose. You win. We work hard to keep the 'bad guys'—an expression I hate—from having that satisfaction."

Education is also a hallmark of a major crimes detective. They are constantly being sent to seminars across the country, from workshops in satanism to autoerotic deaths.

Is a murder investigation exciting? "If you start with an unidentified body, it is," says Scott. "You have to find out who the dead person is. But if you don't have any avenue to follow, it can be very frustrating. That's what'll lead you to sitting at the bar."

From Bogie to Columbo, the Hollywood image of a detective isn't far off from these men, who are truly dedicated to their work. "They can't pay you enough to make it worth what you give up," says Scott. "A good detective works from 8 a.m. until whenever the job is done. There's not a holiday that goes by that half a dozen guys don't get called out. If I call you, I expect you to go. I don't want to hear, 'I'm going to see my daughter who's starring in the school play.' Same with Christmas. You could be just starting to open the presents . . ."

The result of this kind of commitment is an eighty percent success rate, though exceptions include the human skull sitting atop Scott's bookcase. "Found him on the interstate," he explains. "Probably killed in Chicago and dumped here."

According to Scott, the ideal training to be a major crimes detective is to spend several years as an identification man—someone who's first at the crime scene to either snap photographs, dust for fingerprints, or gather evidence. "If you look at enough murder scenes you'll get where you can walk in the room and know what happened from the bloodstains, from where the person had to be standing for the bullet to hit him. Every crime scene has a story. The more you look, the more it reveals. I've had regular detectives tell me the victim's been shot in the head with a .32, when clearly he was killed with a hammer. That's how all the blood got on the walls and ceiling."

As far as letting your work get to you, Scott says: "To me, it's not a person lying there. I can't handle my kid cutting his finger at home, but I can deal with a 747 crashing in the parking lot."

And, as far as being cynical about the evils men are capable of, after all these years, he says, "I would doubt nothing at all."

The Major Crimes Unit has at its disposal such investigative tools as a forensics lab that conducts scientific tests, including blood and hair analysis; a polygraph unit; a voiceprint unit; a ballistics lab; artists who do composite drawings of criminal suspects based on eyewitness descriptions; handwriting and typewriter recognition experts; an Equine Testing Bureau for racehorses and—within the Arson Unit—a Bomb and Explosives Investigation Team that uses two mechanical robots to detonate suspicious-looking devices.

Six days after New York's World Trade Center was bombed on Feb. 26, 1993, by Islamic extremists, five troopers from the New Jersey State Police's Bomb Squad were dispatched to Jersey City to remove and detonate some seven hundred pounds of explosives belonging to the terrorists. The afternoon's haul—mostly unstable nitroglycerine—was two-thirds as powerful as the bomb that tore apart the Trade Center, and was found housed in a densely populated residential neighborhood. The Bomb Squad had not been put to such noteworthy use since April 12, 1989, when Trooper Robert Cieplensky pulled over a motorist for suspicious actions as he left the Vince Lombardi rest area of the Turnpike. The driver turned out to be Yu Kikumuru, a

198 member of Japan's underground Red Army, who was on his way to New York City with three foot-long, explosive-packed cannisters. It's believed that Kikumuru was planning to blow up a downtown Manhattan military recruiting center two days later to commemorate the anniversary of the United States' bombing of Libya.

Because the explosives found in the Jersey City storage area were located on the second floor, the bomb-defusing mechanical robots could not be used. "They can't go down stairs," says Bomb Squad Commander Drew Lieb (Badge No. 2964). "Also, there was too much for them to carry." For those reasons, Lieb and his men—Bruce Dawson, Robert Mazur, Steve McDougall, and Edward Ditzel—had the nerves-of-steel task of physically carrying the boxes and containers of explosive materials downstairs and outside, to the bomb-containment vessels located on a trailer. "We wore our fire-resistant, one-hundred-pound bomb suits," says Lieb. "We went very carefully; and no, nobody slipped. It was night. A storm was approaching, and the temperature was rapidly dropping. Temperature change can cause friction on the molecules of the explosives. As minute as these molecules are, they can rub together and cause a chain reaction. Temperature change can create an explosive atmosphere. There could have been lots of havoc and damage."

The neighborhood was evacuated and roads blocked off as the Bomb Squad transported the explosives to a remote area of Liberty State Park. After FBI members from Washington took representative samples of the materials, it was decided that the explosives had to be detonated immediately. "They were so pure, so unstable, that they couldn't be moved or handled anymore," says Lieb. Before getting rid of them, authorities had to make sure no one could get hurt. The Harbor Patrol, Coast Guard, and FAA all were put on alert. "We couldn't have aircraft overhead, because the explosions would create a blast wave," says Lieb. "We learned there was a troop of Girl Scouts spending the night in the park's new science and technology center, which is practically all glass. They had to be evacuated. The Statue of Liberty was right nearby, and I could just see frags from the blasts knocking her torch off. Around one, one-thirty in the morning, we set off the first four detonations in our four-by-three-foot explosive containment vessel, which we call our bomb pot. It sits atop a two-wheel, double axis trailer. Trooper Ditzel and I climbed up and put in the explosive counter-

Six days after the World Trade Center blast, NJSP Bomb Squad troopers removed explosives from the terrorists' storage area (top). That snowy night seven hundred pounds of bomb-making material was detonated at Liberty State Park, across the harbor from the damaged Twin Towers.

200 charges. The blasts were so powerful that they stressed the seams of the bomb pot. Yes, the noise was quite loud. That was the largest amount of explosives we've ever dealt with."

Nobody was hurt, including Miss Liberty with her carved inscription welcoming the huddled masses to her shores. "It *was* brave, what we did," says Lieb. "When we first arrived in Jersey City, all the federal and county agencies turned to us and asked, What are we going to do? It was a little pucker factor on our part."

"The State Police Bomb Squad has every reason to be proud of the job it did," says Jim Esposito, special agent in charge of the FBI Office in Newark. "I can't be more complimentary. On a larger issue, the State Police and the FBI have been working together to fight terrorism since the eighties. Our terrorist task force has a number of joint endeavors going. The crime problem in New Jersey is of such magnitude that we have to work together in such areas as organized crime, drugs, and counterterrorism. The New Jersey State Police is a very fine group of professionals. Their expertise and talent have brought a great deal to the World Trade Center investigation."

Hailed as "the most significant technological advancement in law enforcement in more than fifty years," is AFIS, an $11 million computerized scanning system used by the Fingerprint and ID Unit. The AFIS computer can compare a set of latents with the 1.9 million on file in New Jersey, providing a suspect in a mere thirty minutes. Manually, that same search would take 167 years. "When we get a hit (meaning a match)," says Joe D'Ercole, principal fingerprint operator, "you can hear us scream down the hall." ("We are desperately trying to get a computer to match a bullet," says Sgt. First Class Carl Leisinger, Badge No. 2666, head of ballistics.)

Often roaming the corridors of the Investigations Section is Buffy, a German shepherd who's trained to sniff out human skeletal remains and gases from decomposing bodies. According to her handler, Det. Sgt. Steve Makuka (Badge No. 3035) of Missing Persons, Buffy's greatest whiffs include "finding a mobster who was wrapped in a blanket four feet underground, finding a baby who was stuffed in a garbage bag and buried three feet deep in the sand under the Atlantic City boardwalk—that took Buffy only two minutes—and locating murdered Exxon executive Sidney Reso."

Major Crime's latest innovation is called HEAT, which stands for

Homicide Evaluation and Assessment Tracking. It's a multimillion-dollar computerized tracking system for murderers and serial killers. When a homicide is committed anywhere in New Jersey, the Major Crimes HEAT Squad can enter into its computer the details of the crime. This information is then entered into the FBI's VICAP files (Violent Criminal Apprehension Program), which checks its nationwide **201**

On the job with Det. Sgt. Steve Makuka and Buffy, who had just located a missing baby buried under the Atlantic City boardwalk.

data base for any similarities with other murders. "HEAT is what the future of law enforcement is all about," says Det. James Kenna (Badge No. 2383) of the HEAT squad. "HEAT allows other law enforcement agencies and municipalities to be in touch with each other, which has historically been a problem in solving crimes."

Besides the Miss America Pageant, tomatoes, and Frank Sinatra, New Jersey, a corridor state, is famous as a dumping ground for dead bodies. From the Roaring Twenties, with its speakeasies, rumrunners, and hoodlums, New Jersey's had a splashy crime history—right up to the recent arrest of Richard Kuklinski, AKA The Iceman, who claims to have shot, stabbed, and poisoned more than one hundred victims, many as a paid hit man for the Mob. A devoted husband and father and a good provider, he got his nickname from stashing body parts in a freezer. Kuklinski's wife and kids say they never knew what he did for a living. Lucky they didn't open the freezer.

With the exception of the Kennedy assassination, no twentieth-century American crime has been as widely investigated as the infamous Lindbergh baby kidnapping, which occurred at the aviator's estate in Hopewell, N.J. The case's 220,000 pages of documents are housed in the State Police Museum at Division Headquarters, along with such artifacts as the baby's nightclothes, ransom notes, and the ladder Bruno Hauptmann used to gain entrance to the nursery. *Will the real Lindbergh baby please stand up?* Since Gov. Brendan Byrne opened the files to the public in 1981, three grown men, all claiming to be the living Lindbergh heir, have found their way to the Museum's door.

Retired Major Hugo Stockburger (Badge No. 504) remembers being in his patrol car on March 31, 1932 "at 8 or 9 p.m., when the call came over the radio that 'the Lindbergh baby was stolen.' They didn't say 'kidnapped.' I spent the rest of the night checking cars on the highway." Stockburger, who would later watch the Hindenberg explode, was assigned to help escort Bruno Hauptmann from New York, where he was arrested, to his jail cell in Flemington, New Jersey. "When we got to Flemington, it was night. We were in four or five cars, so it looked like a parade. We had to fight our way past the reporters and cameramen to get inside the jail." Throughout the entire trial, Stockburger spent four hours a day locked inside Hauptmann's cell guarding him.

Like Hauptmann, Stockburger was German. "We never spoke to each other in German," he says. "I never had a conversation with him about the crime. He'd usually ask what day it was, and what was the weather outside. He was very strong-minded. Very strong-willed. When his wife came, they'd talk about things that happened at home. Once, the warden told him his wife was downstairs with their baby. 'I don't want to see my baby,' he said. 'I don't want my baby to see me behind bars.'"

Hauptmann's widow still insists her husband was innocent, and is trying to get the guilty verdict overturned. Do you believe Hauptmann killed the Lindbergh baby? "I know he did," says Stockburger. "Never any doubt in my mind." Giving key testimony at the trial as to the authenticity of fingerprints found on the ladder was retired Capt. E. Paul Sjostrom (Badge No. 93) of the Outfit's first class, who founded the Identification Bureau. Does he believe Hauptmann deserved to die in the electric chair? "We had all the evidence," he says. Is that a yes? "I could have pulled the switch myself."

The world that existed in those prewar Lindbergh days is far, far removed from today's upside-down goings-on. Sworn to protect the public, state troopers are often the ones who need it the most, especially from trigger-happy drug runners on the highways. For the State Police, as with law enforcement everywhere, no era was as grim as the 1970s and early '80s, when underground revolutionary groups across the country declared war on cops. During that period, the NJSP lost some of its finest.

In 1973, following a routine traffic stop on the Turnpike, Trooper James Harper (Badge No. 2108) was fired upon by Black Liberation Army leader Joanne Chesimard, who was wanted in New York for masterminding an anti-police reign of terror. On this night, Chesimard was a passenger in a car driven by fellow BLA member Clark Squires. Although Harper lived, his backup, Trooper Werner Foerster, died, made to kneel on the pavement before being shot execution-style in the head by Squires. Quickly apprehended, Chesimard and Squires were tried separately and found guilty of murder. While Squires is serving a life term, Chesimard is New Jersey's most wanted fugitive. She broke out of the Correctional Institute for Women at Clinton, New Jersey, and as Assata Shakur, now lives in Cuba with her daughter, whom Squires managed to father during a ten-minute, pretrial conference between codefendants.

In 1981, Trooper Phillip Lamonaco was gunned down on Route 80

204 by members of a white revolutionary group, and in 1984, Trooper Carlos Negron was shot to death on the Turnpike by members of a BLA splinter group after stopping to assist their disabled van.

Of all the State Police's major crime cases over the years, Lindbergh included, it's the hunt for Lamonaco's killers and the subsequent battles to bring them to trial that illustrate detective work at its best. In a most extraordinary way, perseverance, cooperation, mental skill, and forensics all came together to achieve that often elusive result: justice. What follows is the story of that ten-year-long case as seen through the eyes of the New Jersey State Police detectives who, according to everyone involved, "never went home until the job was done."

> *The sun that brief December day*
> *Rose cheerless over hills of gray,*
> *And, darkly, circled gave at noon*
> *A sadder light than waning moon.*
>
> —JOHN GREENLEAF WHITTIER,
> *Snowbound*

December Twenty-first is the shortest day of the year. It should be a festive time, with Christmas so near. As the sun disappeared behind the 1,500-foot-high Kittatinny Ridge of the Delaware Water Gap, Trooper Phillip Lamonaco was completing his last loop on Interstate 80 before grabbing some supper. Heading westbound into the gorge, where Pennsylvania meets New Jersey, he decided to make one last stop.

Shortly after 4 p.m.—at Milepost 3.9, just past the on-ramp for the Truck Stops of America restaurant in Knowlton Township—he pulled over a blue Chevy Nova with two white males inside. Ten minutes later, one of the most highly decorated troopers in the history of the New Jersey State Police lay dying on the shoulder of the four-lane interstate, facedown in the snow, his flashlight and hat lying beside him. Just why he pulled over the car will never be known.

Of the fourteen shots fired at the trooper from a high-powered semiautomatic, nine struck him. So persistent was the volley of shots that Lamonaco had no time to reach into his pants pocket for his back-

To those in the State Police, Super Trooper Phil Lamonaco seemed invincible. His hat and flashlight lie on the shoulder of the highway where he fell, stark testaments to every trooper's vulnerability. As dawn broke, detectives from Major Crimes undertook the grim task of digging through the snow, looking for bullets and other clues.

up snubnosed .38 revolver. The copper-jacketed bullet that killed him entered his body through and under his left arm, a place unprotected by his bullet-resistant vest, and pierced his heart. Within fifteen to thirty seconds, he had lost consciousness. He died at 4:17 p.m., nine minutes to sunset on this winter solstice. Those who saw his body at the morgue say his eyes and mouth were wide open, a death mask of surprise.

A passing motorist who was trained in CPR rushed to Lamonaco's aid. Upon turning the trooper over and finding he had no pulse or heartbeat, the man jumped into the squad car with its flashing overheads and grabbed the microphone. Trooper John Hook was a mile away when he heard a frantic, unfamiliar voice come over the radio: "Can anybody hear me? There's a trooper laying on the ground, and I don't know what's wrong with him. I'm near the truck stop . . . *Somebody please answer . . . Somebody please answer.*"

As the longest night of the year began, a troop car pulled up Lamonaco's driveway in Washington Township. Phil's wife, Donna, who was at home baking holiday cookies with their three small children, just figured Phil had invited some of the guys over for dinner, as was often the case. It wasn't until she arrived at East Stroudsburg General Hospital in Pennsylvania that she was told her husband had been pronounced DOA.

On that day, two opposing forces had come together—the pride of the State Police, and members of a revolutionary group dedicated to the violent overthrow of the United States government. Were these revolutionaries, as their defenders claimed, driven to acts of violence by their profound concern for social injustice? Or were they, as law enforcement members believed, hardened criminals who justified their illegal acts with political excuses?

Statistically, Lamonaco was the ninth New Jersey trooper to be murdered while on duty, the second by an underground group bent on killing policemen. So far, the killers of all nine troopers have been apprehended.

Not since the Lindbergh kidnapping had there been a State Police investigation so involved as the Lamonaco case. So clever was this band of revolutionaries who robbed banks in order to pay for their terrorist bombings that it took police almost three years to track them down. Never before had a State Police department called upon so many

The state trooper and the FBI man can be friends, as witnessed by the Lamonaco trial investigation team. Pooling information are FBI members Andy Dorman (far left) and Jimmy Lyons (fourth from left) and State Police Detectives (l to r) Fred Tavener, Bob Scott, and Richard Jones.

diverse resources to investigate leads, from the IRS to the Little League of America. State Police departments from New York, Pennsylvania, Connecticut, Rhode Island, Vermont, New Hampshire, Massachusetts, and Maine had full-time teams assigned. Superimposed upon the NJSP's investigation was the FBI's separate hunt for the suspects on charges stretching back over a ten-year period.

All of these factions linked to form a dragnet of unprecedented width.

Within an hour of the murder, Dets. Michael Langan, Fred Tavener, Robert Scott, and Ernest Volkmann of the Major Crimes Unit had begun their investigation. With Langan as the primary organizer, the group would spend ten intense years preparing the case for prosecution. From being the first at the crime scene, to attending the final sentencing in a Somerville, N.J., courthouse, they were there.

The basement of a former grammar school building in Knowlton Township, near the murder site, was the unlikely nerve center for the investigation. For the first time in State Police history, an officer from Division Headquarters was assigned to work out of a Command Post until the suspects were caught. "At the beginning, we had hundreds of troopers with blood in their eyes. They were coming out of the woodwork to work on this case," says Maj. Charles Coe, whose first order of business as leader of the Command Post was to handpick ten of the Outfit's best and brightest troopers: Richard Ryan, Tom Evans, Dick Touw, Keith Verheeck, John Gulick, Dave Leonardis, Jack Cole, Dave Gallant, John Leck, and Lester Pagano, Col. Clinton Pagano's younger brother. For almost three years, these men ran down the thousands of leads that came in from across the country. Hanging in the center of a crowded bulletin board was the inspiration that kept these men going through the darkest of days: an eight-by-ten photograph of Lamonaco.

For Col. Clinton Pagano, the Knowlton Command Post was a symbol that justice would prevail. He kept it funded, refusing to shut it down, even when the situation looked hopeless. "It was an image of direction, a place everyone in the country could contact," he says. From the start he made a vow to Donna Lamonaco that justice would prevail. "I gave my word," he says.

The Man Who Could Smell Metal

In winter, the Delaware Water Gap is a pretty bleak-looking place. When covered with snow, the Kittatinny Ridge of the Appalachian chain has been described as resembling a stranded, landlocked iceberg. This seems a strange place for a shootout with revolutionaries.

But not really.

A major link between New York City, Chicago, and the West Coast, Route 80 is a funnel for drugs, guns, stolen goods, and people on the run. As the highway enters the Gap from the Jersey side, it twists and snakes down a steep grade until it reaches the river. Millions of years ago, another irresistible force met an immovable object in this very same spot, meaning, then as now, that something had to give. As the once-

"Watch out for this guy in 1982, whenever you're cruising down Route 80," wrote New Jersey *magazine. By the time the publication hit the stands, the trooper had been killed.*

flat terrain began to rise, the Delaware River refused to alter its course, cutting a downward path through the ascending quartz rock to form a narrow, two-mile S curve in which to flow.

Over a three-year period, on this stretch of Route 80, Lamonaco had made two hundred arrests, recovering $2.5 million in drugs and stolen property. For such distinguished service, Pagano had named him 1979's Trooper of the Year. *New Jersey* magazine even featured his picture on its cover.

They say, Lamonaco could smell metal. That is, he had an uncanny sense for knowing if someone was concealing a gun or a knife. "How many stops had the revolutionaries talked their way out of?" asks Coe. "With Lamonaco, that wasn't possible. He was so thorough." Weapons were not all the trooper could sniff out. The magazine *High Times* warned its readers not to carry drugs on Route 80, because Lamonaco seemed to know just which cars to stop. "He was called the Italian nose," says Donna. "Five cars would go by, and he'd somehow know to pull over the sixth. He was never wrong."

More than anything, Lamonaco liked being on the road. Four years earlier, having been promoted to detective in the Organized Crime Bureau, he made the unprecedented request to go back to patrol work. Everyone agrees, he was miserable behind a desk. "I miss the road," he complained to Donna. "Nobody who's been asked to be a detective has ever gone back." "Since when," she asked, "have you been like everyone else?"

As with the Kennedy assassination, every trooper who was with the NJSP in 1981 can tell you exactly where they were when they heard the news of Lamonaco's death that brief December day. Stationed at Blairstown, Lamonaco was the personification of the breed. If he was invincible, so, too, was every trooper. Within a few hours, an estimated three hundred troopers and local police were combing the area for clues and suspects. Typical was fingerprint expert Sgt. Joe Keely, who spent the night dusting for latents. "I had lunch with Phil the day before. Although I was on vacation, I put myself back on duty," he says.

For Lamonaco, nothing less was expected. "He answered to a higher order," says a former partner who considered Lamonaco his mentor. "I was in a courthouse with him once when a defendant stomped his cigarette out on the floor. Thinking I would impress Phil by emulating

Troopers in their winter dress salute the casket bearing Lamonaco's body.

212 him, I went over and chastised the guy. Instead, Phil took me aside and said that what I had done was wrong, that I should have taken the guy outside and spoken to him privately. Phil said no man deserves to be humiliated in front of his friends."

"His family was everything," says Donna. "He shielded us. Protected us. He came home when his shift ended. Cutting wood was his hobby. He'd stack the logs up, each being exactly twenty-six inches long. I'd tease him, saying, 'How can you burn them, they're so perfect?' After the three-to-eleven shift, the guys liked to go to the Red Barn for drinks. They wanted Phil to come along, too. He finally said he would, but only if he could bring me, which he did. Pretty soon, all the guys were bringing their wives. It became a real fun thing to do."

To this day, Phil's parents, Joe and Grace, well up with tears when discussing their only son, the oldest of three children. A large oil portrait of the trooper wearing his State Police uniform hangs on a wall in their living room in Roselle Park, where he grew up. A Marine who saw combat duty in Vietnam, Phil graduated from the State Police Academy's eighty-third class in 1970, Badge No. 2663.

On the day before Christmas, more than one thousand cars lined the streets outside the Assembly of God Church in Washington, N.J., down the hill from Phil's house, for the 10 a.m. funeral. Five thousand people tried to crowd into the brick church, where, in an open coffin, he was laid out in his State Police uniform. New Jersey Governor Brendan Byrne and Governor-elect Thomas Kean were in attendance, as were troopers from sixteen other states, including two who were flown out by the National Guard Air Patrol from California, with a squad car. One local father showed up with his disabled son, saying Lamonaco would always stop his car and talk to the boy when he was in the area.

Unable to finish his tribute to his partner, Trooper Louis Lepes had to take a walk outside to compose himself. "The spirit of Christmas has palled in the horribleness of that which has happened," said the Rev. Gerald Scott, the pastor. With their comrades saluting, six troopers carried the wooden coffin with a bouquet of roses on top into the hearse. All along the route to the Pequest Cemetery in Great Meadows, where Lamonaco was buried with full military honors, cars pulled off the road in deference as the long entourage approached. "You'd have thought a president died," recalls Lt. Tom DeFeo.

An Extremely Dangerous Force

The first policeman to arrive at the crime scene on that brief December day was Trooper Kirk Trauger, who immediately took statements from passers-by. One man told him that he saw a Puerto Rican male with long brown hair bending over Lamonaco's body.

A few hours later, detectives had their first break.

While checking out a dirt road two and a half miles from the murder site, Det. Nicholas Olenick found the deserted Chevy Nova stuck in a snowbank. In his panic to leave the disabled vehicle, the driver had left his license on the dashboard. The name on it read Barry A. Eastbury, and gave a Bridgeport, Connecticut, address.

Detectives had never heard of him. Did it matter? With so many policemen in the vicinity, some in helicopters, some with bloodhounds, some setting up roadblocks, how could anyone escape? From Trauger's initial information, police had been looking for Hispanics, thus buying Eastbury and his traveling companion time to make a getaway.

That evening, Det. Richard Ryan called a Connecticut Trooper he knew and asked if he'd check out the Bridgeport address. When the trooper called him back to say it was a mail drop, Ryan sent him a copy of the car's registration and insurance, which listed yet a different address. At 2 a.m., Dets. Ryan and Robert Maholland decided to drive to Connecticut to do their own investigating. They had barely fallen asleep at the Howard Johnson in New Haven when Trooper James Cavanaugh pulled up with news. In October the FBI had traced an abandoned car belonging to one of their "Most Wanted" to that city's Hotel Duncan, which just happened to be the address on Eastbury's registration. The owner of the vehicle was Raymond Luc Levasseur, a white, thirty-eight-year-old fugitive who authorities said had master minded a band of New England–based anti-capitalist bombers and bank robbers called the Sam Melville–Jonathan Jackson gang. Levasseur had eluded the FBI for longer than even Baby Face Nelson.

Several months earlier, he had surfaced. While Levasseur was attempting to obtain a dead infant's birth certificate at the town clerk's office in Brattleboro, Vermont, a suspicious clerk, correctly thinking he was trying to obtain an alias, called the local police. Levasseur, who was carrying a gun, managed to disarm the arriving officer and flee, later

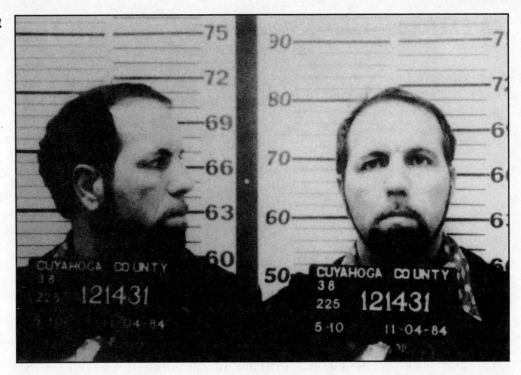

*The "hypnotic" Raymond Luc Levasseur was considered the mastermind behind
the terrorist group, the United Freedom Front.*

ditching his car. Through motor vehicle records, police traced
Levasseur to the Duncan Hotel, where he had stayed during the previous summer under the alias Jack Boulette.

Were Levasseur and Barry A. Eastbury the same man? At 6 feet, 200
pounds, the underground radical was considered an extremely dangerous force. He was wanted by the FBI for bombings, bank robbery, and
the holdup of a Brinks truck.

His green eyes are hypnotic, they say. Tattoos decorate both arms;
one depicting a dragon, the other a panther's head with the word
"Liberation" inscribed above it. While living in Augusta, Maine, in the
mid-1970s, Levasseur worked for a radical bookstore called the Red
Star North. During this period, he helped organize a prisoner's rights

organization known as the Statewide Correctional Alliance for Reform, or SCAR. An ex-prisoner himself for marijuana possession, Levasseur became the leader of a violent SCAR offshoot called the "People's Forces Group," which in turn split off to become the "Sam Melville–Jonathan Jackson Unit." (It was named for two slain radicals. Jackson died in 1970 during a shoot-out in a San Rafael, California, courtroom that eventually led to the famous Angela Davis trial. Melville, a ringleader of a Weatherman-affiliated group, was killed in the Attica prison uprising of 1971.)

By the time the Sam Melville–Jonathan Jackson group went underground in 1976, it had planted at least ten bombs in New England, including one that left twenty-two people injured at the Suffolk County Courthouse in Boston. From 1976 to 1978, the group issued communiqués claiming responsibility for a series of eight bombings and one attempted bombing of multinational corporations on the East Coast.

But when Levasseur's fingerprints were checked with the two sets found on the Chevy Nova, they failed to match. Obviously, Levasseur wasn't the big break the detectives were hoping for. Still, an astute Ryan remembered something: "It seemed to me there was another name on Levasseur's Wanted poster. I thought I had one in my trunk, but I didn't. So I drove from New Haven to the FBI office in Newark to get one." Sure enough, when Ryan looked at the bottom of the identification order there was a warning. Levasseur, it said, may be accompanied by a Thomas Manning, who had helped out on at least one bank job. "When his prints were checked, bingo," says Ryan.

A suspect had been identified.

Catching Thomas Manning would prove a far more difficult task. Over the years he had used a plethora of aliases and disguises to avoid detection. Even his Chevy Nova was equipped with a wraparound rearview mirror and CB radio that picked up police channels.

It was while working at the Red Star North bookstore that Manning had befriended Levasseur. Like him, Manning had served in Vietnam, if only for a month, having been discharged by the Navy for not getting along with others. A year later, he was arrested in Boston for armed robbery, and served three years in prison.

Supporting himself as a handyman and carpenter, Manning met his wife, Carol, through Levasseur. He was a friend of her brother,

216   Cameron Bishop, a known activist who lived in Maine. When Tom married Carol, she was just sixteen, and pregnant. Radicalized by their involvement in SCAR, the Mannings decided to follow Levasseur into the underground. Money "liberated" in their bank holdups was used to sustain them in hiding, financing their campaign of terrorist bombings against such targets as Mobil Oil and Union Carbide.

On December 28, 1981, Thomas William Manning was offically charged with murdering Trooper Phillip Lamonaco.

The Marshall's Creek Safe House

Six days would pass, and a new year would begin, before detectives got another break. It came on January 3, 1982, when an irate Pennsylvania landlord called the State Police about a barking dog that had been abandoned inside one of his rental properties. When the Pennsylvania trooper who was sent to check out the white two-story farmhouse in Marshall's Creek learned that the renters' names were Barry and Diane Easterly, he thought it sounded similar to Eastbury. Thinking that this might turn into a significant lead in the Lamonaco case, he radioed the Command Post in Knowlton Township. Armed with search warrants, troopers rushed to the farmhouse, a few miles west of the Delaware Water Gap. The house sat at the end of a long driveway, on sixty acres. Strategically placed mirrors inside the rooms warned the occupants of anyone approaching.

Dets. Tavener and Volkmann proceeded inside. "As I went up the stairs towards the bedrooms, I had my gun drawn," Tavener says. "I felt as if I were back in Vietnam. I didn't know if I was going to be ambushed, or if the house was booby-trapped to explode. Halfway up the stairs, I froze. I heard voices, which turned out to be a radio that was on a timer."

Among items found in the house were children's toys, crayon dinosaur drawings, a Christmas tree, and a "do list" of things that had to be done when fleeing, including taking a box of family photos that

A barking, abandoned dog led troopers to their first major break, the discovery of Thomas and Carol Manning's rural safe house.

218 had been left behind. Besides the usual household amenities, Tavener and Volkmann found a cache of weapons and ammunition, electronic surveillance equipment, survival gear, radical literature, a makeup kit with mustaches, and a framed pen-and-ink drawing of Black Liberation Army leader, Joanne Chesimard. Also found were receipts for the Chevy Nova and the Bridgeport post office box, both bearing the alias Barry Eastbury. A black address book listed telephone numbers, mostly from the Boston area, alongside nicknames, but no first or last names. In the downstairs bedroom was a framed photograph of a man with a young boy, neither of whom looked familiar.

Thomas Manning's safe house had been found.

Detectives learned that the Manning's oldest child, Jeremy, eight, was enrolled in a private Montessori school under the name Jeremy Collins. No one could ever accuse the Mannings of not wanting the best for their children. The school superintendent believed the boy's father was a long-distance truck driver; that's what the Mannings usually told anyone who asked about his bank robbing absences. Jeremy's mother, he recalled, was a 'strong woman' who, like her husband, was trained in the martial arts. A week before the Lamonaco shooting, Carol had given birth to a girl, Tamara, in the offices of a nearby doctor, with Tom in attendance. Scrawled across a school paper in the safe house were these words: "I love Jeremy with all my heart. I always will. I hope for my son for all your life. Daddy!"

Behind the farmhouse was a tree stump that had been used for target practice. Troopers dug it up and hauled it to the forensics lab at Division Headquarters, so that Sgt. Larry Hillman could examine all of the bullets that were in it. Since the shoot-out, Hillman had been studying the markings on the six bullets and thirteen shells recovered from the crime scene, the two bullets found lodged in the back of Lamonaco's vest, and the bullet that killed him. According to Hillman's microscopic tests, all of these 9-mm metal-jacketed bullets and their spent shells almost certainly had been discharged from the same firearm. Further research strongly indicated that these bullets and shells had come from a Browning high-power semiautomatic.

With hammer and chisel in hand, Hillman spent several painstaking days disassembling the tree stump, scrutinizing the 150 bullets, shot from different guns, that were lodged inside it. Although most of the bullets were badly mutilated from the elements, he was able to positively identify two as having been fired from the lethal weapon. Finding that weapon would be essential for a court case; although, for all anyone knew, it could be at the bottom of the Delaware.

Five days after the Marshall's Creek safe house was found, the Command Post made another important discovery. While checking telephone records of calls made from pay phones on the evening of December 21 in the area where the Chevy Nova had been abandoned, they found a call had been placed to Manning's house from the parking lot of Fink's General Store in Hainesburg. Immediately after that call, another had been placed to a residence in Germansville, Pennsylvania, about twenty-five miles from Marshall's Creek.

Detectives rushed to Germansville, to a white two-story farmhouse.

Too late. The house had just been cleaned out, right down to the stove. All that was left were Christmas present wrappings and name tags on the living room floor. This had been Ray Luc Levasseur's safe house, which he had shared with his common-law wife, Patricia Gros (under the names John and Jeanne Mills) and their three children. Detectives assumed that after killing Trooper Lamonaco and abandoning the Chevy Nova, Tom had called Carol, telling her to grab the kids and immediately head to Levasseur's place in the Poconos. On that snowy night, Manning and his traveling companion probably hiked across a footbridge that spanned the Delaware where, on the other side, they were met by either Levasseur or Gros.

Shortly after the second raid, Det. Evans went to Boston to check out phone numbers from the black address book found at Marshall's Creek. Calling one that had the word "rent" written alongside it, he reached a rental agent, who said he had never personally met any of his clients. A minor roadblock for Evans, who noticed that the owner of the phone book had listed the rent as $275 a month. "Even then, that seemed cheap," Evans recalls. He asked the agent if he had any apartments for that price. "Only coldwater flats in the Back Bay," was the reply. Evans went to Hemenway Street, a dilapidated area where the Boston Strangler once stalked. After showing the photo of the man standing next to the boy to building superintendents, one of them identified the mystery man as Richard Dawkins . . . whoever that was.

Authorities could find no criminal record on Richard Dawkins,

*Troopers just missed catching Levasseur, the Mannings, and other group
members at another safe house in Pennsylvania's Pocono Mountains.*

meaning, the name was probably an alias. According to the building super, Dawkins had moved out in early December. Detectives figured that was probably when he went to live with the Mannings in Marshall's Creek.

One of the numbers found in "Dawkins's" phone book was for one of his old girlfriends, Maureen Ahearn. Evans paid her a visit. Although she wouldn't say who Dawkins really was, she did tell Evans that his mother had recently remarried, and that his stepfather was named Red Riordan. They were living in Gloucester, a seaside town north of Boston. Accompanied by members of the Massachusetts State Police and the FBI, Evans went to visit Riordan, a retired executive. "It was a beautiful town, with granite homes that looked like fortresses," Evans says. "FBI SWAT Teams surrounded the house. I knocked on the door. Red Riordan answered. When a Massachusetts Trooper showed him the picture, Riordan asked, 'Oh no, what's Dickie done now?'"

Using Riordan's phone, Evans called the Command Post to tell them that the second suspect was named Richard Charles Williams, and to check his fingerprints. When Joe Keely compared them to those found on the Nova and on gift items left in the car that had been bought at an Indian trading post on the day of the shooting, they matched.

By researching gun registration records from the Bureau of Alcohol, Tobacco and Firearms, it was learned that a high-powered Browning semiautomatic had been sold to a Richard Dawkins at the Kittery Trading Post in Kittery, Maine, on December 8, 1980. The Firearms Purchase Permit contained the thumbprint of Williams.

On January 19, Richard Charles Williams was officially charged with the murder of Trooper Phillip Lamonaco.

Two days later, Donna Lamonaco and her children, Michael, Laura, and Sarah, did what they always did on January 21: they celebrated Phillip's birthday by going out to eat at his favorite local restaurant. He would have been thirty-three years old.

On January 27, "the tone of the investigation was set," recalls Maj. Coe. That "we mean business" attitude was a blending together of three NJSP elements: diversity, experience, and adaptability. Speaking in Boston before a large gathering of FBI agents and New England State Troopers, Coe announced that his detectives were not taking a backseat to anyone in this investigation. "This was not one of those bear shit in the buckwheat meetings," Coe says. "Up until this case everyone was in awe of the FBI. It had always been a friendly-enemy situation with them. I let them know we weren't going away, so they might as well work with us. The key thing was: We knew what we were doing. We were experienced in homicide, fugitive, terrorist, and under-cover cases. I told the FBI, I don't want to hear you complaining about us sending our men up here. I don't want to hear you telling us to send you an air-tel and you'll check it out. I said, I got news for you, Jack: it don't work that way. When I got through, everyone realized, the New Jersey State Police does its homework. Over the next seven months we hammered out a task force, the first of its kind."

The Attleboro Incident

In his own words, Richard Williams was "a rebel without a cause. Then I found a cause. Imperialism must end." A heroin addict, he served two prison sentences for armed robbery. After his release from New Hampshire State Prison in 1976, he hooked up with SCAR, Levasseur's prison reform group. According to a psychiatric profile done on Williams while he was in NHSP, he's a walking paradox, resentful of authority, and passively dependant. As for growing up with an alcoholic father, Williams told the social psychiatrist, "I don't remember." And as for his wife divorcing him so she could see other men: "I'm not the jealous husband type." The prison shrink did note that Williams expressed strong feelings towards his son, who was the unidentified boy in the safe house photograph.

From the black telephone book found in Williams's bedroom in Marshall's Creek, detectives unearthed one of the suspect's more recent girlfriends, Heather Frost. In late January, Dets. Tavener, Volkmann, and Gary McWhorter went to visit her at her home in Cambridge, Massachusetts. Her poetic, flowery name hadn't prepared them.

Covered from head to toe with tattoos, and so in love with motorcycles that she named her son Harley, Frost had a criminal record that included prostitution. After meeting Williams in a Boston bar in 1980, she had moved in with him for six months.

Frost led detectives to a nearby tree on Magazine Street, where

Richard Williams's girlfriend led detectives to this tree in Boston, where the couple christened the Lamonaco murder weapon.

224 Dickie, as she called him, had taken her to christen a Browning semi-automatic he had bought in December 1980—this, the weapon that police believed killed Lamonaco. When the two bullets that were in the tree were given to Hillman at Division Headquarters for examination, they were found to have the same markings as the bullets found at the crime scene and in the tree stump at Marshall's Creek. This placed the murder weapon in William's possession, and was an important development in building a court case.

January came to a close with Manning and Williams joining Levasseur on the FBI's Most Wanted list.

February roared in, as additional members of the same revolutionary group that killed Lamonaco surfaced.

On February 6, 1982, at 2 a.m., Trooper Paul Landry of the Massachusetts State Police approached a parked car at a rest stop in Attleboro, on I-95, near the Rhode Island border. Sitting in the front seat on this freezing cold night were two men—one white, one black. The white man was in the driver's seat. While Landry was patting down the black man, he felt a bullet-resistant vest. At that moment, the driver slid out of the car and began to run, turning around to fire five shots at the trooper before disappearing into the woods. Landry, who was uninjured, and his backup found a machine gun, shotgun, and a .38-caliber pistol in the vehicle.

As had been the case with Manning, the driver left his license in the car. Again, the name on it was an alias: Salvatore Bella. This was a name used by a West German–born radical, Jaan Karl Laaman, an old friend and prison buddy of Richard Williams. Laaman had served time in the early 1970s for the bungled bombing of a State Police barracks. The bomb, which had exploded prematurely in his hand, had left him permanently disabled. Although Laaman got away this time, his traveling companion, Christopher King, was arrested, and subsequently sentenced to seven years in prison for assault and weapons violation.

What were Laaman and King doing at the rest stop? They were waiting for Laaman's live-in girlfriend, Barbara Curzi, to arrive. She was meeting them there with a van, having decided to join her boyfriend in the underground.

Immediately after King's arrest, Maj. Coe met with him. King refused to cooperate in any way with authorities. Two subsequent meetings proved just as fruitless. "We felt King's capture was a major breakthrough," says Coe. "We had a member of the group we were after. I've dealt with a lot of criminals, and you'll always get something. Even though King was facing some tough time—nothing. He said he didn't know Richard Williams or Thomas Manning. That's how serious these revolutionaries were."

Theory of Prosecution

Over the next few months, more than one million Wanted posters, photographs, and descriptive circulars were distributed to newspapers, gasoline stations, doctors' offices, car dealers, weapons sellers, and other institutions throughout the United States. *Readers Digest* and the *Veterans of Foreign Wars* magazines were asked to run stories about the fugitives, and did. Photographs of Jeremy Manning, Thomas and Carol's son, were forwarded to elementary schools, public and private, across the country. Knowing that Jeremy had played Little League in Pennsylvania, the NJSP sent all of its teams his picture. From the raid at Marshall's Creek, detectives knew that the Mannings' kids took allergy medicines. Pharmacists across the nation were asked to be on the alert for anyone filling such prescriptions.

Just how thorough was the search? It was discovered from a dentist that Jeremy Manning had a rotated incisor. "That was how in-depth our information was getting," says Det. Evans, joking: "We probably knew more about them than they knew about themselves."

Even in those days, before TV's "America's Most Wanted," investigators knew just how important it was to have publicity. "When a policeman's killed, the media goes on about how unfortunate it is. But, after the second or third day, they lose interest. We had to keep the story alive," says Col. Pagano. "We would go to the local papers in New England and tell them members of the group had been sighted in their area, even though they hadn't been," says Coe. "That would get everybody stirred up and excited, and there'd be stories about the fugitives in the local gazettes and on the radio and TV." "It was also my decision, though not an easy one, to publish Jeremy Manning's photograph in newspapers," says Col. Pagano. "No matter how you try to hide, you can't hide kids."

By late summer of 1982, the investigative trial team of the Major Crimes Unit had come up with its theory of prosecution. "By then, we had all the evidence we could develop," says Tavener.

The detectives believed that what happened on that December day, at Milepost 3.9., was this: As Trooper Lamonaco was questioning Manning, he noticed he was carrying a gun. After Lamonaco confiscated it, he ordered Manning to step out of the vehicle. That's when Williams jumped out of the passenger door and opened fire. He shot from behind the car, where palm prints were found, and from the right-hand side. Two of Lamonaco's return shots backed up this hypothesis. One bullet broke the passenger window, where Williams would have been standing. Another penetrated the car's windshield and hit the backseat, the lead portion lodging in the spare tire on the right-hand side of the trunk, where Williams would have been crouched in battle. After Lamonaco had fallen, Manning ran up to him and retrieved his gun. From Lamonaco's wounds and the angle of bullets found in the back of his vest, it appeared Williams had also run up to him to administer the coup de grace, spraying him down the back.

In the early months of the investigation, a major break seemed to be happening every day. But, as time went by, things began slowing up. Except for finding bullets in a log in Vermont that Williams had used for target practice—once again, the bullets matched those from the shoot-out, which placed the murder weapon on Williams at still another location—and for finding the Vermont store in which Williams bought the ammo that killed Lamonaco, there weren't any major developments in the case until late 1982. Not until December 17, to be precise.

That's when, almost one year to the day after Lamonaco was killed, the IBM building in Harrison, N.Y., was bombed. A caller, identifying himself as part of the never-before-heard-of United Freedom Front, gave employees twenty minutes to vacate. According to a communiqué, the bombing was in protest of IBM's involvement with "fascist regimes." A curious detail about the communiqués issued by the group was its logo, a shooting star bisected by a Russian assault rifle. When the New Jersey detectives looked at it, they noticed the similarities between it and one discovered in the Marshall's Creek safe house. Scribbled on a piece of scrap paper was a shooting star, and the words "Think up and draw new logo." Although the FBI was unsure who was involved in this group, State Police detectives were convinced they were the same radicals they were hunting.

When the Lamonaco shoot-out happened, the suspects were in the midst of reorganizing and renaming themselves, from the Sam Melville–Jonathan Jackson unit of SCAR to the United Freedom Front, which had ties to no other group. In 1980, they had added two members, Jaan Karl Laaman and Christopher King, and were in the process of adding Richard Williams. In time, the FBI would pronounce the United Freedom Front "the most dangerous terrorist group operating in the United States."

For a two-year period, the United Freedom Front would remain extremely active, claiming responsibility for eighteen new bombings around the New York City area. Although no one was injured in these attacks, several of the blasts caused extensive damage to the buildings. The UFF's targets included Honeywell, Motorola, the South African Purchasing Office, and a Navy Recruiting district office. During this period they were suspected of robbing at least nine New England banks.

Despite one of the most intense manhunts in law enforcement history, Tom and Carol Manning, Richard Williams, Raymond Levasseur, Patricia Gros, Jaan Karl Laaman, and Barbara Curzi avoided capture. For the detectives, the low point of the investigation came in the summer of 1983. As every lead proved a dead end, pressure mounted to close the Command Post. The cost of keeping it going had already exceeded $1 million, critics pointed out.

On July 18, while following up yet another false tip, Lester Pagano was killed when his car ran off the highway. Lester had been a close friend of Phil Lamonaco, always dropping by his house for spaghetti and crab feasts. Despite having lost the use of a leg as a result of a 1959 gunfight, Lester was a dogged go-getter who refused to slow down, always running out of the Command Post to check out a lead, no matter how farfetched. To Col. Pagano and the Command Post members who served under him, Lester's loss was devastating. "That was a really bad day," recalls Det. Ryan. But, instead of being demoral-

ATTENTION! PHARMACISTS
$100,000 REWARD

For Information Leading To The Arrest and Conviction of the Perpetrators of the

MURDER OF A NEW JERSEY STATE TROOPER

1978 Photo

THOMAS WILLIAM MANNING
AKA:
Steven Carr, Barry A. Eastbury,
Tom Manning, Barry Collins,
Michael Harris, Thomas J. Stockwell,
Anthony Eastbury, Barry G. Easterly,

SEX & RACE ....Male, White

AGE	........................38 Years
DOB	.........................6/28/46
POB	.................Boston, Mass.
HEIGHT	........................5'10"
WEIGHT	....................150 lbs.
HAIR	..........................Brown
EYES	...........................Hazel
COMPLEXION	.................Fair

NO WARRANTS FOR CHILD

JEREMY MANNING
A.K.A.: Jeremy Collins; Eric Carr
SEX & RACE .... Male, White
D.O.B. 11/10/73
HEIGHT .... 5' 1"
WEIGHT ...... (Estimated) 110 lbs.
HAIR ... Brown - EYES ... Brown
PARENTS - Thomas & Carol Manning

MARKS & SCARS - Scar on nose, pierced left ear; TATTOOS: Left upper arm, large cluster of three red roses with background of 'DONNA' darkened and incased in a banner which makes the word 'DONNA' almost indiscernible; Left lower arm, Panther's head; Right upper arm, large green tattoo, not further identifiable; Right lower arm, large green Peacock with red legs and long tail.

WANTED FOR BANK ROBBERY

CAROL ANN MANNING

AKA: Leah Carr, Donna Lambert, Carol Ann Saucier, Dianne Collins, Carol Ann Harris, Dianne Annese, Mrs. Thomas William Manning, Mrs. Michael Harris

SEX & RACE ....Female, White
AGE ....29 Years
DOB 1/3/56

POB ....Sanford, Maine
HEIGHT ....5'6"
WEIGHT ....125 lbs.
HAIR ....Brown

Thomas Manning is wanted for the murder of a New Jersey State Trooper which occurred on 12/21/81. **Carol Manning**, his wife, is wanted for the 12/12/75 robbery of the Bank of Maine, Civic Center Branch, in Augusta, Maine. They may be travelling together and may be accompanied by their children, **Jeremy**, W/M, DOB 11/10/73; **Tamara**, W/F, DOB 6/30/79 and **Jonathan**, W/M, DOB 12/14/81. **Subjects will be utilizing fictitious identification and may attempt to disguise themselves by changing their physical appearances.** The Mannings were residing in the Cleveland, Ohio area until 11/4/84 at which time they fled just prior to their home being raided.

BOTH SUBJECTS ARE MEMBERS OF THE RADICAL UNITED FREEDOM FRONT TERRORIST GANG AND ARE SUSPECTED OF NUMEROUS BANK ROBBERIES AND WANTED FOR TEN BOMBINGS ON THE EASTERN SEABOARD.

NOTIFY	New Jersey State Police Major Crime Unit (609) 882 - 2000, Ext. 2554	N.J. State Police, Fugitive Unit (609) 882 - 2000, Ext. 2436 (800) 792 - 8824	Federal Bureau of Investigation Terrorist Task Force (201) 622 - 5613

USE EXTREME CAUTION - SUBJECTS WILL RESIST ARREST

Both subjects have numerous fictitious identifications and carry automatic weapons.

New Jersey State Police
Printing Unit

Bulletin No. 85-3
Dated: March 18, 1985 (33,000)

RAYMOND LUC LEVASSEUR
AKA

Robert Raymond; Walter Rogers;
Joseph Michael Mocchi; John Joseph
Boulette, John Mills, Jack Mills

White Male
Age . . . . 35 years
Date of Birth 10/10/46
Place of Birth . . . . Portland, Maine

F.P.C. 17AA11C01309AA10P009

(Child, Jeremy, as listed above)

Height . . . . 6' 0"
Weight . . . . 200 pounds
Hair. . . . . Brown
Eyes . . . . Green
Complexion . . . . Ruddy
S.S. No. 006-44-3289
F.B.I. No. 791943G

H.F.C. 17 L 9 A OO 13 Ref 1
        S 2 A 10   2

CAROL ANN MANNING
AKA

CarolAnn Saucier; Dianne Collins;
CarolAnn Harris; Mrs. Thomas
William Manning; Dianne Annese;
Mrs. Michael Harris;

White Female
Date of Birth 01/03/56
Place of Birth . . . . Sanford, Maine
Height . . . . 5' 6"
Weight . . . . 125 pounds
Hair . . . . Brown

MARKS AND SCARS - Scars: on right elbow, outside right eye, right ankle, bottom of left earlobe missing; TATTOOS: Dragon on upper right arm, Panthers head with 'LIBERATION' on left arm.

NOTIFY ►
N.J. State Police, Major Crime Unit
(609) 882-2000 Ext 429

N.J. State Police, Fugitive Unit
(609) 882-2000 (800) 792-8824

N.J. State Police, Blairstown
(201) 362-6128 — 362-9973

USE EXTREME CAUTION — SUBJECTS WILL RESIST ARREST

REMARKS: All three subjects are also wanted on a Federal Warrant for bank robbery. They are alleged members of a terroristic group who have claimed responsibility for several acts of violence. They are known to use automatic weapons and fictitious identifications.

New Jersey State Police
Printing Unit

Bulletin No. 82-3
Dated January 19, 1982 (30,000)

1978 Photo

RICHARD CHARLES WILLIAMS
AKA:

Robert Alan Dawkins,
Jesse Lockman, Robert Farnham
Dickey Williams

SEX & RACE . . . . Male, White
AGE . . . . 34 Years

Date of Photo Unknown

DOB 11/04/47
POB . . . . Beverly, Mass.
HEIGHT . . . . 6' 0"
WEIGHT . . . . 200 lbs.
HAIR . . . . Brown
EYES . . . . Blue
S.S. No. 034-34-5647
F.B.I 257117G
F.P.C. . P074POPO22DIPI172122

1981 Photo

HFC 24 O 13 R 000   ref 13
      I 27 W IOO 22   27

Marks & Scars - Scar on right hand little finger and over right eyebrow, mole on left cheek. Williams is known to use marihuana and cocaine. He has also been known to associate with prostitutes.

Remarks: Both subjects have been charged with the murder of a New Jersey State Trooper, which occurred on December 21, 1981 on Interstate Route 80 in Warren County, N.J. They may be travelling together. Manning may also be accompanied by his wife Carol Ann Manning, WF, DOB 1/3/56, 5'6", 123 lbs. and children, Jeremy, WM, DOB 11/10/73; Tamara, WF, DOB 6/30/79 and Jonathan, WM, DOB 12/14/81. Manning and his wife are also wanted on a Federal Warrant for Bank Robbery.

WANTED FOR QUESTIONING IN CONNECTION WITH ABOVE MURDER

Raymond Luc Levasseur: WM, Age 35 years, DOB 10/10/46, POB Portland, Maine, Height 6'0", Weight 200 lbs., Hair Brown, Eyes Green, Complexion Ruddy, SS No. 006-44-3289, FBI No. 791943G, is being sought for questioning in connection with the murder and is a known associate of Manning. They may be travelling together. Levasseur is also wanted on a Federal Warrant for Bank Robbery.

NOTIFY ►
N.J. State Police, Major Crime Unit
(609) 882-2000 Ext 429

N.J. State Police, Fugitive Unit
(609) 882-2000 (800) 792-8824 Ext 440

N.J. State Police, Blairstown
(201) 362-6128 — 362-9973

USE EXTREME CAUTION — SUBJECTS WILL RESIST ARREST

All subjects have numerous fictitious identifications and carry automatic weapons.

New Jersey State Police
Printing Unit

Bulletin No. 82-5
Dated: February 4, 1982 (30,000)

230 ized, "it really made us determined. We thought, Dammit, we're going to stick this out, no matter what," Ryan recalls. The grief factor—to have lost his most treasured trooper, and now his own brother—only refueled Col. Pagano's determination to catch the suspects: "Lester was heavily involved in this case. Besides my vow to Donna, I also made a vow that day to Lester. We would not give up."

On November 23, 1983, as a result of a painstaking buildup of forensic evidence, including ballistics, firearms registration, finger-prints, blood analysis, handwriting, and pathology, plus testimony from forty witnesses, as well as evidence collected from seven states, a New Jersey state grand jury issued a five-count indictment against fugitives Manning, thirty-seven, and Williams, thirty-five.

Besides Lamonaco's murder, they were charged with two counts of murder during the course of the commission of other crimes, which were robbery and escape. The robbery was Manning's retrieval of his silver gun from Lamonaco after Lamonaco had disarmed him. The escape was flight from custody, which had been established before the shooting. At the time of the murder, Manning was wanted on a federal warrant for bank robbery in Portland, Maine, and Williams was wanted for violation of parole in Massachusetts. Although the indictment iden-tified Williams as the triggerman, Manning was charged as an accom-plice, and under the law was, therefore, equally culpable.

Then, it happened:

Surveillance

"They made one mistake, and we jumped on it," says Maj. Coe.

On August 4, 1984, the FBI got a call from the owner of a self-stor-age warehouse in Binghamton, New York, just across the border from Pennsylvania. After failing to receive payment on a unit for two years, he had obtained a court order to sell off its contents. Upon entering the bin, he found an arsenal of weapons and ammunition, radical liter-ature, and the makings of bombs. He quickly notified the FBI, giving them the owner's name—Salvatore Bella, which was Laaman's alias. Police theorized that the contents really belonged to Levasseur, and had been moved there from his safe house in Germansville shortly after the Marshall's Creek raid. Police figured that after Laaman's encounter with the Massachusetts State Police, he had stopped payment for fear of being traced to the warehouse.

Found among the goods was a two-year-old military surplus magazine that had on it the name Jack Horning and a Derby, Connecticut, address.

"One more rinky-dink lead," thought Connecticut State Trooper Mike Nockunas, who, on October 10, 1984, checked out the address, a duplex in a poor section of town. From the tenants, who'd never heard of Jack Horning, he got the name of their landlady, who lived in California. Five or six years ago, she said, she'd rented to a married couple with that name. Nockunas decided to canvas the neighborhood. Five or six houses down the block, he met an older woman who had known the Hornings, and who put him in touch with their babysitters, two fourteen-year-old girls. One of them just happened to have a picture of their employers. "My mouth dropped to my trousers," says Nockunas. "It was Levasseur and Gros. I never expected the Hornings to be them."

Even though the Hornings did seem like your everyday suburban family, the babysitters had found it odd that Jack and Paula, as they were known, forbade them to go into certain rooms or open certain drawers or footlockers. When Nockunas showed them pictures of Tom and Carol Manning, the girls identified them as the Hornings' friends. They knew Richard Williams as Uncle Dick.

One of the girls remembered having been in a car with Mrs. Horning five years earlier when they were involved in a minor traffic accident. Going through old accident reports, the name Horning didn't show up. Going through them again, the babysitter's name did. Luckily, the officer investigating the accident had taken her name down. The report listed the driver as Judy Hymes of New York.

After Nockunas punched the name into the NCIC computer, which is a national listing of licenses and registration, it came back as being a New York license. Unfortunately, Judy Hymes's address turned out to be an expired mail drop in Yonkers. Inquiring as to why the registration had been cancelled, Nockunas learned that it was because the license had been surrendered in Ohio. When Nockunas checked to see

232 if Judy Hymes had been issued a license there, she had. Her address was a mailbox in Columbus. Box Number 5318 was an active one.

"This was a slipup on their part," says Det. Ryan. "A big slipup. Before, when members of the group left a place, they took all-new ID's. For some reason, she kept her old name."

The New Jersey State Police and the FBI decided to do a twenty-four-hour surveillance on the mail drop. They called upon State Police officers from Massachusetts and Rhode Island to help them with the shift work. A house directly across the street from the mail drop was rented. From the upstairs bedroom of the white frame house, the FBI's Surveillance Team mounted a camera looking out on the building where the mailbox was. A zoom camera was installed inside the building, aimed directly at the mailbox. Surveillance cars and trucks monitored the parking lot and areas around the building.

From the driver's license check, detectives learned that Gros drove a Chevrolet van, and that it was insured with Allstate. After finding the agent who had issued the policy, detectives paid her a call. She identified Gros as her customer. As a double check, detectives had the agent send Gros a letter saying there was a problem with the vehicle's registration, and would she please contact her.

A few days later, the letter showed up in Gros's box.

Three weeks later, on a Saturday morning, July 3, 1984, Gros's red and white van came driving down the street. Dets. John Gulick and Richard Touw had just come off the overnight watch and were in their motel room sleeping, when they got a call from the FBI agents to come back . . . *she's here.*

Since Ohio State was close by, and having a football game, parking was impossible. Detectives sighed with relief when Gros managed to find a spot in front of the mail drop, within camera range. After retrieving the letter from the insurance company, Gros went outside to a pay phone that was out of camera range. She dialed her insurance agent, who put her on hold to look for her file. In reality, the agent was dialing Det. Robert Hopkins at State Police Headquarters in West Trenton to say she had made contact with the fugitive. Hopkins, in turn, called investigators in Columbus, who had lost track of Gros. "She's at the pay phone!" he told them.

The plan was not to arrest Gros immediately, but to follow her, hoping she'd lead detectives to the others. Taking off from a nearby airport at that point was an FBI surveillance plane, which had planned to lock an infrared beam onto Gros's van so that no one could lose track of her. Nobody told authorities that Ohio is the van capital of the world. As Gros was driving through town, she crossed paths with an identical red and white vehicle. At that exact moment, the FBI plane arrived overhead, and mistakenly locked its beam onto the wrong van. As that van pulled onto the Interstate, so did Gros's pursuers. Fortunately, an alert Rhode Island Trooper, Lou Reali, tailed the right van into a shopping center, where Gros had parked. As she sat there looking around to make sure she wasn't being followed, Reali was screaming: "Where are you guys!?" "We're on the Interstate," was the reply. *"No! No! No!"*

Realizing their mistake, the other detectives circled back. For eight hours, a dozen unmarked cars and the surveillance plane shadowed Gros as she led them on a circuitous route to Deerfield, Ohio, one hundred miles away. Before entering the farmhouse, located in a cornfield, she made a phone call to make sure the coast was clear.

Five minutes after Gros entered the house, FBI agents watched suspected triggerman Richard Williams walk out and climb into a car bearing North Carolina plates. "We were on our way to the farmhouse when we heard it over the radio that Williams had been found," recalls Gulick. "No way. No way did we expect that." Agents followed Williams to a row house on a quiet, tree-lined street in southwest Cleveland, about forty miles away.

A farm family that lived across the street from Levasseur and Gros agreed to be taken to a hotel that night so that detectives could set up surveillance in their living room. "At 7 a.m., the newspaper delivery person pulled up and put the paper in Levasseur's mailbox," says Gulick. "A few minutes later, Levasseur came out to get the paper wearing a white T-shirt and jeans. I had goose bumps. After all these years, I was amazed that his tattoos were still so visible. He had made no attempt to remove or cover them."

Later that morning, Levasseur, Gros, and their three children, four, six and eight, climbed into their van, holding wrapped packages and a cake. Obviously, they were going to a birthday party. Since authorities knew that it was Williams's thirty-seventh, they figured the Levasseur

234 family was probably on its way to his place to sing "Happy Birthday." After turning right out of their driveway, police made a decision—based on the weather and the fear of losing them in an urban area—to move in. Other than Levasseur kicking an officer, he and Gros surrendered without a struggle after police quickly surrounded their vehicle. He was carrying a .380 semiautomatic.

Paper boy James Ross was completing his rounds on Station Street that morning when forty law enforcement officers, including a SWAT team from the Cleveland City Police bearing an armored, tanklike vessel, "came down the street, driving slowly, telling us to stay indoors," he says. Neighbors may have thought they were living in Beirut as all of this force was focused upon a white frame house whose polite but standoffish residents—the Owens—could be seen mowing their lawn in the evening or walking their dog. In the front window were the faces of Halloween, a Frankenstein monster, a skeleton, and a werewolf, put up by the couple's three children.

An officer phoned in to Williams to surrender. Police couldn't believe their luck when Barbara Curzi answered. This was Laaman and Curzi's safe house, where birthday boy Williams was staying, and where Laaman's son, Michael, was about to celebrate his birthday, too. The luck quickly turned. At the very moment that the police called in to the house, Curzi was talking to none other than Carol Manning, who was on her way over with her husband, Tom, and their three kids. Thanks to call waiting, the Mannings were spared capture. When Carol asked if it was safe to enter, one can only imagine what Curzi must have told her.

Even though authorities had lost the Mannings, they had pretty much caught their limit for the weekend: Levasseur, Gros, Laaman, Curzi, and Williams.

Face to Face

That afternoon, Det. Ryan had his charge card out at Newark Airport, buying tickets to Cleveland for himself and eight other members of the Lamonaco Command Post.

"He came in with an attitude," recalls Det. Keith Verheeck, who interviewed Williams in jail that night. "When I introduced myself, the blood went right out of him. He started shaking. He said that never in the group's wildest dreams did they think they'd be pursued as they were by the New Jersey State Police. He told us they once rented the movie *Witness*. As they were watching it with Jeremy, they saw a Wanted poster in the background that had his picture on it. Williams said we were relentless. Wherever they went there were fliers."

Of course, Williams refused to answer questions about the group's activities or the Mannings' whereabouts. So, it came as a total shock to Verheeck when "I decided to ask the most obvious question, 'You wouldn't know the Mannings' phone number, would you?'" and amazingly, Williams just blurted it out. "Never expecting an answer, I had to leave the room to get a pen and paper to write it down," he says.

By the time the police located the Manning home in New Lyme, Ohio, about fifty miles east of Cleveland, the family had fled.

Among reams of evidence found in the three houses was a getaway briefcase equipped with false ID and a .357 Magnum handgun, $32,000 in cash, a UFF logo, UFF communiqués taking responsibility for several recent bombings, and a 1,066-page, three-volume record of the group's activities written in Estonian code. A footlocker in the Mannings' bedroom contained five 9-mm Luger caliber firearms—any one of them could be the murder weapon.

Levasseur's farmhouse was a virtual bomb-making factory, where authorities found pocket watches altered in the same way as one recovered from an unsuccessful bombing attributed to "Melville-Jackson" in 1976. A notebook taken from Levasseur's van, meanwhile, was a log of at least one recent bank robbery in Virginia.

Curiously, none of the suspects was linked to any criminal activity in Ohio. They were simply using Ohio as a safe place to live while they conducted their activities elsewhere.

To their communities, they were portraits in family values.

Jeff and Leah Carr (Tom and Carol Manning) moved to Dodgeville Road in the summer of 1984. Neighbors recalled Mr. Carr as a clean-cut man with graying hair who, upon returning from his business trips, dutifully cut the grass on the three-quarter-acre lot with a hand mower, and played for hours with his three children.

Their oldest child, Eric (Jeremy), was an honor student at Pymatuning Valley Middle School; and star pitcher on the New Lyme Dodgers, no less. Although his parents kept to themselves, not allowing neighbors in the house, they once permitted Eric's best friend, Brian Tauche, to spend the night. Their wide-screen TV made up for the health food dinner. The most radical thing uttered in the Carr household was a confidence from Eric to his friend Brian one day that he was a member of a gang in Cleveland and Vermont. "We thought that was pretty cute," recalled Brian's mother, Danette.

The father displayed four guns on the wall, Brian said, but that was not considered unusual in Ashtabula County, where hunting and gun collecting is a way of life.

Eric and Janice Peterson (Levasseur and Gros) sent their oldest daughters to Southeast Primary School in Ravenna. Rachael and Cindy (real names, Carmen and Simone) were described by their teachers as "well-adjusted, well-behaved, well-clothed, attentive to their studies, respectful of authority, and always alert to their aliases." "They were model students who were very polite and not an ounce of trouble in any way," said their principal Richard Archer. "We're as dumbfounded as everyone else," said Assistant Principal, Brian Oglesbee, who said that, in retrospect, there were some curious elements: their parents never came to parent-teacher conferences, and the girls were always absent on picture day.

Laaman and Curzi's older daughters, Lucia, ten, and Nina, nine, attended the Benjamin Franklin School in Cleveland. Known as Chris and Kim Owens, both were academically gifted and enrolled in accelerated classes, including French.

All of the fugitives' children were protective of their parents' lives. After Det. Verheeck interviewed one of Laaman's girls, he realized she had been lying to him the entire time. "She was so good at it," he recalls. "I showed her a picture of Richard Williams and she denied knowing him, even though they had just been in the same house. It was incredible how well programmed she was."

When word of the arrests came, Col. Pagano was at the annual State Police banquet in Atlantic City. On Sunday afternoon, he excused himself, had a trooper drive his wife home, and flew to Cleveland.

Flying out that afternoon was fingerprint expert Joe Keely, who brought with him photographic copies of the latent palm prints found on the Chevy Nova. Upon taking Williams's palm print, a match was made.

Heading out, too, was ballistics expert Larry Hillman, who helped search the safe houses. That night, Hillman and two FBI agents took the five semiautomatic guns found in Manning's footlocker to Washington, D.C., where, in the FBI lab, they discharged four to five bullets from each one. Hillman marked each bullet, bagged each one, then hopped on the next train to Trenton. Going straight to the forensics lab, he began analyzing them. By luck of the draw, the first bullets he inspected matched those from the crime scene, the Marshall's Creek tree stump, the tree in Massachusetts, and the log in Vermont—meaning, the gun that killed Lamonaco had at last been found. For all of the UFF's sophistication, they had violated rule number one of how to get away with a crime: Dispose of the murder weapon.

Despite having gone without sleep for thirty-seven hours, Hillman felt, he says, "absolutely great. That was the culmination of three years of work."

While the Mannings remained at large, the others were held in Cuyahoga County Jail in Cleveland. On November 27, 1984, Levasseur lunged for a deputy's gun and was restrained by eight marshals as he loudly protested a ruling ordering him to give hair samples to the government. Although U.S. District Judge Frank Battisti refused to allow Levasseur to give a statement, Levasseur nonetheless did, claiming that the U.S. was making war on Puerto Ricans and blacks. "I won't cooperate," Levasseur shouted as he was carried by eight marshals from the courtroom, shackled at the waist, wrist, and ankles.

On December 18, Williams was ordered to return to New Jersey. A day later, he was placed in the State Prison at Trenton, with bail set at $5 million in cash.

The Search Was Over

Every object found in the Mannings' house was pored over by the NJSP and the FBI in hopes of finding clues to their whereabouts. Finally, after five months, a major break came when investigators were able to raise a partial serial number on one of the weapons found in the safe house. From a gun dealer in Newport News, Virginia, they discovered that it had been bought by a woman named Debra Fury. The name Debra Fury was new to authorities. When the address on the federal weapons purchase permit was checked, it turned out to be an active mailbox in nearby Virginia Beach. Authorities decided to stake it out, but this time they were more sophisticated in their method. Instead of posting a twenty-four-hour-a-day watch, they convinced the owner of the mailbox business into change his hours to daytime only.

On April 24, 1985, Carol Manning arrived and picked up the mail. Like Gros, she led the surveillance team on a swerving route to her house, which was located on a street in Norfolk, surrounded by tall oak and pine trees, on the banks of a marshy creek.

Authorities always felt that Levasseur was the brains behind the United Freedom Front. Now that he was behind bars, things had gotten very sloppy. Located in a populated area, the Mannings' latest safe house lacked the group's usual high standards of privacy and security. The upstairs portion was a separate unit, rented to a working mother of three. Had next-door neighbor Lucille Thompson unwrapped her April edition of *Readers Digest* she would have seen a full-page photo of the Mannings and notice of a $100,000 reward.

Manning obviously felt hunted. Jeremy had attended school and played Little League in Ohio. He was kept indoors here.

Before authorities could move in, Carol came out of the house and got back in her car. She was followed to the local A&P grocery store. A short time later, her arms loaded with bags, six FBI agents surrounded her. One pushed her against her car, and asked, "Are you Carol Manning?" "I'm fucking Carol Manning," she replied. She was cuffed and arrested.

At the same time, Thomas Manning was on a lawn chair in his back yard, casually sunning himself and reading a newspaper. As he dozed off, a six-man FBI SWAT team came up from the river.

"*Freeze!*" shouted an agent.

In his half-conscious state, Manning tried to comprehend what was going on. Agents tackled him and wrestled him to the ground, where he was cuffed and placed under arrest.

The search was over.

Did the New Jersey State Troopers feel cheated, not having been there for Thomas Manning's arrest? "At the beginning of the investigation, I told my men, in the end, the FBI will be the ones who will make the final capture," says Coe. "I told them, there's no use crying about it. That's the way it always is."

The satisfaction, he says, "is knowing the fugitives were caught because we were such a pain in the FBI's ass. We were always looking over their shoulders. That's why Levasseur, Williams, Manning, and the others were found. Before we came along, the FBI had been looking for these people for seven years and not getting anyplace."

Four months later, the Lamonaco Command Post was closed. "Reality set in," says Det. Ryan. "One day we were special, and the next day we had to go back to our regular jobs, doing everyday work."

But for Langan, Tavener, and Scott, seven years of legal maneuvers to put Manning and Williams behind bars were just beginning.

With flamboyant leftist William Kunstler as his lawyer, Manning fought extradition to New Jersey. To help speed up the process, Col. Pagano took a State Police helicopter to Norfolk to identify Manning as the suspect who had killed his trooper. As so often happened in this investigation, nothing was easy.

"I never told anybody this at the time," Col. Pagano says, "because I didn't want to give Kunstler the satisfaction of knowing what I went through to get there. We were over Chesapeake Bay at 1,700 feet, flying along, when all of a sudden there was a loud bang, and we started diving straight down. Joe Imbriago, our pilot, made the decision to autorotate. Fourteen more seconds, and the blade would have collapsed. We came down, unhurt, on an island that was maybe two hundred yards long and fifty yards wide. We were there for five hours until the Bureau of Coastal Resources found us and took us out by boat."

Before Manning and Williams could stand trial in New Jersey, though, there were federal charges to be dealt with.

First, a trial in Brooklyn, in which the two suspects, along with Carol Manning, Levasseur, Gros, Laaman, and Curzi, were accused of conspiring to overthrow the U.S. government by operating a terrorist ring responsible for a decade of bombings and bank robberies throughout the Northeast. Owing to the unexpected death of her attorney's par-

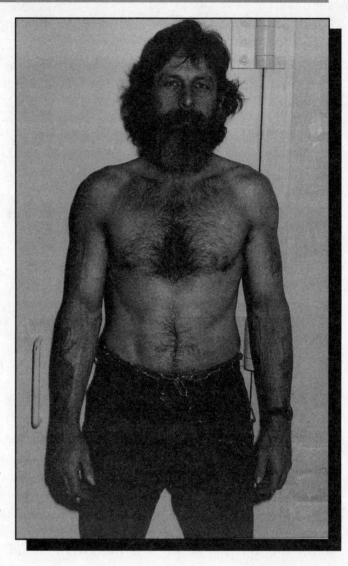

An intense and fit-looking Manning is photographed by authorities following his arrest.

ents, Gros was severed from the case, though she already had a five-year sentence in Ohio for harboring fugitives. The others were convicted in March 1986 on thirty-three counts of conspiracy and bombing. Laaman, who had just been given twenty-nine to forty-five years by a judge in Massachusetts for attempted murder of a State Police Officer at Attleboro, got fifty-three years in a federal penitentiary. Thomas

Manning and Levasseur got forty-five. Carol Manning and Curzi, fifteen, Williams, fifty-three.

After one year of extraordinary preparation by the Major Crimes Unit's trial team—Langan, Tavener, Volkmann, and Scott—who worked with the FBI's Jim Lyons and Andy Dorman, it was decided to try Manning and Williams together.

It was hoped that the terrorist group's diaries found in Ohio would place Williams at the murder scene. But after FBI agent John Markey broke the code—and even after they were again decoded by the aptly named New Jersey cryptographer, Cipher Deavours—"there was no smoking gun," says Tavener. The closest the diaries came to discussing the shooting was an entry from January 4, 1982, in which Manning and Williams held a discussion of "how the situation came about that put us here." Afraid the diaries would weaken their stronger evidence, the prosecution decided not to use them in court. The diaries do provide a fascinating inside look at the group, though. Even the dogs had aliases. Different words have other meanings. For example, "shit" means gun; "candy," ammunition; and "crispies," money.

The Truth Slips Through

The long-awaited murder trial of these two self-described "anti-imperialist fighters" got underway in October 1986, in Somerville, N.J. Prosecutor Anthony Simonetti, deputy attorney general, had the trial team jumping through hoops in his relentless quest for details. "I could shoot you right here in my office, admit I did it, and have it on videotape," says Maj. Coe, "and Simonetti would still say, 'But something's missing.'"

Security was definitely to the max. Escorted by six to eight squad cars and a helicopter hovering above, the prisoners were transported via armored truck each day from Trenton State Prison to the courthouse and back. Because the Somerset County Courthouse Annex wasn't fully built when the trial began, the first six weeks took place in the Somerville Elks Club. More than fifty heavily armed police patrolled the area, while at least two rifle-toting policemen stood inside the courtroom. Although the three defense attorneys, Kunstler, Lynn Stewart, and Ronald Kuby, objected to this display of force, the prosecution felt it was warranted. Especially when Levasseur, before being transported from Marion Penitentiary in Illinois to Somerville to give testimony, was found to have in his possession a drawing of how the courtroom was laid out. Authorities believe it was smuggled to him by a spectator at the trial.

The defense claimed Williams was not at the scene, and, therefore, could not have killed Lamonaco. They further argued that the 9-mm semiautomatic Browning used to kill the trooper did not belong to Williams. Manning took the entire rap, claiming he shot Lamonaco in self-defense after the trooper, allegedly realizing Manning was a fugitive, tried to execute him. During the ten-week trial, in which eighty witnesses testified and more than five hundred pieces of evidence were presented, Williams refused to take the stand. To do so, he claimed, would be an act of betrayal against his brother-in-arms.

In fact, in solidarity with their clients, the defense team refused to stand when Judge Michael Imbriani entered the courtroom.

Of all the emotional moments in the trial, the most grueling came when Lamonaco's bullet-riddled, bloodstained vest was put on a mannequin. Lamonaco's wife, Donna, who was seated up front, burst into tears and bolted from the courtroom.

If Williams wasn't at the crime scene, who was the other person or persons witnesses all supposedly saw with Manning? Although they could not produce them, the defense claimed they were two Puerto Rican hitchhikers, a man and a woman. Manning testified that he went gift shopping with Williams earlier in the day at the Trading Post near Budd Lake, N.J.; hence, Williams's fingerprints on the car and its contents. Afterwards, Manning said, he dropped Williams off so that he could catch a ride elsewhere with revolutionary compatriots. On Manning's way back to Marshall's Creek, he claimed to have picked up the two strangers. Although Manning was with them for a half hour, he said he never learned their names.

When passing motorist Donald Longyhore took the stand on November 19, he was asked by the defense about the Puerto Ricans he saw at the shooting site. Longyhore threw the defense a shocking blow when he said he didn't mean to convey that the suspects were Hispanics by describing them to police as Puerto Ricans. "I don't mean they had to be Puerto Ricans. They don't even have to be colored. It's just an expression I have. What's so horrible about it? Why are you trying to make a big deal out of it?" he asked. ("We learned a great deal from this," says Bob Scott. "An announcement came over police radios that the Hispanics we were looking for were in a car heading east on 46. We believe that announcement came from Williams and Manning, who we think were monitoring us on their radio. We learned, when you get a sighting, don't everybody go the same way. That's how we got screwed in the beginning. Manning and Williams were less than a mile away.")

On January 14, 1987, Prosecutor Anthony Simonetti presented his summation to the jury, claiming: "The truth slips through the tale in two slipups made by Manning during his testimony." Simonetti noted Manning's Freudian error when he said that he went to retrieve his "gun" from the fallen trooper's body, rather than his driver's license. Simonetti further pointed out that Manning said he was in the driver's door when the shooting started, rather than the passenger door, where he claimed he had gone to get his gun from the glove compartment.

Simonetti told the jurors an armed fugitive would never pick up two strangers: "Never happened. Never would happen. Never could happen." Manning's claim that Lamonaco tried to kill him in front of two hitchhikers, he said, "defies logic." (Besides, had they been in the backseat as the shooting was going on, as Manning claimed, they would have been directly in the line of fire.)

On January 20, 1987, after five days of deliberations, the jury convicted Manning of killing Trooper Lamonaco in the course of committing the crimes of robbery and escape. He was acquitted of knowingly committing murder or manslaughter as the jury did not believe the shooting was premeditated.

Despite Manning's conviction, this was not going to be a day of celebration for law enforcement or Lamonaco's family. The jury split seven to five on Williams, which meant a mistrial was declared. Despite the setback, the suspected triggerman could at least be retried.

"Venceremos!" ("We shall conquer!") shouted a jubilant Manning upon hearing the verdicts read. "A momentous victory for our clients and all revolutionaries in the United States and for all juries," announced Kunstler. "A victory for the armed clandestine movement," declared Williams.

On February 18, 1987, Judge Michael Imbriani sentenced Manning to life in prison, specifying that he would not be eligible for parole for thirty years. The judge ordered that the term follow, rather than be served concurrently with, the fifty-three-year federal sentence for his bombings. "You have spoken of your concern for the poor and down-trodden. I have searched the record in vain for evidence," Imbriani told Manning. "Everything I've read about you portrays a man who has resorted to violence and crime for your own personal machinations."

A New Method and a New Trial

Before a decision to retry Williams could be made, UFF members faced yet another messy legal battle, this time in Springfield, Massachusetts The U.S. government charged the radical group with seditious conspiracy and racketeering under the RICO laws, for ten bank robberies and several bombings, including the blast that had injured twenty-two people at the Suffolk County Courthouse in 1976. It was estimated that the group had obtained $900,000 from bank holdups.

"We are charged with conspiring to overthrow the government of the United States, an honorable thing to do," stated Kunstler.

Following ten months of jury selection, the enormously complex Springfield trial dragged on for more than two years. Basically, when it was all over, it was a clean sweep for the defense. By copping an Alford plea (a form of plea bargaining), Carol Manning was given a reduced sentence and let off early. Laaman and Curzi were severed from the trial on a technicality. Williams, Manning, Levasseur, and Gros all were acquitted of charges of seditious conspiracy.

Seeing as Williams had racked up a hefty prison sentence from the federal government in the Brooklyn trial, Lynn Stewart, his attorney, felt it a waste of taxpayers' money for the state of New Jersey to retry him. "A lot of people were for giving Williams a deal," says Col. Dintino, who by now had succeeded Col. Pagano as superintendent. "I wasn't for that. I wanted to send a message: if you kill a trooper, we'll go to the end to find you and convict you. I even made up my mind that if a second trial ended with another hung jury, we'd go for another trial. Still, I went to Donna Lamonaco and asked her what she wanted. She wanted a trial."

The NJSP trial team also felt Williams had to be brought back to court. "Without a murder conviction, he would be eligible for parole in about twenty years," says Tavener.

This time around, the trial team felt it had a much stronger chance of conviction. Since January 1987, a new method of blood examination for forensic identification purposes had been introduced in the United States. By the spring of 1990, this test, which involves DNA testing of dried bloodstains, had been accepted as legal evidence—although not in New Jersey. The first trial tests showed only that the blood found on the inside front door panel and armrest could have come from Manning or Williams, but not Lamonaco. The two suspects had the same protein markers, which are found in about thirteen percent of white Americans.

In July 1990, State Police chemist Fran Gdowski traveled to Richmond, California, to meet with Dr. Edward Blake, who had done the pioneer work in the field of testing bloodstains through a process known as polymerase chain reaction, or PCR. These tests require a very small amount of genetic material, and can be performed on blood samples that have been contaminated or exposed to elements over a long period. Successful tests have even been carried out on Egyptian mummies. Using ten-year-old bloodstains from the West Trenton forensic lab that had come from the Chevy Nova, Dr. Blake was able to determine that they did not come from Manning, and could have come from Williams. The chances of someone else having those identical markings was between one and three percent.

The next step was to get the court to allow them as evidence. In the spring of 1991, Judge Imbriani held hearings in Somerville on that very matter. But before those hearings could even take place, prosecutors had to wage a legal battle—which they won—to get fresh blood samples from Williams and Manning. After a month of hearings in which numerous geneticists, including Dr. Blake, swore to the validity of PCR testings, Judge Imbriani said he would allow them. "This hearing included the most complex, complicated scientific testimony I've ever heard in fifteen years on the bench," he said.

Delayed by the hearings, the retrial finally began on September 23,

1991, with Judge Imbriani again presiding. Again, Williams refused to testify. Except for the blood testings and Kunstler's absence from the courtroom following his client's conviction, this trial was pretty much a rerun of the original. It was, however, big on verisimilitude. On Oct. 8, the trial was moved to the carport of the Somerset County Jail in Somerville to enable jurors to see the actual blue Chevy Nova that Lamonaco had pulled over. For the first time, Phil's father, Joe, and two sisters came to the courtroom. They watched the prosecution and defense act out their son and brother's murder in an eerily realistic manner.

There, under direct examination by Lynn Stewart, Thomas Manning—or Tommy, as his lawyers affectionately called him—ran, crawled, crouched, and even dove to the ground while demonstrating how the incident supposedly occurred on that December day.

His retelling of the event had a lot more flourish than it had in the first trial. Manning testified, he was "dragged" from the car by Lamonaco, who, he said, was holding a gun to his head. Once outside, Manning said, the trooper "pushed" him onto the car roof, at which time his "gun went off right next to my ear." Manning said he pushed the trooper into the door and then ran, dove, and crawled around the car, with Lamonaco pursuing and firing at him. Eventually, Manning said, he managed to crawl through the passenger-side door and retrieve his gun from the glove compartment. He demonstrated how he fired three "volleys" of multiple shots toward the front of the vehicle and "into the haze of blue smoke" that was coming from Lamonaco's revolver.

On Tuesday, December 10, the eight-woman, four-man jury began deliberations. On Friday the 13, just eight days shy of the ten-year anniversary of Lamonaco's death, the jury reentered the courtroom. As the verdict was read—*guilty*—Donna Lamonaco began shaking and sobbing, putting her hand to her mouth. Because of the PCR blood testings, the jury believed that Williams was without a doubt the triggerman. He was found guilty of murder, felony murder and escape. "He can finally rest in peace, " said Donna.

A somber-looking Williams leaving the courtroom during the first murder trial.

Honor, Duty, Fidelity

For the February 8 sentencing, the courtroom was packed with the people who had helped to bring this day about. It was a bit like a curtain call, since so many of the players of both major roles and bit parts— including the Major Crimes Unit trial team, the Command Post detectives, FBI men, and Paul Landry, the Massachusetts Trooper who had been shot at by Laaman—showed up to see the final curtain ring down.

As Donna Lamonaco read a presentencing statement, a female security guard wept. "I won't make a plea for mercy," an unemotional Williams told the judge. "I expect none, nor will I give any."

Despite the defense's likening of Williams to Nelson Mandela, Judge Imbriani showed no mercy, handing down the maximum sentence. Williams would have to serve at least thirty years in State Prison before being transferred into federal custody to serve his previous forty-five-year sentence for bombings. He would not be eligible for parole until 2029.

"The politics are nothing more than a cloak to hide your true purpose, which is to rob and steal the hard-earned money of others. There is no record of you ever having spent any of the money you stole in a way that would benefit others. The record shows all the money went for your personal benefit," declared the judge.

"God bless America," said Grace Lamonaco, who sat in the back row of the courtroom with her husband and two daughters. For Phil's mother, this was the first time she had set eyes on her son's killer.

Sadly, the fatal bullet that lodged itself in Trooper Lamonaco's heart on that brief December day produced an emotional richochet that tore apart a family. In the fall of 1989, Joe and Grace turned on their TV set to see footage of their son's funeral on a political ad for a gubernatorial candidate. The ad featured a voiceover by Donna. Joe and Grace, who had never spoken publicly about the murder, issued an angry press statement, saying that all they wanted was for their son to rest in peace.

The years immediately after Phil's death had been turbulent ones for Donna, who suffered an emotional breakdown and, upon remarrying in October 1985, lost Phillip's pension. The marriage lasted only ten months. ("He said he couldn't live with all this," said Donna, showing off a wall in her house that has Phillip's awards and honors on it. Donna has since become active in Survivors of the Triangle, a rights group comprised of families of slain officers.)

After the sentencing, for which the stylishly coiffed Williams wore ironed jeans, a celebratory lunch was held at a nearby Italian restaurant. Even the snipers from the roof attended.

Although there was plenty of food and drink, it was not a merry affair. Maybe, after ten years, everyone was too worn out to be excited.

An exhausting job well done: Members of the Lamonaco investigative team.

250   Maybe the reality hit: now that it finally was over and justice at last had prevailed, nothing could bring Phil Lamonaco back.

If any good has come out of Phil's death, it's that other troopers' lives may have been saved. After his murder, the State Police replaced the traditional six-shot revolver with a much faster 9-mm semiautomatic handgun capable of firing forty-one rounds in twenty-five seconds. All road troopers were issued shotguns, and bullet-resistant vests became standing operating procedure.

In honor of Phillip Lamonaco, the New Jersey State Assembly voted to name the portion of Route 80 heading in and out of the Delaware Water Gap after him. All year round, the east- and westbound signs bearing the trooper's name and badge number are covered with a colorful array of flowers, crosses, and ribbons, put there by policemen, friends, family members, and strangers.

On a bleak winter's day, they make a brilliant contrast to the desolate landscape where he gave his life.

If there's a single hero in the solving of this crime, it is Phillip Lamonaco, even though he appears in spirit only. His passion for perfection, his unswerving commmitment to honor, duty, and fidelity, inspired an entire State Police department to do some of its finest detective work ever, to be as relentless in its pursuit of justice as the Delaware River was in wearing down a mountain.

13 / Characters with Character

Almost everybody I interviewed for this book is a working trooper. Along the way, I met some retired ones who represent other eras, from horses to motorcycles to black-and-whites. These were some of my favorite people, whose vivid stories brought to life other days and other chases. I thought they belonged in this book, too.

"I Had to Make Them Afraid of Me"

The first person I interviewed for *TROOPERS* was Capt. Albert Varrelman (Badge No. 159), who graduated from the second class, and since has died. Our meeting was scheduled for noon at the State Police Museum and Learning Center, though when he arrived, he said, "I was

251

Varrelman must have been a good teacher, as witnessed by Trooper William Codd's dazzling display of trick riding. Thanks to Varrelman, troopers were also skilled in pyramid riding, though purely for theatrics, and not for apprehending criminals.

Everyone agreed, riding master Capt. Albert Varrelman was a strict disciplinarian. Old-timers say they still have the saddle sores.

promised lunch. I get to eat first." And he did.

When the Outfit began, the State Police had sixty-one horses, which were the preferred means of patrol. Varrelman was the feared riding master who taught Academy recruits pyramid and Roman riding to develop confidence in themselves and their mounts. "It's true, I was tough on them," he told me. "But there was a reason. I had to make them afraid of me so they wouldn't be scared of the animals."

It seems inconceivable that a trooper on horseback could stop a speeding car. "Not at all," said Varrelman. "You hopped on the running board of a passing automobile and said to the driver, 'Chase that car!'" And people obliged? "Oh, yeah. They'd take you. No question about it. I don't know of any cases where men were refused." And if you were on horseback and came to an accident where someone was hurt? "You'd tie the horse to a tree, taking off the saddle because he might roll and hurt himself. Then you'd hail a car and say, 'Hey, take this guy to Doctor so-and-so. He lives at such-and-such a place . . .'"

"Back then," Varrelman said, "riding horses was a good way to get dates. They had one-room schoolhouses in those days. You'd ride down at recess and talk to the kids. The teacher was always a good-looking girl who you wanted to impress and ask out. The kids would say to you, Hey, Trooper, can you do this? or do that? Like pick up a handkerchief, do an overmount or some trick riding. You made a big hit with them, and, of course, with the teacher."

"We Lived by the Rules. We Didn't Complain"

"If you want to know more, just call me. Have memory, will travel," said Sgt. First Class Phillip O'Reilly (Badge No. 733), who, with his wife, Helen, came to my house one day for a visit. No trooper more exuded the authoritative look of a motorcycle cop—with his high leather boots, gray sweater, scarf, flared breeches, chin strap and goggles—than O'Reilly, who joined the Outfit in 1941, and rode a Harley-Davidson for fifteen years. An opera and ballet buff, he was known as "Gentleman Phil." "I was considered a pretty boy until too many spills took their toll," he says.

"The patrols were beautiful," he went on to say. "On a spring day, there was nothing lovelier than riding through the countryside. Or going out in the evening during a gorgeous sunset. You had great rapport with the people. The two-way radios didn't come in until 1943. If you were wanted by your sergeant, the dispatcher would call a designated place, such as a gas station or private house, and the owner would hang out a red flag. That's how we communicated then. Since you couldn't ride a cycle nonstop all day, you'd get off to see people. In the rural country areas we got to know everybody on the route. Around Great Meadows, the old Russian and Polish farmers who wore those traditional caps would tip them as you passed. All their kids would wave. In those days it was so unusual to see a trooper that everybody waved. We were really somebody in our uniform and boots.

"You knew everything that went on in your area. Instead of locking kids up, I'd hold court myself. I'd bring them home to their parents and tell them what they did. It was the humane way to do things.

"We didn't have sirens on the cycles. If you wanted somebody to pull over, you motioned them with your hand. In the winter it was impossible to write tickets because your hands were so frozen. You could get caught in the ice and snow, but they'd never send you out in it. We carried a raincoat attached to a little carrier on the back. Today, troopers have so much equipment. Back then all we had was a small book which acted as our notebook for investigating crimes and as our summons book. You put everything in that book. It was part of your uniform. You stuck your pencil in your boot.

"Some of the cycles had sidecars, which had no winter fronts. The sidecar was just a thin sheet of metal. So, when the senior man took you out for a ride, and it was zero degrees, you froze to death.

"We rode the cycles during the day, not on night patrol. If you were riding when it got *really* cold out, or night came, you'd stop and buy a magazine or newspaper to put under your coat. Riding during Japanese beetle season in the summer was the worst, though. They'd hit you on the nose and lips. I knew a fellow trooper who was all dressed and going to inspection when he was hit by a pheasant. It was

*A smiling "Distinguished Gentleman Phil," days before his
bone-cracking crash.*

all over him.

"We lived in the barracks, which were like boarding houses. Often
families ran them. We had two, three, sometimes four cops in a room.
We ate our three meals there. You'd get up at 6:30 and the sergeant
corporal would assign you your patrol for the day. You'd line up and
stand at attention. Invariably, the day you didn't have your long johns
on was when you got the cycle, and the day you did wear them, you
got desk duty.

"We were off four days and six nights a month. All the rest of the
time, we were at the barracks. Besides your four days and nights off,
you got two other night passes. But if you had reports, they could take
that pass away from you. If you left your collar open on a hot day you
could lose a night pass for that. You got one holiday off a year,
Christmas or New Year's, but not both. Vacations were two weeks, and

had to be taken during the winter.

"Today, troopers say no one understands them. Yeah, they only work eight hours a day and get overtime. They don't know what it's like to have so little time off and then lose it because of a hurricane or a train wreck. There was nobody to tell you your eight hours were up. You just stayed. We lived by the rules. We didn't complain.

"Even though troopers were seldom at home, you never heard of divorces. When you were off, you were with your wife. If you were divorced you were almost ostricized. It was just not the thing.

"In those days, we had to pass an oral exam to get into the Academy. You were judged by how you spoke. If you stuttered they might disqualify you. They wanted a certain image and look."

"Tall and handsome," says Helen.

"I was a good rider," says Phil. "I respected the cycle while I was afraid of it. But once I thought I was pretty good—it's true with all the troopers—that's when I'd crash. Most of your old-time troopers had broken bones from the spills. My worst crash was Easter weekend, 1945. I was stopped at the Amoco station putting in a gallon when this car went by, *whooooom!* I cranked it up and started off. There was a long hill, and it took me a while to get over it. I caught up with him on the top of it, and started down it wide open, at 90 mph. As I went into a slight curve, the cycle went into a high-speed shimmy, and threw me off. I landed on my head, and we didn't wear helmets then. I slid 153 feet down the concrete. I cracked my skull, broke my collarbone, my shoulder blade, eleven ribs, my hand and nose. But I was back on duty in eleven weeks.

"In twenty-five years with the Outfit, I only lost three days to sickness. You never let the other fellows down by taking time off. We were a pretty healthy group from being out in the open air all of the time. Of course, we were pretty rugged when we came in. That's why we've all lived to be in our eighties and nineties. One time, I got real sick and refused to stay home. Fortunately, they put me on desk duty and not on a cycle. The next morning I was in such pain I had to be driven to the hospital. I went into a coma for three days and was given last rites. My appendix had burst. But I healed fast. The big thing the Outfit looked for was attendance. They didn't want any sugarbabies."

"He thinks he's tough," says Helen.

Helen, he's tough.

258 "Whoa, Whoa, Whoa. Let's See Your License"

All through my research for this book, troopers would ask, "Have you met 'The Font'?" Arthur Fontanella (Badge No. 1400) patrolled the Turnpike during the fifties and sixties before retiring in 1986, as a lieutenant in Organized Crime. His career has had more turns, spins, stops, and gos than a high-speed chase. No, he wasn't exactly what Col. Schwarzkopf had in mind—irascible and often impossible. Still, he makes for colorful stories, especially his tales of the Turnpike. At the seventieth anniversary banquet for the NJSP, The Font was named the 1950s Co–Trooper of the Decade, and they're still talking about it. "I didn't want the other guys to see, but I was crying like a jerk," he says. One only has to look at The Font's checkered history to see how heart-felt those tears were.

If The Font believed a fellow trooper had gotten an unfair deal, he became Don Quixote—politics be damned. "He'd go to his death defending a guy," recalls one of his secretaries, Kay Lewis. "A great guy, but you have to realize he has this quirk," says a trooper and longtime friend. "You can tell him anything. Just don't touch him. It makes him nuts."

During his career The Font managed to be thrown out of four troops—"for mouthing off," he says. In 1955, after just eight months on the job, the ex-Marine was suspended for insubordination. "I had a sergeant who was an extremely difficult man, a tyrant. One morning, I felt him grab me and rip my jacket. Well, I lost it. I called him a few names. I didn't hit him, though I came close. There was a court mar-tial and I was fired, but later reinstated."

Even Dick Tracy would have trouble catching up with The Font, who, though retired, still teaches self-defense at the Academy. "The recruits can't keep up with him," says P.T. Instructor Tim Fogarty. "Nobody can." "I'll meet you at the Asbury Park service area of the Garden State," says The Font, "on my way to the gym."

Sitting on a bench in the hot summer sun, he looks, for a man of sixty-one, a decade or two younger, with arms like Popeye's after the spinach. In his shirt pocket The Font keeps a piece of crumpled paper that's his trademark. "It's true, I write down everything I eat," he says,

"The Font" (standing on the first step, second from the left) at the Colt Neck Station's annual inspection, 1964. (Unseen, in his jacket pocket, is his food list.)

pulling it out. "I always have. That way, I know when to cut back on my calories." Those lists should be left, if not to science, then to the Ripley's Believe It Or Not Museum. The Font loves raw pork sausage, often a pound and a half for lunch. "I like the Italian kind you get at the deli, with extra fennel," he says. He's been known to wolf down entire jars of hot peppers in one sitting. Ex-barrackmates recall how he got up for breakfast one day and put away forty eggs and three pounds of bacon. "He used to take me to lunch at Colonel Sanders," recalls another one of his secretaries, Barbara Jackman. "He never left a mess. That's because he'd eat the chicken bones."

Pity the all-you-can-eat seafood restaurant he once visited, devouring 278 steamer clams. "I know because I wrote each order down," he says. Later that night, The Font wound up in the hospital with iodine poisoning. His appreciation of food seems to be hereditary. "My father and grandfather worked together in a Newark factory," he says. "I remember them eating thirty-eight sandwiches for lunch one day."

His appetite for life was no less ravenous. When he worked in Organized Crime, no one could keep him behind a desk. "I loved the action, being out with the guys doing the surveillance, executing the search warrants. I thought I should be out there backing 'em up in case they got roughed up." On days he couldn't get out of the office, The Font would work off his caged energy with a weighted jump rope, his other trademark. "He'd jump up and down the halls for hours on end. You always knew when The Font was around," says Jackman.

When doing surveillance, The Font provided escape valves. "It was 93 degrees outside, and we were in back of a van," he recalls. "Things were getting real tense, so I went to the trunk of my car, got out a heavy winter coat with a hood on it, and put it on. Then I put on a pair of glasses that had no lenses in them. I put 'em on my face upside down. Then I started walking real funny, back and forth, in front of the house we were watching. Those wiseguys would never take me for a cop. Nobody would. I looked like some poor old simpleminded idiot. One of my guys said, 'Font, you're so crazy!' Everyone got to laughing so hard the tension busted right up.

Tales of The Font still haunt the Turnpike. In 1962, he got his picture in the newspaper for one of his arrests. "It began," he says, "on a cold-as-a-bastard February morning. I was driving south on the

Turnpike around New Brunswick when I saw what I thought was a jet go by. Now, I know this car was going over 100 mph. So I spun around, crossed the island, foot to the floor. I had a Chrysler that could really move, and I could barely catch the guy. When I did, I told him to get out of the car. That's when he started yelling, 'I'm a congressman! I can't be inconvenienced! Here are my credentials! I'm leaving now!' I says to him," *'Whoa, whoa, whoa. Let's see your license.'* That really got him screaming and hollering. I had no idea how important he was. Chairman of the House Appropriations Committee. Then his wife starts in at me: 'This is worse than Nazi Germany!' She was really a knockout, too, like a showgirl. He, however, was fat and bald. He gave me such a bad time that I had to arrest him as a disorderly person."

Then "Mr. Special Privilege" made his fatal mistake. "He grabbed ahold of my jacket," says The Font, thus violating the Please don't touch the you-know-who rule. "That was it. Boom. Bang. Cuffs on, everything. Then he passed out on the road. That's when his wife went crazy, so I had to cuff her, too."

Ever the maverick, The Font later that year gave a ticket to the Turnpike's head purchasing agent, a bigwig who was in charge of buying the patrol cars. "A friend who worked at the maintenance yard told me that the purchasing agent wasn't afraid of getting a summons from a trooper. 'That'll be the day,' he bragged to my friend. When I heard that, I knew I had to get him. So I waited by the East Brunswick exit. Sure enough, he came by doing 80 or 85. Out I pulled." The Font, who was married and living in northern Jersey, claims that was the reason he was reassigned to the southernmost end of the Turnpike, near Delaware. His job: to sit in a service area in an unmarked car every night from 6 p.m. to 2 a.m., looking for drug dealers. But don't cry for Fontanella. In typical Font style, the situation quickly reversed itself. "About 11:30 one night, I was about to doze off in my car, when I see two guys in overcoats break into a Chevy with a crowbar and drive off," he says. "So I followed 'em to South Brunswick where I pulled 'em over. Turns out they were Santoro and Klein, two New York car thieves who'd been working the Turnpike, cleaning it up. Everyone was after them. I caught them . . ."

"They say I was my own worst enemy," says The Font. "I was too vocal, and very, very set in my ways. Sometimes you shouldn't express your opinions, and I always do. If I don't like a guy, I can't be two-faced with him. I can't shake his hand. I just walk by him like he's invisible. I recently ran into the sergeant who fired me back at Howell Station. He's eighty-five now. He came over to say hello, and I just walked away. You know, Johnny, sometimes it's good to be a little tactful; and I'm not."

But who would expect correct social behavior from such an all-or-nothing guy? Here's what you'd want: "When a guy's in trouble," says The Font, "and you go in his corner one hundred percent, when you doggedly defend him right to the end, when you give a guy who's in pain some compassion, when you do something for him that's not conducive to your going up in rank, he'll always remember that. Guys still come up to me and say, 'Font, I'll never forget what you did for me. Never.' That's the best reward of all. When I'm dead and gone, I'd like people to remember me by saying, 'If you needed him, he was there. The Font would never let you down.'"

Looking Down the Road

Having written about the present and the past of the New Jersey State Police, I figured no one would have a better insight into its future than Col. Dintino, who's spent more than forty years in law enforcement, starting with his graduation from the Academy in 1952. Throughout my research for this book, people who know the colonel all told me the same thing: he has always been one to look ahead. I asked Col. Dintino if he would reflect a bit on some of the changes that he sees coming. Sitting at his desk at Division Headquarters, he talked enthusiastically about "a new era that I feel is breaking in State Police history." He boasted of recent developments in crime fighting, and talked of those that are on the verge of happening.

For starters, I asked him who he thinks the trooper of tomorrow will be. "As we move into the twenty-first century, our troopers must be equipped to use their intellect," he said. "Our troopers are the ultimate

Col. Dintino began his career in 1952, patrolling the highways of South Jersey on a Harley-Davidson.

weapon in our arsenal to fight the war on drugs, street crime, domestic violence, and terrorist attacks. We no longer live in the twenties, thirties, forties, or fifties, when a trooper could rely on brute strength to get the job done. Today's criminals are sophisticated, intelligent, cunning and shrewd individuals. They use their skills to steal billions of dollars annually, never once raising their voice, let alone a gun. Still, a trooper's self-defense training can never be compromised. There are, unfortunately, times when the basic instincts of man prevails, and a weapon must be drawn.

"In our continual efforts to maintain the highest standards of training for our troopers, we recently purchased three FATS machines, which stands for Firearms Training Simulator," he added. "A FATS machine is like a video arcade game. They cost $70,000 each, and have been installed at our Academy in Sea Girt. Twenty-nine different deadly force scenarios are presented on a ten-foot screen, with lifesized images. For example, in one scenario, you have a drunk on a park bench who pulls a knife on another officer. By using a special gun, a trooper can shoot a laser beam at the screen. An instructor can then analyze the trooper's marksmanship and whether he or she made the right decision to use a weapon. All of our troopers will be trained on these machines as part of our in-service program."

In this computer age, the State Police use a state-of-the-art system called CAD (Computer Aided Dispatch) that ensures rapid response to all types of general police calls, as well as the statewide 911 system. I asked the colonel, In what other areas will computers be used in law enforcement? "They're beginning to play a larger role in police investigation reports," he said. He further predicted "a day where all of these reports will be entered into a main regional computer. That computer will then analyze the type of crime that's been committed, who the suspects are, how it was carried out, where it took place, and what was the MO, or modus operandi. The crime would be further compared to similiar ones in different jurisdictions. In police work, the sharing of information with other agencies is invaluable. That hasn't generally been the case, but it is definitely the future of crime fighting."

According to the colonel, computers will be mounted inside troop cars to provide officers knowledge about traffic, weather conditions, and general police information. "These mini computers will be able to transmit instantaneous data to an officer on such things as wanted vehicles, stolen cars, and missing persons," he said.

"Just as we now employ the computerized AFIS fingerprint system to identify suspects, tests are currently being done that will allow an officer who's on patrol in his vehicle to do the same thing with an individual's thumb print," he said. "By using a screen that's attached to an in-car computer, an officer will be able to transmit the print to a computer in Washington, D.C. If the individual has ever been fingerprinted, all available biographical data, his or her criminal history, and a photograph, will be sent back to the computer screen."

As for future advancements in electronic surveillance, "our need to have the latest high tech equipment is an ongoing process," the colonel said. "With communication satellites beaming messages across the world to portable cellular telephones or digitial message receivers, our ability to intercept these transmissions is never-ending." With that he issued a challenge: "Let me just give a word to the astute businessman, investor, scientist, and entrepreneur: We are always in need of better technology. I would like to see the development of electronic sensors that can detect the odor of narcotics in a vehicle as it passes a certain checkpoint. That would definitely enhance our efforts to win the drug war. I would like to see a device that can uncover narcotics or explosive devices that are secreted in baggage, cargo, or machinery at our airports, train stations, and ocean ports. Also, how about a simple, nonintrusive instrument to reveal motor vehicle drivers who are under the influence of narcotics or alcohol? To me, this would be a really great, lifesaving, humanitarian invention."

To close the book, I asked the colonel if there was anything he could say to someone considering a career in law enforcement. "We recently built a State Police Museum and Learning Center at Division Headquarters, which he or she should visit," he said. "Through its displays and video presentations, it gives a lively, in-depth history of the NJSP. I can't see how the Museum wouldn't be an inspiration for any young person interested in joining the State Police."

And, finally, any words for the five thousand members of the NJSP? "I would simply like to thank the men and women, enlisted and civilian, who make up the State Police family," he said. "All of you have made the NJSP what it is today, the finest police organization in this state if not the nation. As the world we live in becomes more and more complex, your responsibility to ensure the safety and well-being of our

266 citizens continues to expand. You must be articulate, informed, and sensitive to the needs of the people you've been sworn to protect. At the same time, you must be able to take command of a dangerous situation, apprehend a violent criminal, or breathe life into a dying person. The future of the New Jersey State Police has to be your ability to exhibit the strength, character, and fortitude to adapt to these difficult needs. If we wish to be a police force for the twenty-first century, this is our challenge."

Index

A

Acevedo, David, 51-52, 53-58
Addonizio, Hugh J., 84
Adonis, Joey, 83
Adonis, Joey, Jr., 108
Aeromedical program, 175-181
Affirmative action, 46
AFIS computerized scanning
    system, 200
Ahearn, Maureen, 221
Aleshire, Donald, 79
Algor, Jeff, 33-39
Anastasia, Albert, 83
Anderson, John, 21
Andreychak, Chris, 157
Aramini, Patsy, 102, 109-113,
    113-114, 114, 117
Arce, Louis, 151
Archer, Richard, 236
Armellino, John, 96
Arroyo, Rick, 175, 177, 178-179,
    181

B

Bananas, Tony, 122
Bank robbery, 184-187
Battisti, Frank, 237
Baum, Bill, 102, 104
Bishop, Cameron, 215
Black troopers, 10, 41-42, 46-47
    affirmative action and, 46
    in undercover drug operations,
    144-148, 150-151
Blake, Edward, 245
Blakey, Robert, 90, 94
Blue Max, 184
Bochiccio, Felix, 89

Boero, Sean, 22
Boiardo, Ruggiero "The Boot,"
    84, 85, 86, 87, 96
Bomb Squad, 197-200
Bonanno family, 127
Bordentown (New Jersey), 24-25
Brennan, William III, 91-92, 100
Bridge jumpers, 28-29, 31
Brinamen, Thomas, 191, 192
Bruno, Angelo, 89
Bruno/Scarfa crime family, 97,
    119-121, 122, 124, 125
Buono, Ralph, 104, 115, 117
Bureau of Alcohol, Tobacco and
Firearms, 146
Burke, Todd, 72, 73
Byrne, Brendan, 202, 212

C

CAD (Computer Aided
    Dispatch), 264
Cadmus, Charles, 135, 137, 148,
    150, 152, 153
Caffrey, Brian, 159, 162-166
Cali drug cartel, 134, 135, 137
Cameron, Gail, 42
Camiso, Jerry, 153
Caramandi, Nicholas, 97
Carhart, James, 74, 79, 80
Carhart, Louis, 79-80
Car wrecks, 31-33, 38, 172, 177
Castillo, Benny, 4, 8-9
Cavanaugh, James, 203, 213
CERB. See Criminal Enterprise
    and Racketeering Bureau
    (CERB)
Cherry, Isiah, 41-42

Chesimard, Joanne
    (Assata Shakur), 203, 218
Child abuse prosecution, 6
Chirico, David, 168, 171-175
Churm, Larry, 162
Cieplensky, Robert, 197-198
Civil Forfeiture Act, 140
Civil liberties, 95, 134
Clark, Ramsey, 95
Codd, William, 254
Coe, Charles, 208, 210, 221, 224
    225, 230, 239
Coffin, Greg, 52-53
Cole, Jack, 208
Commission on Organized
Crime, 99
Comprehensive Drug Reform
    Act of 1987, 143
Computers, 264-265
Confessions, 25
Consent to search form, 54, 62
Constructive force, 36-37, 48-49
Cooper Medical Center, 175,
    178, 180-181
Cosa Nostra, La
    initiation ceremony of, 121,
    130-131
    vs Mafia, 89
    proof of existence, 96
    See also Organized crime, in
    New Jersey
Coyle, Cliff, 184, 190-194
Coyle, Shannon, 177
Crime. See Cosa Nostra, La;
    Major Crimes Unit;
    Organized crime, in New
    Jersey
Criminal Enterprise and
    Racketeering Bureau (CERB),
    99, 133-166

267

268 *(Criminal Enterprise and Racketeering Bureau, continued)*
busting drug dealers, 159
DARE program, 142-143
drug raids of, 148-153, 162-166
formation of, 133, 134
informants, 160-162
narcotics dogs of, 140-142, 151, 152-153
Operation Roadside, 136, 138-142
racketeering as priority of, 134-135
undercover operations, 143-148, 160-162
wiretaps and surveillance in, 135, 137-138, 154-159
Criminal Justice Act of 1970, 94
Criminal Justice Division, 94, 134
Curzi, Barbara, 224, 227, 234, 236, 239, 244

D

Dalpe, Donald, 168-171
Dalrymple, Dave, 56
Dancisin, Richard, 75-78
DARE (Drug Abuse Resistance Education), 142-143
Dawson, Bruce, 198
Deavours, Cipher, 241
DeCarlo, Angelo "The Gyp," 85
DeCavalcante family, 121
DeFeo, Tom, 212
Delaney, Robert, 102
Delaney, Robert, Jr., 102-106, 107-109, 113, 114, 115, 116, 117
Delaware Water Gap, 204, 209, 216, 250
DelGiorno, Tommy, 97
Deltieure, Genevieve, 181
Del Tufo, Robert, 1, 3
D'Ercole, Joe, 200
DiGilio, John, 91, 102, 104, 106, 115, 116-117
DiNorscio, Jackie, 102, 104, 106, 107
Dintino, Justin J., 1, 3, 46, 89, 95-96, 97-98, 133, 134, 142, 244, 262-266
DiSalvatore, Anthony, 4, 6, 52,
Ditzel, Edward, 198
DNA testing, 245
Dogs
Major Crime Unit, 200, 201

narcotics, 140-142, 151, 152-153
Dorman, Andy, 207, 241
Douglas, Karl, 150-151
Drug cartels, 134
Cali vs Medellín, 137
corporate structure of, 135, 137
money couriers of, 140
in New Jersey corridor, 138-142
ship transport, 139-140, 190-194
tractor-trailer transport, 135, 139, 191, 192
See also Criminal Enterprise and Racketeering Bureau (CERB)
Drug Enforcement Agency (DEA), 150, 190-194
Drug laws, 143
Drug raids, 148-153, 162-166
Drunk drivers, 30-31
Duranik, Alan, 112

E

Eastbury, Barry A., 213, 214
Eden, James, 143
Einwechter, Chris, 22-23
Electronic surveillance, 90, 92-97, 265
Electronic Surveillance Act, 90 91, 92, 95
Ellington, Danny, 36
Esposito, Jim, 200
Evans, Tom, 208, 219, 225

F

FATS (Firearms Training Simulator), 264
Federal Bureau of Investigation (FBI), 88, 106, 150, 198, 213, 230
in Lamonaco case, 207, 208, 222-222, 227, 230, 232, 233, 239
VICAP files, 201-202
Ficke, Marty, 96
Fingerprinting, 265
Firearms Training Simulator (FATS), 264
Fire rescue, 168-171
Fiumara, Tino, 102, 104, 106, 107

Five Percenters, 29
Flaherty, Joann, 47-50, 144
Foerster, Werner, 203
Fogarty, Tim, 6-7, 258
Fontanella, Arthur, 258-262
Forsythe, Ed, 90
Fort Dix Barracks, 33-39
Fortunato, John, 54
Francis, Robert, 56
Fresolone, George, 97, 119-132
Friedland, David, 91
Frost, Heather, 222

G

Gallagher, Thomas, 9-10
Gallant, Dave, 208
Galloway, Wendy, 10-12, 14
Garden State Parkway, 19, 21, 22, 27-33
Gdowski, Fran, 245
Genovese crime family, 97
Genovese, Vito, 83, 96
Godfather, The, 108
Goldstock, Ron, 94
Gonzalez, Nelson, 54, 55, 56, 57
Goss, Tim, 145-148
Gotti, John, 94, 97
Granitzski, David, 8
Grant, Annemarie, 141-142
Grant, Jack, 78-81
Grant, James, 24-27
Grant, Tim, 138
Gravano, Sammy "The Bull,' 97
Gros, Patricia, 219, 227, 231-234, 236, 240, 244
Gulick, John, 208, 232, 233

H

Hanratty, Thomas, 22, 23
Harper, James, 203
Hartigan, Matthew, 138, 139
Hauptmann, Bruno, 202-203
Hay, Bruce, 13-14
Hay, Rufus, 13, 14
Healey, Kevin, 36
HEAT (Homicide Evaluation and Assessment Tracking), 200-202
Heim, Ted, 181, 177. 179
Helicopters, 73-74, 175-181
Henderson, Peter, 112
Henfey, Brian, 76

Hennon, Lori, 21, 42
Herrerra, Alfonso, 54-55, 56, 57
Highway patrol. See Road patrol
Hillman, Beverly, 45
Hillman, Larry, 218-219, 237
Holba, Dennis, 79, 80
Homeijer, Charlie, 73-74
Hook, John, 168, 169, 206
Hopkins, Robert, 232
Horse era, 251-254
Huertas, Carmelo, 4, 5, 6-7, 8,
    12, 13
Hughes, Richard, 91
Hyland, William, 115

I

IBM bombing, 226
Identification Bureau, 200, 203
Imbriago, Joe, 239
Imbriani, Michael, 242, 244, 245,
    246
Informers, 97, 98-99, 119-130
Intelligence Unit
    Brennan and, 91
    formation of, 88-89
    identification of crime families,
        89-90
    See also Organized Crime
        Bureau
Irizarry, Victor, 160

J

Jackman, Barbara, 260
Jacobs, John, 52, 58-60
Jesch, Ernest, 20
Johnson, Ed, 97
Johnson, Lyndon, 90
Jones, Richard, 207

K

Kean, Thomas, 212
Kearns, Chris, 151, 152-153
Keely, Joe, 210, 221, 236
Kelly, David, 88-89, 91, 92
Kelly, Pat, 104, 106, 108
Kenna, Jim, 78, 79, 81, 202
Kikumuru, Yu, 197-198
Kineran, 49
King, Christopher, 224-225, 227
Kitson, Richard, 72, 73-74
Kuby, Ronald, 242
Kuklinski, Richard, 202

Kunstler, William, 239, 242-244
    246

L

Laaman, Jaan-Karl, 224, 230,
    235, 236, 240, 244
Lamonaco case, 203-250
    aftermath of, 250
    arrests in, 234-236, 238
    FBI and, 207, 208, 221-222,
        232-233, 239
    federal trials, 239, 244
    fugitive families, 235-237
    indictments, 230
    manhunt, 225, 230-237
    murder trials, 241-248
    murder weapon in, 218-219,
        222-224, 230, 237-238
    organization of investigation,
        206-208
    sentencing, 244, 247, 248
    suspects in, 213-221, 222-225,
        227, 230
    theory of prosecution, 225, 230
Lamonaco, Donna, 206, 208, 210,
    212, 221, 242, 245, 246, 248
Lamonaco, Grace, 212, 248
Lamonaco, Joe, 212, 246, 248
Lamonaco, Phillip
    funeral of, 211, 212
    killing of, 203-205, 226-227
    posthumous honor to, 248,
        250
    reputation of, 210-212
Landry, Paul, 224, 248
Langan, Michael, 208, 240, 241
Lauther, Gerry, 164-165
Leck, John, 208
Leisinger, Carl, 200
Leonardis, Dave, 208
Leonetti, Phil, 97
Lepes, Louis, 212
Levasseur, Raymond Luc, 213-
    215, 216, 219, 222, 227, 230,
    231, 233, 234, 236, 237, 238,
    239, 240, 241, 242, 244
    State Park, 198, 199
Licata, Joseph "Scoops," 126,
    127-128
Liddy, Jack, 102, 108, 115
Lieb, Drew, 198, 200
Life magazine, 84-85, 88, 90, 91
Lifesaving, 167-181
    aeromedical program, 175-181
    drowning, 171-175
    fires, 167-171

Likus, Paul, 185
Lindbergh baby kidnapping,
    202- 203
Linden, Bob, 164
Longyhore, Donald, 242-243
Lyons, Jimmy, 207, 241

M

Mackin, Joseph, 94
McConnell, Harry, 79
McCormick, Jim, 195
McDougall, Steve, 198
McLemore, Paul D, 43
McSorley, Jim, 9
McWhorter, Gary, 222
Mafia, vs La Cosa Nostra, 89
Maholland, Richard, 213
Major Crimes Unit, 195-251
    AFIS scanning system, 200
    bomb squad, 197-200
    detectives of, 196-197
    dogs of, 200, 201
    HEAT squad, 200-202
    investigative tools of, 197
    in Lingbergh baby kidnapping,
        202-203
    responsibilities of, 196
    See also Lamonaco case
Makuka, Steve, 200, 201
Mallen, Albert, 163. 165
Manetto, Pete, 151, 152, 153
Manning, Carol, 215, 216, 217,
    218, 219, 227, 231, 234, 235,
    237, 238-239, 241, 244
Manning, Jeremy, 218, 225, 229,
    236, 238
Manning, Thomas, 215-216, 217,
    218, 219, 226-228, 230, 231,
    234, 235, 236-237, 238-239,
    240-241, 241, 243, 244,
    245, 246
Markey, John, 241
Marr, Matty, 192
Martens, Fred, 160
Martin, Randy, 11
Martirano, Pasquale "Patty Specs,"
    121, 122-123, 124, 125, 128,
    130, 131
Mason, Don, 190
Mattos, Juan, 159, 160-162
Maximo (drug dealer), 148, 150-
    151, 152, 153
Maziekien, John "Zeke," 27-33
Mazur, Robert, 198
Medellín drug cartel, 137
Medical service, emergency, 175

Mercer County Prosecutor's Office, 150
Meritorial Service Award, 184
Mid Atlantic Air Sea Transport, 104
Mihalik, Mike, 151, 152
Milano, Nicholas, 97
Miranda, John, 151, 152
Modarelli, Vince, 100, 134, 137, 140, 142, 143-144, 155
Money couriers, 140
Monte, Frank, 126
Motorcycles, 22, 254-257
Mountainside (New Jersey), organized crime meeting at, 84-85
Moure, Joe, 24
Mursheno, Rich, 163, 164

N

Narcotics Bureau, 99, 133, 134,143
  See also Criminal Enterprise and Racketeering Bureau (CERB)
Natale, Richard, 74
Negron, Carlos, 204
Newark Port, 140
New Hampshire State Prison, 222
New Jersey magazine, 210
New Jersey State Police
  and affirmative action, 46
  commands of, 19
  Distinguished Service Medal, 52
  founding of, 25
  future of, 262-266
  links with organized crime, 84-85, 88
  Museum and Learning Center, 202, 265
  ninety-sixth experiment, 42, 44
  Picnic, 8
  reputation with organized crime, 121
  in World Trade Center bombing case, 197-200
  See also Intelligence Unit; Major Crime Unit; Organized Crime Bureau; Police Academy; Troopers
New Jersey Turnpike, 19, 22, 258, 260-261
Newsome, Billy, 119-120, 121, 132

New York Organized Crime Task Force, 94
Ninety-sixth class, 42, 44
Nixon, Richard, 95
Nockunas, Mike, 231

O

Oglesbee,Brian, 236
Olcheski, Arlene, 45
Olenick, Nicholas, 213
Omerta, myth of, 98, 123
Omnibus Crime Act of 1966, 90
O'Neill, Charles, 168-169, 171
O'Neill, John, 73
Operation Alpha, 101, 102-109, 114, 115
Operation Broadsword, 97, 119-121, 126
Operation Intrepid, 96-97
Operation Marat, 124
Operation Omega, 96
Operation Roadside, 136, 138, 142
Operation Tigershark, 97
Operation Waterjack, 101, 110, 113, 114
O'Reilly, Phillip, 254-257, 259
Organized crime, in New Jersey, *See also* Cosa Nostra, La
Organized Crime Bureau, 84, 90, 100, 134, 210, 258
  electronic surveillance, 92-97
  informers and, 97, 98-99
  See also Criminal Enterprise and Racketeering Bureau (CERB)
Organized crime, in New Jersey
  code of silence, 98, 123
  electronic surveillance of, 92-97
  extent of, 83-87, 89-90
  informers on, 97, 98-99, 119-130
  legislative hearings on, 90-91
  links to New Jersey State Police, 84, 85, 88
  links to state legislature, 91-92
  Mafia vs La Cosa Nostra, 89
  Mercer County Grand Jury investigation of, 91
  narcotics and, 99-100
  See also Undercover operations
Organized Crime Institute, 94
O'Riordan, Tim, 25
Orman, Stumpy, 89

P

Pacillio, Anthony, 106
Packwood, Guy, 42-43, 46
Pagano, Clinton, 115, 208, 226, 230, 244
Pagano, Lester, 208, 227, 228
People's Forces Group, 215
Pereira, John, 91
Perski, Walter, 168
Pecznik, Ira, 94
Piccolo, Anthony "Tony Buck," 121, 123, 128
Piperata, Al, 96
Point, Bobby, 191, 192, 193
Police Academy, 1-14, 33, 167, 173, 264
  bonding of recruits, 9-10
  campus of, 6
  clothing of recruits, 12-13
  curriculum, 5, 6
  dress, 12-13
  focus/concentration training, 8, 13-14
  graduation, 1-4, 14
  mess, 13
  ninety-sixth class (all-women), 42, 44
  physical demands of, 4-5
  physical training, 5, 6-8, 9-10
  punishment techniques, 8-9
  requirements for entry, 5
  residency requirement, 12
  training in focus and concentra tion, 8, 13-14
  weeding out process, 9
Potter, Nancy, 45
Presidential Organized Crime Commission, 90- 91
Project Alpha, 96

Q

Quirk, Eddie, 119, 121-132

R

Reali, Lou, 233
Red Star North bookstore, 214, 215
Repsha, Jack, 157
Revolutionary groups
  murders of troopers by, 203-204, 206

See also Lamonaco case
Richards, Peter, 92, 95
Riggi, John, 121, 126, 127, 128
Riordan, Red, 221
Road patrol, 17-39, 263, 264
  bridge-jumpers on, 28-29, 31
  cars on, 18-19, 20-21
  car wrecks on, 31-33, 38, 172, 177
  chasing suspects, 37
  constructive force on, 36-37
  deer injuries on, 35-56
  domestic fights on, 34
  drunk drivers on, 30-31
  excuses offered, 25, 28, 35
  Fort Dix Barracks assignment, 33-39
  high-risk stops, 29-30, 51-68, 184-188
  home base, 19
  liars caught in, 30
  mileage records in transporting women, 24
  physical force on, 36
  predawn hours, 27-28
  radio communication system, 19
  service areas, 29
  sexual assault victims on, 32
  training period, 17, 19, 22, 37-38
  uniform and gear, 19, 29, 250, 264
  vehicle searches, 19, 134, 210
Road troopers, 17-39
  cars of, 18-19, 20-21
  emotional stress on, 24
  home base, 19
  injuries and death, 22
  mileage records in transporting women, 24
  radio communication system, 19
  shift work, 22
  training period, 17, 19, 22
  uniform and gear, 19
  vehicle inspection, 19
Robbins, Norman, 91
Roberts, Richard "Archie," 183, 184-187
Robert Wood Johnson University Hospital, New Brunswick, 175
Robinson, Ronnie, 81
Rodriguez Orejuela, Gilberto, 135
Rogers, John, 175, 177, 179-181
Rohrbach, Rick, 181
Rookie troopers, on highway patrol, 17, 19, 22

Russo, Tony "Little Pussy," 85
Ryan, Richard, 208, 213, 230, 24

S

Sam Melville-Jonathan Jackson gang, 213, 215, 227
Satz, David, 92
Scarfo, Nicodemo, Jr., 120
Scarfo, Nicodemo, Sr., 97, 120-121
SCAR (Statewide Correctional Alliance for Reform), 215, 222
Schiavo, Dominick, 164, 165
Schwarzkopf, Norman, 3, 4, 25, 88
Scott, Bobby, 103-104
Scott, Gerald, 212
Scott, Robert, 196, 207, 208, 241, 243
Self-defense classes, 5, 260
Semon, Thomas, 126
Sempkowski, Anthony, 27-28, 30-33
Service areas, 29, 263
Sexual assault intervention, 6
Sherman, Victor, 145-146, 148-150
Siegel, Bugsy, 83, 96
Sills, Arthur, 88, 91, 92
Simonetti, Anthony, 241, 243
Sjostrom, E. Paul, 203
Sniper incidents, 74-81
Sodano, Joe, 121
South Jersey Hospital/Cooper Medical Center, Camden, 175, 178, 180-181
South Regional Narcotics Bureau, 162-166
SPEN, 188
Springfield (Massachusetts), UFF trial in, 244
Squires, Clark, 203
State Commission of Investigation (SCI), 90, 91
Steelman, Ralph, 22-23
Stewart, Lynn, 242, 244, 247
Stier, Edwin, 89, 92, 93, 94, 95
Stockburger, Hugo, 202-203
Swimming-lifesaving, 172-174

T

Tactical Patrol Unit, 75
Tauche, Brian, 236

Tavener, Fred, 195, 207, 208, 216, 218, 241, 245
TEAMS (Technical Emergency and Mission Specialists), 69-81
  in helicopter rescue, 73-74
  physical test for, 72-73
  skills of, 69-70, 72
  in sniper incidents, 74-81
  special equipment of, 72
Tice, Lester, 8
Tormey, Kevin, 183-184, 188-190
Torowicz, William, 10
Touw, Richard, 208, 233
Trauger, Kirk, 213
Trenton (New Jersey), drug raid in, 150-153
Trooper of the Year, 183, 210
Troopers
  black sense of humor, 38
  body language/demeanor of, 6, 24-25
  death of, 22, 23, 74, 165, 203-204, 206,
  See also Lamonaco case
  emotional stress on, 24
  fitness requirements of, 22-23
  of horse era, 251-254
  injury to, 22, 52-53, 58-59, 63-68, 74, 185-187
  marital problems of, 26-27
  of motorcycle era, 254-257
  organized crime, and. See Organized crime, in New Jersey
  positive aspects of job, 27, 38-39
  public scrutiny of, 12, 22
  shift work, 22
  See also Black troopers; Lifesaving; Road patrol; TEAMS (Technical Emergency and Mission Specialists); Women troopers

U

Undercover operations, 101-117
  bonding with criminals, 113-114
  courtroom trials and, 114, 116-117
  in drug enforcement, 143-148, 154-159
  fear of reprisal, 116, 117

272 (*Undercover Operations, continued*)

Operation Alpha, 101, 102-
109, 114, 115
Operation Waterjack, 101,
109-113, 114
Union City (New Jersey), under
cover drug operations in,
154-159
United Freedom Front, 226, 227
U.S. Attorney's Office, 150
U.S. Customs, 140, 190
U.S. Justice Department, 150
University Hospital, Newark,
175

V

Valachi, Joe, 88
Van Doren, Al, 177
Van Tassel, Thomas, 126
Varrelman, Albert, 251-254
Verheeck, Keith, 208, 235, 236
VICAP (Violent Criminal
Apprehension Program),
201-202

Volkmann, Ernest, 208, 216,
222, 241

W

Walker, Thomas, 187
Walsh, Brian, 160
Washburn, Dean, 78
"Weed and Seed," 150
Weisert, Robert, 102, 105,
106-107, 109, 114, 115,
116, 117
Wetzelburger, Bobby, 189
Whittier, John Greenleaf, 204
Whitworth, Linda, 177, 179-
180, 181
Williams, Richard Charles, 219,
221, 222-224, 227, 230, 231,
233, 234, 235-236, 237, 239,
242-243, 244, 245, 246,
247, 248
Witness, 235
Witness Protection Program,
104, 119

Women recruits
in physical fitness class, 5, 7
special problems of, 10-11
Women troopers, 45
chauvinism and, 49
constructive force and, 48-49
ninety-sixth class (all-women),
42, 44
physical strength of, 5, 7, 47-48
role of, 11-12
social life of, 49
special problems of, 10-11, 48
in undercover drug operation,
144
World Trade Center bombing,
197-200

Y

Yakup, Joseph, 3, 4

Z

Zicarelli, Joseph, 85, 95-96